*Cigarette Wars*

Poster distributed by the Our Boys in France Tobacco Fund, 1918
(Hoover Institution Archives, Stanford University)

# Cigarette Wars

THE

TRIUMPH

OF

"THE LITTLE

WHITE SLAVER"

Cassandra Tate

New York     Oxford     Oxford University Press     1999

Oxford University Press

Oxford   New York
Athens   Auckland   Bangkok   Bogotá   Buenos Aires   Calcutta
Cape Town   Chennai   Dar es Salaam   Delhi   Florence   Hong Kong   Istanbul
Karachi   Kuala Lumpur   Madrid   Melbourne   Mexico City   Mumbai
Nairobi   Paris   São Paulo   Singapore   Taipei   Tokyo   Toronto   Warsaw

and associated companies in
Berlin   Ibadan

Published by Oxford University Press, Inc.
198 Madison Avenue, New York, New York 10016

Oxford is a registered trademark of Oxford University Press

Library of Congress Cataloging-in-Publication Data
Tate, Cassandra.
Cigarette wars : the triumph of
"the little white slaver" /
Cassandra Tate.
p.   cm.
Includes bibliographical references and index.
ISBN 0-19-511851-0
1. Cigarette habit—United States—History—20th century.
2. Antismoking movement—United States—History—20th century.
I. Title.
HV5760.T38   1998
362.29'6—dc21      97-50571

1 3 5 7 9 8 6 4 2

Printed in the United States of America
on acid-free paper

# *Acknowledgments*

*T*his project began life as a magazine article and grew into a doctoral dissertation. That it is now a book is due in part to the chairmen of my dissertation committee at the University of Washington in Seattle: professors William J. Rorabaugh and the late Robert E. Burke. Each read innumerable drafts of the manuscript, offered unfailingly good advice, and provided both encouragement and occasional skepticism (when I skated too far onto thin ice), along with countless newspaper clippings and suggestions about sources. I am also grateful to my other committee members, professors James C. Whorton and Richard R. Johnson. They asked challenging questions and otherwise helped push me beyond my comfort zone, and my work is the better for it.

I might still be staring out the window, surrounded by drifting piles of notes, were it not for the members of what I hereby christen the Compulsive Footnoters Club: Alexandra Harmon, Julia Eulenberg, Mary Wright, and Jane Merritt. As fellow graduate students, they forced me to meet deadlines and tried to improve my thesis paragraphs. Thomas LeBien at Oxford University Press picked up where they left off. His keen eye and enthusiasm (to say nothing of his willingness to laugh at my jokes) helped ease the metamorphosis from dissertation to book.

I owe a great deal to scores of archivists and librarians who responded to my written inquiries by digging into their records to do research that I could not do in person. Among those who were most generous with their time (and their copying machines) were David Carmichael at the Young Men's Christian Association Archives, University of Minnesota, Minneapolis; Alfred E. Epstein at the Frances E. Willard Memorial Library in Evanston, Illinois; Jo Ann Rayfield, archivist at Illinois State University, Bloomington; the staff at the Illinois State Archives in Springfield; Henry Ilnicki, senior librarian at the New York State Library in Albany; and Patricia White, archivist specialist at the Department of Special Collections, Stanford University Libraries.

*Smithsonian Magazine* financed research trips to the Arents Collection at the New York Public Library, repository of virtually everything written about tobacco since the sixteenth century; and to the Library of Congress, the National Archives, and the Smithsonian Institution itself. A grant from the American Historical Association sent me to the tobacco country of North Carolina and Virginia. Archivists in the manuscript collections at Duke University, the University of North Carolina, and the University of Virginia helped me make the most of my research time (and directed me to great local barbecue spots). A dissertation fellowship from the University of Washington helped me complete the writing.

I am going to borrow a line from Sarah Sharbach and say that I am surprised to find that I have any friends left at the end of this long and isolating experience, but she is one of them. I have profited not only from her friendship, but from her considerable skills as an editor. Rosemary Adang spent part of her limited time off from teaching at Highline Community College to copy newspaper articles for me and, later, to critique a draft of the entire manuscript. Dolly Katz sheltered, fed, chauffeured, and entertained me during a research trip to the Bentley Historical Library at the University of Michigan in Ann Arbor; prodded me to hone some of my arguments; and then meticulously edited parts of the manuscript.

My interest in the history of cigarettes comes from my mother, Mary E. Haggerty, a member of what may be the Last Great Cigarette Generation, who tolerated my questions even when they made her uncomfortable. She smoked her first cigarette in 1936 and her last one in 1994, shortly before her death. In later life she was a defensive smoker, but she never lost her sense of irony or her appreciation for a good story. If the seed was planted by my mother, it was nurtured by my husband, Glenn A. Drosendahl, and daughter, Linnea Tate Rodriguez, and by the rest of my family. Individually and collectively, they have been the sustaining influences on this project, from conception to delivery.

# *Contents*

*Cigarette Wars*

# Introduction

My mother—Mary Elizabeth Haggerty—smoked her first cigarette in 1936. She was 14. It was a Kool, with a filter tip made of cork.

In more than fifty years as a smoker, she never forgot that cigarette. The occasion was her first formal dance, on the roof of a hotel in Dallas, Texas, some 400 miles from her home in the small town of Dumas. She remembered the feel and the rustle of the apple-green taffeta dress she was wearing, how the city lights looked from the roof of the hotel, the promise of adventure that seemed to hang in the night air.

She had gone to the dance with three friends, one of whom, it turned out, had relieved her parents of a pack of Kools before leaving home. The friend pulled the cigarettes from her beaded evening bag and passed them around. A group of young men stood nearby. Striving to appear uninterested, the girls casually lit up. After a minute or two, one of the boys made an observation: "You girls haven't been smoking very long, have you?" They assured him they had been smoking quite a while. "Well, you ought to learn to light the right end," he suggested. In the dim lighting on the roof, all four of the girls had managed to light their cork filters. My mother did not smoke another cigarette for some time after that.

She became a regular smoker in the early 1940s, a golden age for the cigarette, when it seemed as if "everyone" smoked. In fact, cigarettes have never been a habit of the majority in the United States. Even at the height of the Cigarette Age, in 1965, only 42 percent of American adults smoked them. However, for people like my mother—members of the generation that came of age during World War II—cigarettes were embedded in the

3

cultural landscape. They were almost everywhere: on billboards, in the movies, on the radio, in magazines and newspapers and novels. The heroes of detective novels, in particular, could scarcely move from one page to the next without searching for, taking out, lighting, inhaling deeply on, grinding out, or tossing away a cigarette. Even among nonsmokers, cigarettes were accepted as emblems of modernity and sophistication. Their place in American culture was symbolized by the president himself, Franklin D. Roosevelt, whose cigarette was as much a part of him as his confident grin.[1]

The world was one big smoking section back then. My mother remembered going to dinner parties where each place setting would include an individual ashtray with three cigarettes in it. Guests were not obligated to smoke them, but no one would dream of objecting to those who did. Certain conventions limited smoking to a degree: "nice" girls did not smoke while walking on the street; a gentleman always lit a lady's cigarette before his own; it was bad form to smoke in elevators; smokers always sought permission ("Mind if I smoke?") before lighting up. Still, there were few places where smoking was not permitted. College students smoked in classrooms; passengers smoked on airplanes (some airlines even provided complimentary cigarettes); patients smoked in their hospital beds; broadcasters smoked on television.

By the time my mother was smoking her last cigarettes, shortly before her death in 1994, she was part of a shrunken and increasingly troubled minority. The number of smokers in the adult population had dropped to about 25 percent, and nonsmokers were becoming ever more assertive in defending their rights to breathe unpolluted air. There seemed to be only two kinds of smokers left: the young and defiant, and the old and defensive. They retreated to the back of the plane, to the back stairs at the office, to the back porch at the dinner party—and then found even some of those venues closed to them. My mother stopped traveling by air after smoking was banned on domestic flights. When she went to a dinner party, if the hostess provided any sort of ashtray at all, it was likely to be a tuna can, outside.

Cigarette smokers encountered just as much hostility a century ago. Respectable men smoked pipes or cigars; respectable women did not smoke at all. The cigarette was new, in a society that had not yet come to value novelty for the sake of novelty; it was associated with immigrants, in a xenophobic age; it seemed to be habit-forming, at a time of growing concern about addictive drugs; its suffix implied either femininity, when women were not supposed to smoke, or effeminacy, which was even worse. The ethos of middle-class America condemned the sensuous and suspected the foreign. The cigarette represented both.

Cigarettes were legally restricted as well as socially stigmatized. Between 1890 and 1930, fifteen states enacted laws to ban their sale, manufacture, possession, or use, and no fewer than twenty-two other states and territories considered such legislation. By 1920, minors could legally buy cigarettes only in Virginia and Rhode Island. Many municipalities imposed further restrictions, from making it illegal for women to smoke in public, to outlawing smoking in or around school buildings, to banning certain kinds of advertising. Cigarette smokers faced discrimination in the court-room, in the workplace, and in daily life. In 1904, for example, a New York judge ordered a woman to jail for thirty days for smoking in front of her children. A few years later, a Seattle woman won a divorce on the grounds that her husband was "a cigarette fiend." A New York woman took the precaution of requiring her fiancé to sign a prenuptial agreement promising never to smoke cigarettes (he also agreed to be kind to his mother-in-law and to beat the carpets every spring without grumbling).[2]

Many companies, large and small, refused to hire cigarette smokers. Workers who indulged even on their own time could lose their jobs. When a rural Washington school board found out that one of its teachers had been smoking in the school yard after class, it fired him; the teacher sued for reinstatement but lost. Likewise, a teacher in Secaucus, New Jersey, failed to get her job back after she was fired for cigarette smoking in 1923, despite an appeal that reached the state supreme court.[3]

Congress rejected several petitions to prohibit cigarettes at the federal level, but in 1892 the Senate Committee on Epidemic Diseases agreed that they were a public health hazard and urged the petitioners to seek remedies from the states. Although a number of lower courts held that anti-cigarette laws were unconstitutional, the United States Supreme Court affirmed their validity in an important decision involving a Tennessee statute at the turn of the century. Decades before the surgeon general began labeling ciga-rettes as hazardous to health, an anti-cigarette activist proposed that each package be stamped with the word "poison" in capital letters above a skull and crossbones. The Food and Drug Administration was first petitioned to investigate the content of cigarettes in 1912. In the court of public opinion, a cigarette suggested either insipidity, insolvency, or depravity. It was at best "a miserable apology for a manly pleasure." The *New York World* could offer no greater insult to the young Theodore Roosevelt than to describe his followers as the sort who smoked cigarettes. No other form of tobacco attracted such sanctions, legal or social.[4]

This book tells the story of how America overcame its initial qualms and embraced the cigarette, despite the determined efforts of such influ-ential reformers as Frances Willard, president of the Woman's Christian Temperance Union; David Starr Jordan, first president of Stanford Univer-sity; and Harvey W. Wiley, author of the Pure Food and Drugs Act of 1906. It examines the dimensions and context of the first anti-cigarette crusade, assesses the degree to which it succeeded, analyzes the reasons for its eventual failure, and suggests some lessons that might be learned from it. Previous writers, when they have taken any notice of this cam-paign at all, have generally dismissed it as the work of a few crackpots firing from the lunatic fringe. The legislative record alone shows that it was far more important politically than has been recognized. In promoting their cause, the first generation of anti-cigarette crusaders articulated virtually every issue that is still being debated about smoking today. Theirs was not a failure of rhetoric or determination, but of timing.

The underlying premise of this book is that patterns of tobacco use are influenced less by physiology than by culture. The presence of an addictive psychoactive substance (nicotine) in cigarettes is clearly part of their appeal. It was also an important element in the development of opposition to them. Early reformers described nicotine as both poisonous and enslaving. Although they did not understand the precise mechanisms of cigarette addiction, they intuitively recognized the effects. Simple observation suggested that cigarette smokers were more dependent on their habit than were users of other tobacco products. Even so, one of the most striking things about cigarettes is not that they have addictive properties, but that social status has always been the single most important determinant of who smokes them and who does not.

Until the era of World War I, cigarette smoking was largely confined to the fringes of American society. It was most common among recent immigrants, especially those from southern and eastern Europe; working class, single men; self-assertive youth; women of the demimonde; and members of the avant-garde, of both sexes. The habit spread into the middle classes after the war and then, beginning in the mid-1960s, slowly receded. By the 1990s, for every person in the United States who was still smoking, there was one who had quit; and blue-collar workers with less than a high school education were far more likely to smoke than college-educated professionals. If behavior were governed strictly by physiology, socioeconomic patterns would not figure so largely in the history of cigarettes.[5]

War, luck, feminism, and a few notable individuals all play a part in this story. It begins with James B. Duke, founder of the American Tobacco Company. It was Duke who, in 1885, obtained the rights to a cigarette-making machine and then proved both that the machine was workable and that people would buy what it produced. As the young industry expanded, it encountered growing opposition from religious leaders, temperance workers, health reformers, businessmen, educators, eugenicists, club women, and even a few traditional tobacconists (who resented the competition). Duke himself began to wonder if his fledgling enterprise would be strangled in its infancy.

Anti-cigarette sentiment continued to build during the Progressive Era—roughly comprising the first two decades of the twentieth century—when the spirit of reform flourished to a degree that would not be matched until the 1960s and 70s. The industry's key challenger during this period was Lucy Page Gaston, founder of the Anti-Cigarette League of America, who maintained that cigarette smoking was a dangerous new habit, particularly threatening to the young, likely to lead to the use of alcohol and narcotics, and thus part of a social miasma that included gambling, crime, and prostitution. If this argument seems extreme, it should be remembered that cigarettes became widely available at a time of expanding awareness of the interlocking nature of social problems. By halting the advance of what Henry Ford called "the little white slaver," the reformers hoped to promote the health, morality, and productivity of society as a whole.[6]

Support for the cause was broad but shallow, and it collapsed during World War I. The United States entered the war in April 1917 under the banner of moral reform. Its leaders were determined to "make the world safe for democracy" with a "clean" army—meaning one that was untainted by alcohol or prostitution. Many organizations that had once been hostile to cigarettes (including the Young Men's Christian Association and the Salvation Army) reluctantly accepted them as allies in the battle against greater sins. They actually encouraged soldiers to smoke them, in the interest of chastity and sobriety. Men who were offered the comfort of a cigarette, it was argued, would be less likely to seek more harmful diversions. Congress included cigarettes in the rations issued to soldiers overseas and it subsidized their sale at post exchange stores at home and abroad. People from all walks of life contributed to private "smokes for soldiers" funds. Those who protested found their patriotism questioned.

The amount of tobacco consumed in the form of cigarettes rose from less than 2 percent in 1900 to 40 percent by 1930. Many writers have attributed this growth to the influence of national advertising. Manufacturers themselves had faith in advertising, as reflected by the increasing amount of money they devoted to it. Duke once said that if manufacturers would simply advertise extensively enough, they could make smokers out of all Americans. Historian Allan M. Brandt has suggested that advertising helped change the belief system of the American middle class, from one that condemned pleasure seeking and self-indulgence to one in which pleasure was sought after ("Indulge yourself with a Lucky"). Advertising may have made cigarettes more acceptable simply by making them appear to be more commonplace. A person smoking a cigarette was once unusual enough to excite comment (invariably censorious) even in urban centers. By the late 1920s, images of smokers in newspapers and magazines and on billboards and posters were inescapable, from the smallest towns to the biggest cities. Still, these are indirect, secondary influences; in themselves, they do not account for the swift advance of the cigarette after the war.[7]

In fact, the war itself was far more significant than advertising or any other factor in promoting cigarettes and undermining the campaign against their use. Millions of American soldiers smoked cigarettes during the war, at the behest of their government and fellow citizens. This alone helped erode the unsavory images that had limited the acceptability of cigarettes in the past. Even nonsmokers began to connect them with positive virtues, such as freedom, democracy, and modernity. In addition, the war accelerated certain social changes that favored increased cigarette smoking, including urbanization and broader economic opportunities, especially for women.

Women were the fastest growing segment of the cigarette market after the war, and also the focus of a final rally by the demoralized anti-smoking forces. Many people who were willing to accept cigarettes when smoked by men were still deeply offended by the habit in women, even though tobacco use had not been uncommon among women earlier in American history. Foes of the cigarette regrouped in the early postwar period in an effort to save female smokers from themselves. Theirs was a quixotic, rear-guard action that ignored both historical precedent and the feminism of the day.

Although many Americans remained ambivalent about cigarettes in the late 1920s, particularly when it came to their use by women, organized opposition was clearly on the wane. Yet at the same time, the seeds were being planted for a new, more vigorous, and ultimately more effective campaign. After years of disinterest, medical researchers began to give serious attention to the effects of smoking on health. Their work attracted little notice initially, but it led to the eventual revival of the anti-cigarette movement.

The early opposition to cigarettes was first spawned and then undercut by the reform impulses of the Progressive Era. Cigarette smoking was a sensual indulgence that became an addiction, and thus clashed with the progressives' admiration for the rational control of merely physical appetites. In addition, the first significant groups to smoke machine-made cigarettes in the United States were immigrants living in cities. Daring members of the upper classes smoked expensive hand-rolled brands. Progressives tended to view with nearly equal suspicion the habits of the foreign-born, the wealthy, and the citified.

However, it is an oversimplification to see the first anti-cigarette movement as simply an exercise in social control by people seeking to return to an idealized past. It was, instead, the result of a contradictory mix of religious fundamentalism, social progressivism, a search for efficiency, and a conviction that human behavior could be governed by the force of law and the weight of public opinion. While it was led by evangelical Christians and driven by concerns about morality, it was not divorced from issues of health (with the notable exception of lung cancer, which was largely unknown until the early 1920s). Early reformers identified cigarettes as a cause of virtually every health problem now linked to smoking, including heart disease and emphysema.

Likewise, the current campaign against smoking, while ostensibly more concerned with public health than private rectitude, remains entangled in moralism. Anti-smoking activists today speak of the need to wage "war" against the "merchants of death" who have brought about "the tobaccoism holocaust." They use militaristic terms, pressing for "victory" in the "battle" against their opponents. This is the classic language of moral reform.[8]

The first generation of cigarette activists differed from their successors primarily in the matter of emphasis. They gave more attention to state legislation than to federal regulation; they concentrated on saving individual smokers rather than protecting the rights of nonsmokers; and their rhetoric was focused on morality more than health. Like the current reformers, they attempted to use the power of government to institutionalize their objections to cigarettes; to a limited degree, they succeeded. However, in advancing their case, they made claims they could not support, such as this one from a 1913 tract published in Virginia: "Babies have been killed by inhaling the nicotine expelled from the cigarette, or from the lungs of a cigarette smoking father; and many infants not actually killed have been seriously injured for life—and often their mothers become sickly from inhaling cigarette fumes." In this and many other instances, they anticipated arguments that would be made later. But they spoke from a platform braced more by speculation than by science, in a world that increasingly put its faith in science.[9]

Today, the pursuit of health has become something of a national obsession, and physicians and scientists carry the kind of authority once reserved for religious leaders. Few weeks go by without yet another report on the hazards of cigarettes or yet another restriction on their sale, advertising, or use. Courts have denied custody of children to parents who smoke; in some companies, workers who smoke, on or off the job, risk being fired. Less concrete but perhaps more telling is the symbolism attached to the cigarette. For much of middle-class America, it has become a social liability. As the humorist Garrison Keillor put it, "When a man lights up a cigarette in America these days, people look at him as if he had spit on the floor, or stuck a pin in his cheek, or pulled out a dead rat and started chewing on it. They back off and look away and try not to stare at the long black tail hanging from his mouth."[10]

Middle-class America took up cigarettes around the time of World War I and then, after the Vietnam War, began to put them down again. Even more remarkably, the nonsmoking majority began to withdraw its consent to smoking. In the late nineteenth century, people who did not smoke cigarettes regarded those who did as weak, addicted degenerates. Later, even nonsmokers associated cigarettes with glamour and sophistication. Now cigarettes have been restigmatized; once again, they are identified with weakness and addiction. The answer to the question "Mind if I smoke?" is likely to be "Yes."

My mother groused about the degree to which her smoking had made her an outcast late in her life, but she appreciated the irony. She remembered that her father (a pipe smoker) had expressed doubts about the masculinity of any man and the virtue of any woman who smoked cigarettes. He told her that "coffin nails" were bad for her health; that they would "hook" her; and that lots of people would not hire her if she smoked them. "So it's not as if we haven't heard all this before," she said.

Hostility to cigarettes has been strongest during periods of economic uncertainty. A century ago, the upheaval came from a massive influx of immigrants and a shift from agriculture to industry as the basis of the economy. Today, the shift is from industry to information and service; it is accompanied by another wave of immigration. Cigarettes may catch the eye of the reform-minded in part because they appear to be more manageable than other problems. As one commentator pointed out a few years ago, "The mannerly middle class may not be able to outlaw assault weapons or rap music or violent movies, but it can shove smokers (usually the working class, the minorities and the young) into the pariah class, right next to the serial killers." A cigarette is more than just a smoke: it is an important symbol, deeply entwined in much larger social issues. That was as true during the first anti-cigarette campaign as it is today.[11]

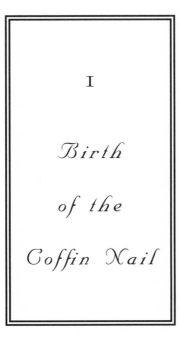

I

*Birth*

*of the*

*Coffin Nail*

With new devices for dissipation,
new means are required for reform.
*Nelson Sizer (1883)*[1]

*J*ames Buchanan "Buck" Duke, father of the modern cigarette industry, detested cigarettes himself. He never smoked them, and he refused
to permit any women in his family to smoke them. As a young man, he
preferred chewing tobacco. Later in life, in concession to his position as
one of the richest men in America, he took up cigars. The larger-than-life
bronze statue that honors his memory at Duke University in his hometown
of Durham, North Carolina, depicts him with a cigar in his hand, not a
cigarette.[2]

Nevertheless, in 1881, Duke bet his future on the cigarette, a lowly,
disreputable product few of his contemporaries would have expected to
become either socially acceptable or commercially successful. Americans
chewed far more tobacco than they smoked, and the amount they smoked
in the form of cigarettes was negligible. Even snuff—never more than a
minor part of the tobacco industry in the United States—was more popular
with Americans than cigarettes. Chewing tobacco accounted for about 58
percent of the total quantity of tobacco consumed in the United States in
1880; pipes and cigars, about 19 percent each; snuff, less than 3 percent;
and cigarettes, barely 1 percent. Cigarettes were oddities, rarely seen outside a few eastern cities, smoked by people who were considered morally

suspect for one reason or another. The *New York Times* summed up the prevailing attitudes when it warned, in 1884, that "[t]he decadence of Spain began when the Spaniards adopted cigarettes, and if this pernicious practice obtains among adult Americans the ruin of the Republic is close at hand."[3]

As Duke remembered it later, a key factor in his decision was a bill pending in Congress to reduce the federal cigarette tax from $1.75 per thousand to 50 cents. The bill was introduced as a measure to cut the revenue surplus then bedeviling the government. Duke recognized that its passage would greatly reduce the cost of manufacturing cigarettes, making such a venture more profitable. As a further incentive, the Duke family's pipe tobacco business was making few inroads against its competitors. The market leader was W. T. Blackwell and Company, also based in Durham, manufacturers of the famed "Bull Durham" tobacco. The Dukes seemed doomed to sit in the shadow of the Durham Bull, symbol of the competing brand. "My company is up against a stone wall," Duke reportedly said. "Something has to be done and quick. As for me, I am going into the cigarette business."[4]

Cigarettes of sorts date back to the Aztecs and the Mayas, who smoked tobacco in hollow reeds, corn husks, leaves, or, less commonly, paper. Members of a Spanish expedition to Mexico in 1518 reported being offered "a small cane lit at one end, which are so made that after they are kindled, they are consumed gradually without giving out a flame." In seventeenth-century Spain, poor people smoked crude cigarettes made from cigar butts and scrap tobacco. These "beggar's smokes" eventually spread to Portugal, Italy, and southern Russia. Later, paper cigarettes made by hand from choice tobaccos gained favor among the upper classes in southern and eastern Europe. The Crimean War (1853–56) introduced thousands of British soldiers to the cigarettes smoked by their Russian enemies and Turkish allies. Britain's Prince of Wales (later King Edward VII) took up the habit in the 1880s, giving it an aura of glamour in England.[5]

In the United States, however, cigarettes were relatively unknown, and what notice they did attract was largely negative. One of the first published references came in an anti-tobacco tract written in 1854 by Dr. Russell T. Trall, a noted temperance and health reformer, who reported with disgust that a few "ladies" in New York City were "aping the silly ways of some pseudo-accomplished foreigners, in smoking Tobacco through a weaker and more *feminine* article which has been most delicately denominated *cigarette*." Shortly after the Civil War, in the first recorded mention of a cigarette in the tobacco-growing regions of the South, a prominent Virginian named Samuel Schooler reported that he had seen "Capt. H——d. Knew he did not belong about here—he was smoking a cigarette wh: is unheard of in these parts—."[6]

The earliest American-made cigarettes were produced by hand by a predominantly immigrant labor force working in rudimentary factories in New York City. They were common enough by 1864 that the federal government began to tax them. Still, tax records show that fewer than half a billion were manufactured in 1880. An inventory from a general store in Dayton, in the eastern part of the Washington Territory, demonstrates the relative position of cigarettes compared to other tobacco products around the time that Duke entered the business. The store's stock included 179 boxes of cigars; 188 boxes of pipe tobacco; so much plug (or chewing) tobacco that the enumerator did not bother to count it; and only ten boxes of cigarettes.[7]

Given their relatively insignificant share of the American tobacco market, cigarettes attracted a surprising degree of antagonism. In 1892, the Woman's Christian Temperance Union (WCTU) organized the first of several nationwide petition drives to convince Congress to outlaw their sale, manufacture, and importation. The Senate Committee on Epidemic Diseases responded sympathetically, saying it was "satisfied that the cigarette is an evil," but concluding that Congress had no constitutional power to intervene within the borders of individual states. However, if the petitioners could convince enough state legislatures to ban cigarettes, "the committee ventures to express the opinion and the hope" that Congress would prohibit all imports, along with manufacturing and sale in the District of Columbia and in the territories. By 1900, four states (Washington, North Dakota, Iowa, and Tennessee) had passed such laws, and at least twelve others had considered doing so.[8]

The legislative activity suggests that public attitudes were hardening, as does the proliferation of denigrating slang for cigarettes: coffin nails, dope sticks, devil's toothpicks, Satan sticks, coffin pills, joy pills, little white devils, and so forth—epithets associated with either death or immorality. No other form of tobacco encountered such hostility. The reasons for this are deeply rooted in the social, political, and economic currents of the Gilded Age. Duke was searching for a simple business opportunity, but what he found was a focal point for concerns about health, morality, and the very shape of American society.

In 1881, when Duke started making cigarettes, he was twenty-four years old; tall and ruddy, and innocent of higher education except for a six-month term at a business college in Poughkeepsie, New York. He was known as someone who worked hard but was not averse to enjoying himself, particularly when it came to women. According to one perhaps apocryphal story, a family member once took him aside and scolded him about an alleged liaison with a particularly notorious paramour, saying, "That woman has slept with every man in Durham." Duke reportedly thought for a moment and then replied, "Well, Durham's not such a big town."[9]

Duke began working in the family tobacco manufacturing business (established by his father, Washington Duke, after the Civil War) when he was, in his father's words, "a little bit of a fellow, just big enough to put a bridle on a horse." He was put in charge of production when he was only fourteen. A studio photograph from this period presents him as a serious-looking young man, gazing into the distance, a cowlick at the back of his head defying the obviously firm hand that had slicked down the rest of his hair. By 1878, when the business was incorporated as W. Duke, Sons, and Company, he was supervising both production and sales. When his father retired in 1880, Duke became president of the company, in partnership with his two older brothers and two outside businessmen.[10]

Duke did not leave much of a paper trail. As a businessman, he had a penchant for secrecy, often communicating in code. He may have been self-conscious about his rudimentary writing skills (although he was far from being the illiterate boob depicted in a posthumous profile in H. L. Mencken's *American Mercury*). Very few of his personal letters are known to survive. But one of them, written to his brother, Benjamin N. Duke, during an extended trip to Tennessee to "drum up the trade" right after he took over the family business, offers revealing glimpses of the man who would soon come to dominate the cigarette industry. It shows him to be diligent and shrewd in business matters, and a bit of a rake in his personal life.[11]

Duke reported that he was "very much discouraged" by the results of the trip to date, and he vowed to "put in some very hard work from now until I reach home." He had "studdied up" a new way to process tobacco, by drying it thoroughly and then dipping the leaves in rum, which he hoped would "make it smoke sweet and uniform." He told his brother that the tobacco "must be doctored in some way" to make it sell more rapidly.

Duke was not solely occupied with business during this trip. About half of the long letter is given over to the hijinks he enjoyed during a three-day visit at the home of his uncle in Milan, Tennessee. The gathering included several young female cousins and their friends, among them "the liveliest girl I think God ever put breath in." There was plenty of wine, which "kept the crowd jolly all the time" (and would have dismayed his teetotaling, Methodist father had he known about it). As a lark one day, Duke passed out "Ciggarretts" to everyone, commenting, "It was a big sight to behold." It is clear from the context that Duke regarded cigarettes as something of a joke in 1880—good for a laugh, but not much more.[12]

His attitude began to change the next year, when Congress began debate on the bill to cut the cigarette tax. Expecting the bill to pass and thereby reduce the cost of doing business, Duke hired 100 skilled cigarette-rollers from New York City (most of them recent Jewish immigrants from eastern Europe) and set them to work in a factory in Durham. Total production for that first year was under one million cigarettes. Even so, Duke had some trouble selling them. As he recalled later, "our brands were not in public favor." The company accumulated such a backlog of unsold cigarettes that it temporarily closed the factory. Prospects looked grim until March 1883, when Congress approved the long-debated tax reduction. Duke immediately cut the price of his cigarettes in half (from ten cents to five for a package of ten). This "gave us an immediate big market for the goods." He sold them at a loss for several months, but he secured a foothold in the market.[13]

Duke's cigarettes were not only cheaper than competing brands, they were easier to smoke. When he entered the business, it was dominated by brands made with strong Turkish tobaccos. Duke used the milder tobacco grown in North Carolina and Virginia. A new method of curing the domestic leaf, developed as early as 1810 but not widely used until the 1870s, enhanced its inherent mildness. The process involved drying the tobacco with indirect heat from flues run through storage barns. Flue curing changed the biochemistry of the leaf, making its smoke slightly acidic and therefore easier to inhale than the alkaline smoke produced through older methods.[14]

Duke further revolutionized the industry by mechanizing it. Although several cigarette-making machines had been developed in the early 1880s, major manufacturers had shown little interest in them. Consumers had firmly rejected machine-made cigars, and the conventional wisdom held that they would also reject machine-made cigarettes. In addition, the early machines were troublesome: they jammed frequently and produced cigarettes of uneven quality even when they were working more or less properly. As Duke put it, other manufacturers "could not make them go and they were also afraid that . . . the public would be prejudiced against cigarettes made on the machines."[15]

The Promethean spark that gave life to the modern cigarette industry was a machine invented by a Virginian named James A. Bonsack. In the spring of 1884, Duke installed one of Bonsack's creations at his factory in Durham. Theoretically, the machine was capable of producing as many cigarettes in one day as forty-eight skilled hand-rollers. In practice, its performance was sporadic and imperfect. Correspondence between W. Duke, Sons, and Company and the Bonsack Machine Company indicates that the problems persisted for several years. Nonetheless, in 1885 Duke demonstrated his faith in the machines by negotiating a contract that gave him almost exclusive use of this new technology during a critical period.[16]

Mechanization remained a gamble, however, and he and his partners hedged their bets by expanding their labor force. By 1885, W. Duke, Sons, and Company employed about 500 hand-rollers at its factory in Durham and another 200 to 300 at a recently opened factory in New York City. The next year, the company advertised in Durham for "[f]ive hundred white boys and girls, from 14 to 21 years of age to learn cigarette making. The work is light and very profitable to those who are willing to apply themselves diligently." In the race-conscious South, a manufacturer already concerned about the image of his product would not have risked further censure by producing it with a racially mixed labor force.[17]

As the mechanical problems were resolved, the major vexation for Duke and his partners was Bonsack's failure to supply as many machines as they wanted. "Our trade is suffering on account of our inability to turn out goods fast enough to meet the increased demand for our cigarettes," Duke's brother Benjamin, vice president of the company, complained in 1886. Duke added new brands to his lineup (most notably Cameo, Cross

Cut, and Duke's Best) and hired an aggressive sales force to peddle them all over the country. Duke himself promoted his goods to jobbers and retailers in the New York market. By the summer of 1886, D. B. Strouse, president of the Bonsack company, was crowing, "Your house has a success without a parallel in this country, and all due to the use of our machines!"[18]

Duke's nearly exclusive rights to a workable cigarette-making machine gave him the leverage to dominate the industry. Later, while unsuccessfully defending himself against charges of violating the Sherman Anti-Trust Act, he blandly denied that he had attempted to limit distribution of the machine. However, his surviving correspondence with the Bonsack company proves otherwise. In 1885, the company agreed not to place any additional machines with any other manufacturer and to remove any existing machines as soon as possible. Duke worked assiduously over the years to hold Bonsack to these terms. He not only insisted that the company not provide any of its machines to any of his competitors in the United States, he also objected to Bonsack's efforts to do business with overseas manufacturers. Meanwhile, he steadily added new machines, exponentially increasing production.[19]

Without mechanization, the cigarette could never have been more than an inconsequential part of the tobacco business. The machines reduced the costs of production, keeping prices low. They also made it possible to supply a mass market. Access to this market was aided by the thickening network of railroad lines linking Durham to the rest of the country. The number of major lines serving Durham quadrupled between 1885 and 1890, due in no small part to lobbying and financial support from the Dukes. This allowed the company to open more channels of distribution, assuring that potential consumers could see Duke cigarettes in retail outlets all over the country.[20]

By 1889, W. Duke, Sons, and Company was the largest cigarette manufacturer in the United States, producing nearly as much as all its competitors combined. The next year, Duke convinced his four major rivals to join him in organizing the American Tobacco Company, with himself as president. The move gave him control of more than 90 percent of the industry. Duke had envisioned "a concentration of the business" as early as 1885; evidently, it had taken more time and effort than he initially expected. Asked about his motives in organizing what quickly became known as the Tobacco Trust, he said, simply, "I thought we could make more money and handle the business to better advantage by establishing a larger concern."[21]

For a young industry, producing an inexpensive product with a slim margin of profit, the trust offered considerable advantages. Like Andrew Carnegie, whom he greatly admired, Duke attempted to integrate his monopoly vertically; that is, to control the sources of essential raw materials, from tobacco to paper to pasteboard. Agents for the trust bought leaf tobacco directly from the farmers at auction ("Sold American!"), bypassing the leaf dealers. This created some enemies but kept prices down. Monopoly control also put an end to the ruinous price wars that had lowered profits for both manufacturers and retailers in the mid-1880s.[22]

By 1890, the cigarette industry was poised for tremendous growth. Mechanization had brought nearly unlimited capacity for production. The trust had "rationalized" the industry (as the economists put it), improving efficiency. The continuing flood of immigration, much of it from countries where cigarettes were already popular (such as Italy, Spain, and Russia), helped enlarge the potential market. The expansion of railroads in the South made it possible for Duke to supply that market.

Additionally, the rapid urbanization of the late nineteenth century gave cigarettes advantages over other forms of tobacco, particularly chewing tobacco. Once so ubiquitous that European visitors suggested the spittoon replace the eagle as the national emblem, chewing tobacco had few friends in urban areas. It was a relic of the time when an American "could stand in his doorway, bite his morning 'chaw' and spit eighteen feet without trespassing on his neighbor." Frances M. Trollope, the English travel writer (and mother of novelist Anthony Trollope), was appalled by the "incessant, remorseless spitting" she observed during an extended visit to the United States in the 1820s. "The air of heaven is not in more general use among the men of America than chewing tobacco," she wrote. Charles Dickens left Iowa in the 1840s convinced that frontiersmen were so addicted to chewing tobacco that "they expectorate in dreams." By 1890, however, more than a third of the American population was living in cities. Urban standards of hygiene and decorum discouraged spitting, a necessary adjunct to tobacco chewing. The market for "chaw" began to decline, leaving an opening for something new.[23]

The perfection of inexpensive, safe, reliable matches also helped promote cigarettes. Early matches, made by dipping a thin piece of wood into melted sulfur, could only be lighted by sparks created by striking a flint against a piece of steel. Friction matches ("Lucifers"), invented in England in 1827, were somewhat easier to light, but they were coated with poisonous white phosphorous, creating problems both for the workers involved in their manufacture and for any consumers who inhaled their residue. Few smokers used them to light tobacco. Nonpoisonous "safety matches" were developed in the late 1860s, but they were unstable—sometimes exploding with a shower of sparks, endangering clothing and any other flammable material within reach. Cardboard matches, tucked into small paper matchbooks (similar to those in use today) were invented in 1892. They allowed smokers to light up easily and safely, anytime, anyplace. This helped transform the act of smoking from deliberate action to almost unconscious habit.[24]

For Duke, all that was lacking was widespread public acceptance of his product, and that proved harder to secure than he may have expected. Although cigarette production doubled between 1880 and 1885 (from about 500 million to 1 billion a year), and then doubled again by 1890,

Americans still overwhelmingly preferred other forms of tobacco. Further-more, the industry's very success in increasing production brought it to the attention of reformers. The American Tobacco Company was a mo-nopoly, operating at a time of growing concern about monopolies; man-ufacturing a morally suspect product, in an era of moral rectitude. This was the stage for a cultural conflict whose outcome would remain in doubt for nearly thirty years.

The cigarette was a tempting target in part because it was new to the American market and thus less entrenched than other tobacco products. Indeed, some of the most vigorous opponents of cigarettes were themselves users of tobacco in other forms. For example, Thomas A. Edison—who believed cigarettes were poisonous and refused to hire anyone who smoked them—smoked ten to twenty cigars a day. The author of a 1903 bill to ban the sale of cigarettes in Washington State was an incessant cigar smoker who once started a fire in a hotel room by gesturing too freely with a match. The organizer of an anti-cigarette group in New York City was a dedicated pipe smoker.[25]

In addition to being new, the cigarette suffered from its associations. The first significant consumers of machine-made cigarettes in the United States were immigrants from southern and eastern Europe, where cigarette smoking was already common. Cigarettes were popular with such immi-grants because they were both familiar and cheap. In the 1890s, a nickel could buy a box of ten cigarettes: the price of one cigar. New York City alone—with its large foreign-born population—accounted for 25 percent of the cigarettes sold in 1895. To middle-class Americans of Anglo-Saxon heritage, cigarette smoking was just one more discomfiting habit of the newcomers who began crowding into the nation's cities in the late nine-teenth century. One reformer described it as "an infection from inferior breeds of people." John L. Sullivan, Boston-born prizefighter and occasional social commentator, once observed, "It's the Dutchmen, Italians, Russians, Turks and Egyptians who smoke cigarettes and they're no good any-how."[26]

The cigarette market in the 1890s was divided into two tiers. At the bottom were the cheap machine-made brands, manufactured with domes-tic tobacco and sold mostly to the working classes. Imported, hand-rolled brands and those made with a high percentage of Turkish tobacco were more expensive; they appealed to adventurous members of what writer Stephen Crane called "the kid-gloved" set. For some of the rich, the ciga-rette was an expression of distance from middle-class morality. In Crane's novel *Maggie: A Girl of the Streets*, published in 1893, the only cigarette-smoking character is a wealthy young man "with a sublime air . . . and a look of ennui," who ventures into the Bowery in hopes of meeting a woman of indifferent virtue. The hosts of one fashionable party in New York City in the 1890s offered their guests cigarettes wrapped in hundred-dollar bills. Middle-class Americans in the xenophobic hinterland found the habits of the wealthy nearly as disturbing as those of the foreign-born. "The doings of the rich and fashionable should not be aped too closely," warned Edward Hyatt, superintendent of public instruction in California in the early 1900s. "When all is said, they do not as a class represent the best of American manhood and womanhood, and the taking up of one of their bad habits will not raise poor people to their material station in life."[27]

The case against cigarettes included the charge that they were unhealthy, even fatal. Newspapers published stories with headlines such as "CIGARETTES KILLED HIM" and "CIGARETTE FIEND DIES." Both lay-people and physicians understood that tobacco smoke contains nicotine, an alkaloid first isolated in 1828. Although they did not specifically recognize its addictive properties, they regarded nicotine as highly poisonous. As early as 1879, the *New York Times* reported that science had proven "the disastrous effects of nicotine upon the human system." Even defenders of tobacco believed nicotine could be dangerous. The author of one handbook for smokers, while mocking the reformers' penchant for grisly tales about nicotine-induced deaths, also recommended a detailed regime to reduce exposure to the substance. Many commentators speculated that cigarette smokers absorbed more nicotine than users of other forms of tobacco because they were more likely to inhale. "The 'accomplished' cigarette smoker," one writer explained, "draws the smoke into the depths of his lungs, holds it there a moment, and then expels it though his mouth and nose. The poison is thus allowed to penetrate to every portion of the lung cavity, and, by absorption, is taken into the blood." According to another school of thought, the paper used in making cigarettes prevented the evaporation of nicotine, leaving the "poison" to flow into the smoker's body instead of burning off harmlessly.[28]

Concerns about nicotine led to the marketing of several filtered cigarette brands in the 1880s and 1890s. Among the more unusual were Dr. Scott's Electric Cigarettes, which were advertised as being both safe and self-lighting ("NO MATCHES REQUIRED; THEY LIGHT ON THE BOX"). The manufacturer promised that "[n]o Nicotine can be taken into the system while smoking these Cigarettes, as in the mouth-piece of each is placed a small wad of absorbent cotton, which strains and eliminates the injurious qualities from the smoke." Later, various scientists and entrepreneurs tried to develop nicotine-free tobacco. Notwithstanding the lack of scientific evidence, there was a sense of popular wisdom that cigarettes were not conducive to health, as indicated by the fact that they were commonly known as "coffin nails."[29]

However, the people who waged war against cigarette smoking a century ago were not primarily concerned with its effects on health. After all, relatively few people smoked cigarettes, and those who did tended to be on the social borderlines. The critics were far more concerned about issues involving morality. Thus, a New Jersey doctor, in a letter to the *New York*

*Times*, could report in all earnestness that cigarette smoking "increases sexual propensities and leads to secret practices" (meaning masturbation), an effect he clearly thought was more serious than its tendency to cause "disorders of the heart."[30]

Anti-cigarette sentiment was fed, instead, by broader social and political forces. The depressions of the 1870s and 1890s; the violent confrontations between labor and management; the enormous increase in immigration from non-Protestant, non-English-speaking regions of the world; the shift of political and cultural power from the countryside to the city; the increasing gap between the wealthy and the poor: all these factors produced an undercurrent of uneasiness that reverberated throughout the Gilded Age and into the Progressive Era. Most middle-class Americans were aware that the world was changing. The cigarette provided a convenient focus for anxiety about those changes.

Part of the framework for the opposition to cigarettes was provided by the tenets of Social Darwinism, which were deeply implanted in middle-class culture by the late nineteenth century. As interpreted by writers such as Josiah Strong, a Congregationalist minister and author of the best-selling *Our Country* (1885), Charles Darwin's theory about the "survival of the fittest" proved that Americans of white, Anglo-Saxon, Protestant heritage were destined to rule the world. Strong claimed that Anglo-Saxons had been "divinely commissioned" to prevail over other races. Since the United States had been settled by the most vigorous and capable of the Anglo-Saxons, it would surely become the center of Anglo-Saxon power. Despite these inherent advantages, America faced a number of perils, including the possibility that it could be "devitalized by alcohol and tobacco."[31]

Although Strong later lent his name to the Anti-Cigarette League, he did not initially single out cigarettes as being more "devitalizing" than other forms of tobacco. However, many other writers did. As evidence, they pointed to the sorry state of Spain, which had embraced cigarettes earlier and with more enthusiasm than any other country. In an era of rapid industrial growth and imperial expansion, Spain was being eclipsed by nations in which custom favored the pipe or cigar.[32]

The outcome of the Spanish-American War seemed to offer further proof of the debilitating effects of cigarette smoking. American news services quoted a member of the British Parliament as saying, flatly, that Spain had lost the war because of its national appetite for cigarettes. In publishing this story, the editor of the *Chicago Daily News* hastened to add, "The argument is, of course, directed against cigarettes, not against smoking generally." William Randolph Hearst reprinted the British report, along with the Chicago editor's comments, in an anti-cigarette tract that concluded Spain "might not have reached its present state of deterioration" if it had prohibited cigarette manufacturing "before it became a national occupation and misfortune." The tract was written by Mrs. John A. Logan, widow of a prominent Illinois politician (and Civil War hero); she called for anti-cigarette legislation to protect the United States from "the inevitable decadence" of "this monstrous vice."[33]

Middle-class attitudes toward cigarettes were also influenced by eugenics, an offshoot of Social Darwinism. The 1880 census had shown that the birthrate among Americans of Anglo-Saxon ancestry in the United States was declining. Meanwhile, nearly a million immigrants were arriving every year, most from the supposedly inferior racial stocks of southern and eastern Europe. To many opinion-shapers—educators, ministers, physicians, and others with access to communications media, from Theodore Roosevelt to Henry Ford—this population shift suggested that Americans of Anglo-Saxon heritage were on the verge of "race suicide," to use the terminology of the day.[34]

These concerns helped focus attention on the reproductive health of both men and women, but particularly on women, as the bearers of children. If Anglo-Saxons were to achieve their proper destiny, they must have larger and healthier families. Many eugenicists categorized tobacco as a "race poison," one that was especially harmful to women, whether they used it themselves or were merely exposed to the exhalations of others. This was in keeping with the Victorian assumption that the female constitution was inherently weak and thus more vulnerable to damage than the male. Anticipating arguments that would be advanced by medical science in the late twentieth century, eugenicists attacked tobacco as a cause of infertility in adults and of infirmity in any children who somehow managed to be born to tobacco-using parents.[35]

If tobacco was bad, cigarettes were worse. Dr. John Harvey Kellogg—a prominent health reformer, best remembered now for having established a breakfast-cereal dynasty—was among those who were convinced that cigarettes were eugenically disastrous. He believed they were more hazardous than other kinds of tobacco because their smoke was more likely to be inhaled and thus could cause greater damage to internal organs, including those involved in reproduction. Although Kellogg thought smoking was harmful for both sexes, he said that women had certain biological shortcomings that put them at greater risk than men. Cigarette smoking would "unsex" women by producing "premature degeneration of the sex glands." As evidence, he pointed to France, where the "feminine mustache" was "becoming noticeably more frequent" because of the prevalence of cigarette smoking among French women.[36]

Kellogg was a tireless advocate of what he called "biologic living." In addition to eugenics, its principles included temperance, vegetarianism, frequent bathing, Fletcherizing (the art of mastication), and diligent monitoring of the bowels. His base was a sanitarium founded at Battle Creek, Michigan, by Ellen White, so-called "prophetess of health" of the Seventh-Day Adventist Church. Although he held a degree from one of the better medical schools in New York, Kellogg had embraced a variety of unconventional therapies by the time he became medical director of the sanitarium in 1876. A charter member of the Race Betterment Foundation, he was one of the first to label tobacco a "race poison." He refused to allow its use in any form at the sanitarium. White herself preached that tobacco was even more sinister than alcohol.[37]

Not all of those who accepted the principles of eugenics believed that tobacco in general was harmful. For example, in his phenomenally popular novel *Looking Backward* (1888), Edward Bellamy envisioned a utopian world that had preserved "the better types of the race" but had not banished tobacco. Significantly, however, it was only the men who smoked in Bellamy's utopia, and they smoked only cigars. In the late nineteenth century, few voices were raised in defense of cigarettes, and virtually none in defense of smoking by women.[38]

Although American women did not begin to smoke cigarettes in substantial numbers until after World War I, reports about the few who did received wide circulation in the popular press. This publicity led to the perception that women were being enticed by a degenerate habit at the very time when they should be protecting the "vital force" of the Anglo-Saxon race.

Ironically, tobacco use had not been uncommon among women earlier in American history. One colonial writer reported that women "smoke in Bed, Smoke as they knead their Bread, Smoke whilst they're cooking." While that account was surely tinged with poetic license, records of colonial court proceedings in New England include numerous casual references to women smoking, with no indication that the practice was out of the ordinary. Testimony in several rape cases indicated that it was acceptable for women to smoke at their own hearths or doorsteps but not in taverns, particularly in the company of strangers. In rural areas, midwives often prescribed an analgesic pipe for women in childbirth. The pious Mary Rowlandson, wife of a Puritan minister, came to regret her fondness for tobacco and gave it up after being captured by Indians in Massachusetts in 1676. In her earlier life, "when I had taken two or three pipes, I was presently ready for another." Benjamin Ferris, a Quaker traveling in western New York 150 years later, was dismayed to find women so infected by the "tobacco plague" that "they sit smoking their pipes by the half dozen without the least attempt to conceal it, or the least apparent sense of its indelicacy."[39]

Smoking by women may have been even more common in the South. Archaeologists have found tobacco pipes specifically designed for women at Martin's Hundred, a settlement on the James River near Williamsburg, Virginia, that was founded in 1619. Durand de Dauphine, a French Huguenot traveling in Virginia and Maryland in 1686, noticed women smoking everywhere, even in church. Anecdotal evidence suggests that southern women held on to their pipes long after their northern sisters gave them up. Tobacco was found at all levels of female society in the antebellum South, from the backwoods to the White House. The wives of Presidents Andrew Jackson and Zachary Taylor were both ardent pipe smokers. Dolley Madison also enjoyed an occasional pipe, although she preferred snuff and often used it publicly during her tenure as First Lady. The diary of Gertrude Clanton Thomas, born into the planter class in Georgia and a charter member of the WCTU in Augusta, suggests she was accustomed to smoking a cigar after dinner. W. S. Kimball, a Wyoming pioneer, vividly recalled "many good women" who smoked corncob or clay pipes in his native Kentucky during the Civil War era.[40]

In Victorian America, however, respectable women did not smoke, and respectable men did not smoke in their presence. The spheres occupied by men and women had diverged, at least among the middle and upper classes. With the advance of industrialization, the center of production shifted from the family to the factory. Women acquired new social roles, replacing older economic functions. The "canon of domesticity" made them the guardians of public and private morality and the inculcators of values in the young. It would not do to have the fingers on the hand that rocked the cradle be yellowed with tar and nicotine.[41]

Tobacco was one of the markers that separated the morally superior world of women from the earthy world of men. In her 1889 autobiography, Frances Willard—the guiding force behind the WCTU—called tobacco a "fleshly indulgence" that lured men away from the elevating society of women. "Drink and tobacco are today the great separatists between women and men," she wrote. "Once they used these things together, but woman's evolution has carried her beyond them; man will climb to the same level some day, but meanwhile he thinks he must have his dinners from which woman is excluded and his club-house with whose delights she intermeddleth not." Women could indulge themselves only by sacrificing their moral superiority: "[N]o man would ever be seen with a woman who had the faintest taint or tinge of tobacco about her . . . it isn't thinkable." Willard's mother, incidentally, had used snuff.[42]

The cigarette represented a threat to these new standards. It was presumed to be more tempting to women than other forms of tobacco because it was "weaker and more feminine." In fact, most of the cigarettes that were available in the late nineteenth century offered considerable challenges to delicacy: they were loosely packed, fell apart easily, and tended to shed part of their contents onto the lips or into the mouth of the smoker. While developments in the cultivation and processing of cigarette tobacco had made it milder and easier to smoke, women had proven themselves perfectly capable of smoking, snuffing, and chewing all kinds of tobacco. Still, the perception remained that the "finer sensibilities" that had led women to eschew tobacco in general were not sufficient to protect them from the allure of cigarettes.[43]

These attitudes suggest something of the Victorians' deep ambivalence about the nature of women. Women were innately virtuous and yet easily led astray. They were not only more vulnerable to the harmful effects of cigarettes on health, but more likely to take them up in the first place.

Almost as soon as cigarettes began to be noticed at all in the United States, they were linked to women and wickedness. The author of an 1877 anti-tobacco tract reported that he had personally seen young girls smoking in "dancing saloons," in a "striking exhibition of depravity." While it was occasionally whispered that a proper lady here or there had ventured upon a cigarette, for the most part the habit was considered the province of chorus girls, actresses, prostitutes, and other women of doubtful reputation. As the *New York Times* observed in 1879, "[T]he practice of cigarette-smoking among ladies seems to be generally regarded as the usual accompaniment of, or prelude to, immorality." In one of the earliest extant photographs of anyone with a cigarette, taken around 1850, Lola Montez—the Irish dancer and self-styled adventuress—was shown holding one between languid fingers as she cast a seductive look over her shoulder. Lillie Langtry, the Victorian actress (and mistress of Britain's future King Edward VII), scandalized respectable society by posing with a cigarette in her mouth. As seen in these and other examples, cigarette smoking was at least a token of, if not a direct conduit to, the demimonde.[44]

Georges Bizet's opera *Carmen* (first produced in New York in 1878 and very popular with American audiences in the 1880s and 1890s) helped reinforce the connections between women, cigarettes, and sin. Bizet's heroine, who worked in a cigarette factory in Spain and freely partook of the fruits of her labors, was both sensual and vulgar—qualities that were identified with female smokers for decades. The association was potent enough that in a production of *Carmen* on the Chautauqua circuit in Kansas in 1914, the heroine worked in a dairy instead of a cigarette factory, and made her entrance carrying a milk pail instead of a smoke.[45]

Even in the heart of cigarette country, respectable women shunned any link to cigarettes. In 1899, the American Tobacco Company offered a donation of 3,000 cigarettes to a women's group that was organizing a bazaar in Raleigh, North Carolina. The women refused to accept the gift, saying they could not countenance the sale or use of cigarettes in any way. According to Josephus Daniels, then editor of the *Raleigh News and Observer*, later a member of Woodrow Wilson's cabinet—who recounted this incident in his autobiography—"If anyone had indicated in that year, that any North Carolina lady would ever smoke what [were] popularly called 'coffin nails,' it would have been regarded as slander of the good women of the State."[46]

Particularly when smoked by women, cigarettes seemed to unleash a disquieting sexuality. Although there is an element of sensuousness in the use of any kind of tobacco (the mouth and hands being intimately involved whether it is chewed, snuffed, or smoked in pipes, cigars, or cigarettes), the effect seems more pronounced with cigarettes. Perhaps this has something to do with the frequency with which cigarettes are brought to the mouth, with the smoke being deeply inhaled, suggesting a titillating degree of intimacy. Leaders of the WCTU were greatly alarmed by the prospect of "young ladies with cigarettes between the lips, inhaling the smoke." To devotees, the distinctive physicality of cigarettes offered "a swift sensuous pleasure that neither pipe nor cigar can supply." A thirty-two-line tribute to "My Cigarette" by the poet Charles F. Lummis lingered on its potential as an aid to seduction. The cigar was reflective; the pipe, contemplative; the cigarette, sybaritic.[47]

The association between cigarettes and sex may have been enhanced by the use of women's pictures on cards inserted as stiffeners in cigarette packages in the 1880s and 1890s. The cards usually included a lithograph on one side and explanatory text on the other. Each was part of a numbered series, aimed at motivating consumers to collect all the cards in a series. The subjects ranged from "Great Americans" to "Perilous Occupations," but the perennial favorites were "Actresses" and "Beauties." One of the most popular series was Duke's "250 of the Most Beautiful Ladies in the World," distributed in Cross Cut cigarettes. Although the models were modestly dressed by today's standards, they showed more skin than was customary at the time. To Daniels, who thought cigarettes threatened the sanctity of the home, these were "pictures of naked women," pure and simple.[48]

Among those who objected to the inclusion of what he called "lascivious photographs" in cigarette packages was Washington Duke. A deeply religious Methodist (a faith that had traditionally condemned tobacco as being as deadly as alcohol and dancing), Duke asked his son to discontinue "this mode of advertising" after receiving a letter of protest from a minister. The elder Duke said such advertising had "pernicious effects" upon young men and women, and, furthermore, would be used to strengthen the arguments against cigarettes "in the legislative halls of the states." James B. Duke's response, if any, to his father is not known, but the pictures of curvaceous coquettes remained in cigarettes packaged by his companies.[49]

Aside from the advertising, there was something about the cigarette itself that suggested licentiousness. Observers noted that smokers seemed unduly preoccupied with their habit, lighting up far more often than pipe or cigar smokers. "The typical cigarette smoker wants to smoke all the time," one writer commented in a letter to the *New York Times*, voicing an oft-heard complaint. In an age that valued self-restraint, cigarettes represented unbridled physical appetites.[50]

Oscar Wilde portrayed this quality in his 1891 novel, *The Picture of Dorian Gray*. Wilde himself was a dedicated smoker whose cigarette was as much a part of his equipage as his fresh-cut flower. One of his novel's central characters is the dissolute Lord Henry Wooton, who lives by the philosophy that "[t]he only way to get rid of a temptation is to yield to it." Wooton is rarely without a cigarette. He describes it as "the perfect type of a perfect pleasure. It is exquisite, and it leaves one unsatisfied." The thin blue wreaths of smoke that curl from Wooton's cigarettes symbolize release: the smoker has cut himself free from conventional ties in order to pursue pleasure and dissipation.[51]

For the reform-minded, this was a dangerous freedom. One writer warned darkly that cigarette smoking, especially by women, would lead to "degradation [sic] altogether beyond what comes of being a slave to the vile weed." A somewhat less circumspect writer claimed that cigarettes were "an ally to the white slave traffic" because they could be easily drugged and thus employed in the ruination of young girls. According to another, "The boy who smokes at seven, will drink whiskey at fourteen, take to morphine at 20 or 25, and wind up with cocaine and the rest of the narcotics, at 30 and later on." Like today's anti-smoking activists— who depict the cigarette as a "gateway" drug, leading to alcohol, marijuana, and harder drugs—earlier reformers saw connections between cigarettes and other social problems.[52]

In the 1890s, cigarettes were often called "dope sticks" or "paper pills" (pill was a common term for opium after it was prepared for smoking); people who smoked them were "cigarette fiends"; people who manufactured and sold them were engaged in "the cigarette traffic." These pejoratives implied that cigarettes were part of a mélange of vice, including prostitution, crime, and drug abuse. The "cigarette traffic" was part of a cloth that included the "white slave traffic" and other unsavory enterprises; "cigarette fiends" were on the same ladder to perdition as "dope fiends."

The increasing availability of cigarettes coincided with growing public awareness of the problems created by opium and coca and their derivatives, heroin, morphine, and cocaine. Until the passage of the Harrison Act in 1914, narcotics were essentially unrestricted in the United States. They were widely used in proprietary ("patent") medicines, including those intended to soothe fretful children or ease the monthly "distress" of delicate women. They were freely dispensed by prescription and even added to some soft drinks. Although such practices received relatively little attention from newspapers (perhaps reflecting the high profile of patent medicines in newspaper advertising columns), popular magazines such as *Collier's* and *Ladies Home Journal* pointed out the dangers of addiction and deplored the pervasiveness of the drugs. Medical journals carried reports about overdoses, violence, and collapsed careers stemming from drug use. The *Union Signal* (weekly newspaper of the WCTU), *Survey* (published by the Charity Organization Society of New York), the Boston *Independent*, and *Century Magazine* were among the many reform publications that reported on the problems and demanded legislative remedies. Fiction writers, too, contributed to the impression that "dope fiends" were undermining the fabric of American life. In Upton Sinclair's *The Jungle*, for example, the hero's cousin Marija was lost to a brothel through drug addiction.[53]

Because cigarettes became more available to American consumers at a time of heightened concern about drugs, they came under suspicion as agents of drug use, either directly or indirectly. In 1887, the *New York Times* took it as a matter of common knowledge that "[t]he wrappers of some Turkish cigarettes are impregnated with opium." The next year, the *Chicago Tribune* reported that tests conducted by a local chemist on eleven brands of cigarettes showed that two—Old Judge and Sweet Caporal— contained opium. (The chemist reportedly also found "a squirming grub" in a package of Lone Jack cigarettes.) The *Saturday Review* described cigarette smokers as "poor creatures" whose tastes had been vitiated by "hemped" or "opiated" tobacco (meaning tobacco that had been laced with marijuana or opium). A public health official in Indiana, recalling his childhood in the 1890s, remembered his father pointing out a cigarette smoker at a baseball game, in a tone of voice that implied the man was holding a hypodermic of morphine instead of a cylinder of tobacco. "I was utterly horrified and felt that I had seen the very dregs of sin," he said. His father, he added, was probably smoking a pipe at the time.[54]

Cigarettes were grouped with narcotics partly because they seemed to have the same addicting qualities. Although little scientific evidence was available, simple observation suggested that cigarette smokers were more dependent on their habit than other tobacco users. Modern science attributes this to nicotine, a psychoactive substance that stimulates brain cells and triggers the release of endorphins, the brain's natural opiates. Cigarette smokers typically absorb more nicotine than users of other forms of tobacco and hence become more habituated to it. Contemporaries noticed only that cigarettes seemed to produce a suspicious contentment followed by agitation—the same qualities produced by drugs freshly recognized as addicting. Many people assumed that cigarettes had those properties because they contained opium, cocaine, or some other narcotic. In the words of one writer, "The main reason why the cigarette obtains so fatal a power over young men is because of the opium in it."[55]

This notion persisted until well into the twentieth century, despite frequent scientific reports to the contrary. In 1892, for example, Harvey W. Wiley—then chief chemist for the Department of Agriculture and later the first director of the Food and Drug Administration—directed a series of studies by prominent chemists who tested cigarettes purchased from retail outlets around the country. None found any evidence of narcotics. One scientist pointed out that it made little sense on the face of it to add expensive opium to cigarettes, which sold for about half a cent each. Wiley reported that he himself had tested the thirteen most popular brands of cigarettes and found no trace of opium or its derivatives in any of them.[56]

Nonetheless, between 1889 and 1907, four states took the rumors seriously enough to prohibit the sale of cigarettes that were "adulterated" with drugs, and two others passed laws that defined cigarettes as narcotics. A United States Supreme Court justice, in a 1900 decision upholding an anti-cigarette law in Tennessee, commented that "there are many (cigarettes) whose tobacco has been mixed with opium or some other drug." The WCTU, which had created a Department for the Overthrow of the Tobacco Habit in 1883, replaced it with a Department of Narcotics in 1885. The department's priorities are reflected in the 1887 annual report of its Kentucky division, which distributed 9,000 pieces of literature on cigarettes and tobacco and only 100 on opium.[57]

Even those who supposed that cigarettes themselves were free of drugs associated them with drug use. No less an authority than Wiley claimed that people who smoked cigarettes would "more readily become victims of alcohol, cocain[e], opium, and other narcotic drugs." He speculated that cigarettes somehow blunted the nervous system and thereby interfered with moral restraints. Charles B. Towns, a prominent anti-drug crusader, believed "[t]he relation of tobacco, especially in the form of cigarettes, and alcohol and opium is a very close one. . . . Cigarettes, drink, opium, is the logical and regular series." Dr. Winfield S. Hall, professor of physiology at Northwestern University Medical School in Chicago, expressed similar sentiments. Hall smoked for years before deciding that he was forming a "drug" habit and quit. The practice, he said, "paves the way to other dissipation."[58]

The allegations about cigarettes and drugs were repeated so often and in so many venues that they acquired the aura of the self-evident. They helped to place cigarettes in what historian John C. Burnham has called "the constellation of bad habits." To Willard, president of the national WCTU, "the fuming cigarette" belonged in a symbolic grave with "the bar room, the decanter, the pack of cards, the pool room, the haunt of infamy." Even people with little interest in reform suspected that cigarette smokers were more likely to use drugs, drink to excess, and otherwise misbehave. Cigarettes came to be defined as part of an interlocking web that included not only drugs but alcohol, prostitution, crime, abuse of women and children, and other social problems—even insanity.[59]

Ultimately, this connection proved to be a mixed blessing for the anti-cigarette movement. On the one hand, it attracted powerful allies; on the other, it meant that their agendas were crowded. Cigarettes were never more than a secondary issue for most of those who supported the campaign against them. As time went on, their objectives narrowed. This pattern was typified by David Starr Jordan, Stanford University's first president, an ardent reformer whose interests included prohibition, eugenics, female suffrage, world peace, education, conservation (he was a founder of the Sierra Club), and, to a lesser degree, cigarettes. After World War I, he greatly reduced the scope of his activities in order to concentrate on the issue of peace. Responding to yet another plea for money from an anti-cigarette group in 1927, he protested, "I have long since come to the bottom of what I can afford to spend each year for various good purposes." He sent a small check anyway, but provided nothing further after that.[60]

The primary concern for most of those who joined the early battle against cigarettes was alcohol. They acted out of the conviction that "[s]moking leads to drinking and drinking leads to the devil," as the WCTU put it in 1885. This was a refinement of an argument developed nearly a century earlier by Benjamin Rush, surgeon general of the American Continental Army, the most eminent physician of his day, and an early advocate of temperance. In two essays published in the 1790s, Rush contended that tobacco dried out the mouth, producing an unnatural thirst that could be satisfied only by alcohol. His ideas influenced the debate about tobacco for generations. For example, William A. Alcott (cousin of

Bronson Alcott, a famous Transcendentalist, who was, in turn, father of the still more famous author Louisa May Alcott) cited Rush in arguing that tobacco was "among the larger, more efficient tributaries to the ocean of Intemperance." Alcott's anti-tobacco treatise, first published in 1847, was reissued in 1883, with an introduction by Nelson Sizer, a temperance worker and health reformer. Sizer pointed out that a new, more deadly form of tobacco had appeared since Alcott's day: the cigarette. "With new devices for dissipation," he added, "new means are required for reform."[61]

The opening wedge in the organized campaign against cigarettes was the charge that they corrupted the young. Many people who accepted other forms of tobacco disapproved of cigarettes simply because they seemed so easy to acquire and so seductive to the young. Price was a factor in this availability: cigarettes were often sold individually, two for a penny, putting them within the financial reach of youngsters with just a little pocket money (perhaps earned selling newspapers, shining shoes, or working in the factories of industrializing America). Manufacturers earned enmity by distributing free samples to young people. Scores of parents objected when a California company sent gift packages to every household in Sacramento, since some of the packages were opened, and the contents presumably tried, by children. (On the other hand, in 1891, officials at the Bingham School, a military prep school in North Carolina, expressed thanks for a donation of American Tobacco Company cigarettes, "which were greatly enjoyed by the cadets.") The sight of "[e]rrand boys and school boys smok[ing] on the street with an abandon belonging to their elders" shocked even a gnarly Seattle editor. "Their dwarfed bodies and yellow, inebriated faces tell a story which ought to make any passer-by feel his duty toward the race," he wrote.[62]

Adults seldom approved of tobacco use by children—as Tom Sawyer could attest—but their disapprobation of cigarettes verged, at times, on hysteria. Even the *New York Times* was given to hyperbole on the topic. Cigarettes, according to one early editorial, were "[doing] more to demoralize and vitiate youth than all the dram-shops of the land." By 1905, according to another editorial, the cigarette had "an appalling hold on American youth beyond anything which the public at large has dreamed of." To illustrate a 1909 article on the anti-cigarette movement, the *Times* published two photographs of indolent, smirking boys with cigarettes. Meanwhile, its news columns were peppered with shocking stories about children smoking at very young ages. An eleven-year-old boy had been "KILLED BY CIGARETTE SMOKING"; an eight-year-old who had died "in frightful convulsions" had smoked cigarettes since age five; an eighteen-year-old had been reduced to imbecility by his "insatiable taste" for cigarettes, acquired at age fourteen.[63]

These stories, whatever their relationship to the facts, reveal something about contemporary notions regarding both the potency of cigarettes and the nature of childhood. As a result of decreases in the birthrate and other changes in middle-class family life, "childhood" was being extended well into the teens; for middle-class parents, cigarettes may have been discomfiting badges of premature adulthood. A cigarette dangling from the lips of a young boy—or, worse, a girl—was an affront to romantic images of children as innocent and dependent. It also represented rebellion. In his autobiography, Lincoln Steffens remembered seeing groups of boys sitting hatless in front of synagogues in New York in the 1890s, busily smoking cigarettes, while their orthodox fathers attended services inside. The cigarettes served as a visual declaration of independence from parental values.[64]

By 1890, no fewer than twenty-one states and territories had outlawed the sale of cigarettes to minors, defined for the most part as persons under age sixteen. Penalties for violating the laws varied widely, with the average being a fine of $20 to $25. South Carolina provided that half the fine ($25 to $100) be paid to "the informer of the offense." The law (later imitated by several other states) was written in such a way that a juvenile could buy a package of cigarettes and then collect a reward for turning in the seller. Some states ordered youthful smokers to reveal the source of their cigarettes on pain of a fine or jail term. Whether bracketed with bribes or threats, the laws did not eliminate the problem, at least as indicated by the speed with which reformers moved to prohibit the sale and manufacture of cigarettes entirely.[65]

The first calls for cigarette prohibition came from the WCTU. Willard, who had become national president of the organization in 1881, had long abhorred tobacco in general. Her older brother Oliver smoked; she apparently felt this had contributed to his death in 1878 at age forty-three. She had a close relationship with John Harvey Kellogg and his wife, Ella, and with others in the health reform movement, most of whom advocated abstinence from tobacco. She frequently complained, in her journals and other writings, about the offensive effluvia of smokers. For example, commenting on her meetings with the resolutions committee during the Republican National Convention in 1884, she wrote, "I do not think that any member smoked in our presence, but the room was thoroughly distasteful, almost sickening to us, by reason of the sight of the many much-used spittoons and the sight and smell of the blue cloud of smoke."[66]

However much she disliked tobacco, Willard seemed to recognize the futility of attempting to dislodge the "accursed weed" altogether. Speaking to the National Convention of the WCTU in 1891, she merely said it might be feasible "some day." In a note written on the flyleaf of her copy of Walt Whitman's *Leaves of Grass*, she conceded that the idea of a world free of meat-eaters, drinkers, and smokers was "utterly crazy for the 19th century." A world free of cigarettes seemed more attainable, since so many people already detested them.[67]

At Willard's behest, the WCTU began to campaign for the prohibition of cigarette manufacturing, sales, and imports. In her last annual address to the WCTU, a few months before her death in February 1898, she broadened the attack and urged the abolition of the entire tobacco industry. For the most part, however, the WCTU merely expressed disapproval of other forms of tobacco. Its legislative efforts were confined almost exclusively to cigarettes. Eliza B. Ingalls, longtime superintendent of the WCTU's Anti-Narcotics Department, explained in her annual report for 1900 that "[w]ork against other narcotics has gone steadily on, but the cigarette habit is of such great importance that other things seem to sink almost into insignificance."[68]

This dedication may have been fortified by the appearance of success. Reports from the Bureau of Internal Revenue showed that cigarette sales, as measured by collections of federal excise taxes, dropped almost by half in five years, from 4.2 billion in 1896 to less than 2.3 billion in 1901. The decline is even more dramatic when measured against the rapid population growth of that period. While cigarette sales fell by nearly 50 percent, the population increased by about 10 percent, primarily because of immigration. "Everything points to the death of the little coffin nail," Ingalls reported. "The sentiment against this habit is at a fever heat; now is the time to strike." She was confident that "[a] few more years of active, earnest work and this evil will be outlawed."[69]

The reasons for the five-year depression in the cigarette business are not clear, although Ingalls and her fellow "agitators" (to use the contemporary term) did not hesitate to claim the credit for themselves. Writers for journals as disparate as the *Forum* and the *U.S. Tobacco Journal* thought the decline had less to do with reformers than with the increasing popularity of the bicycle; people were said to be so busy riding, they had little time to smoke. Certainly, members of the WCTU were busy and well organized in attacking cigarettes: they generated a prodigious quantity of literature; distributed it through schools, churches, and other venues; encouraged businessmen not to hire cigarette smokers; and lobbied Congress and the states for anti-cigarette legislation. They staged public demonstrations, often involving school children who were invited to do things such as jump up and down on piles of cigarette butts. They pushed for restrictions on smoking in public and on the use of cigarettes by public employees, including teachers and policemen. And they vehemently protested the use of "obscene pictures" in cigarette boxes and advertising, even sending delegations to plead their case directly to prominent manufacturers. These and other activities were extensively, and often sympathetically, reported in the mainstream press. Still, the dimensions of the early anti-cigarette campaign are easier to measure than its effects.[70]

Organized opposition was just one of the influences on cigarette sales in the 1890s. Another factor to consider is the economy. During the depression that began in 1893, Americans bought fewer cigars and more cigarettes: per capita consumption of cigars slid by 25 percent, while that of cigarettes increased by 35 percent. The hard times may have encouraged some pipe and cigar smokers to switch to cigarettes. If they gave up the cheaper smokes when the economy revived in 1897, their behavior could explain the subsequent drop in cigarette sales.[71]

The decline also coincides with increases in the federal excise tax on cigarettes, from 50 cents per thousand in 1896 to $1 in 1897 and $1.50 in 1898. Manufacturers responded by raising prices. This increase eliminated the cheapest brands, which had shown the greatest growth in earlier years. Cigarette sales began to recover in 1902, when taxes were reduced to 54 cents per thousand. By and large, however, retail prices did not return to their previous level after the tax decrease. The correlation between price and consumption is thus not as tidy as it could be.[72]

The laws themselves probably had minimal effect, since cigarettes were not particularly popular in the states that banned them; furthermore, enforcement tended to be haphazard. However, the legislation had the incidental effect of convincing Duke that "the paper cigarette was going to be knocked out." As a result, his American Tobacco Company expanded into other tobacco products and reduced its advertising and promotion of cigarettes. Testifying during the 1908 anti-trust suit that eventually resulted in the breakup of the company, Duke attributed the five-year slide to a shift in sales tactics. People bought fewer cigarettes because "we sort of let up on our activity to push the cigarette business and pushed other lines of tobacco." It should be noted that Duke's testimony was not given entirely in the interest of unvarnished truth; he was attempting to defend his company's methods and justify its domination of nearly every aspect of the tobacco trade.[73]

More significant, and less amorphous, than the causes of the decrease are its effects. For one thing, it energized the "agitators," giving them what they took to be proof of their effectiveness. At the annual meeting of the WCTU in 1900, delegates were cheered not only by the sales figures but by reports that the National Weather Bureau and the Chicago, Burlington, and Quincy Railroad had prohibited the use of cigarettes by employees while on duty. The Weather Bureau, additionally, warned that employees who smoked cigarettes at all, even on their own time, would be "mentioned" in confidential memoranda to department heads. Delegates also applauded the news that the United States Supreme Court had upheld the constitutionality of a law banning the sale of cigarettes (and cigarette papers) in Tennessee. They vowed to seek similar legislation in all the states, demonstrating faith both in their own power and in the power of laws to regulate behavior.[74]

James B. Duke responded to these developments with a combination of aggression and retreat. His surviving correspondence indicates that he closely monitored the progress of restrictive legislation and directed the efforts to defeat it, using methods that were not always within the bounds of legality. It is possible, although not provable, that some of his legendary philanthropy was intended to deflect criticism of his business. Meanwhile, he busily invested in nontobacco endeavors.

In fending off legislative attacks, Duke preferred using emissaries not directly connected to the American Tobacco Company. He relied on local businessmen to defeat ordinances that would have imposed prohibitive license fees on cigarette retailers in Marion, Indiana, and Springfield, Illinois, in 1896 and 1899, respectively. When the Springfield City Council considered a proposal to ban cigarette sales altogether in 1904, Duke commissioned the same agent he had used earlier, telling him, "Of course, we should dislike to have such an ordinance passed, and I assure you that we will appreciate your efforts to defeat it."[75]

Duke also kept his corporate legal staff busy. Williamson W. Fuller, the company's chief counsel from its organization in 1890 until its court-ordered breakup in 1911, filed dozens of lawsuits challenging what one of his friends recalled as "a temporary but widespread and vehement objection to the consumption of cigarettes, which found expression in statutes . . . to prohibit their sale." These cases took Fuller into courthouses around the country.[76]

In court, the company rarely addressed the merits—or lack thereof— of cigarettes themselves. The defense rested instead on the narrow issue of state police power, arguing that only the federal government had the power to regulate interstate commerce. This was a safe position, since the federal government had shown no inclination to restrict the commerce in cigarettes.

Elsewhere, however, Duke sought to defend cigarettes on a broader basis. In an uncharacteristically long letter to W. C. Purdy, president of the Chicago, Rock Island, and Pacific Railway, he insisted that "cigarette smoking is no more injurious than smoking in any other form." Purdy had announced that any employees who smoked cigarettes, on or off duty, would be fired; he apparently believed that such people were unproductive and inattentive. Duke grumbled that the policy was "entirely unjust," likening it to forbidding the use of coffee while permitting tea, or outlawing baking powder made with cream of tartar while accepting that made with alum. He insisted that any discrimination against cigarettes was at odds with American notions about fair play and tolerance.

Duke was obviously concerned that anti-cigarette policies adopted by large employers could undermine his business. He could discount, at least publicly, attacks made by what he called "irresponsible agitators, or professional so-called reformers." Those that came from railroad presidents and other prominent businessmen were harder to ignore. He sent Purdy a copy of *The Truth About Cigarettes*, a 48-page booklet absolving cigarettes of any ill effects; asked him to read it; and offered to arrange a meeting in the hope of "a modification of the order which you have made." In case Purdy needed additional persuasion, Duke also pointed out that some of the same people who had invested in the Chicago, Rock Island, and Pacific Railway had also invested in American Tobacco, and "[t]hese investments would be made less profitable, and less secure, with the diminution of the cigarette business." Duke thus deftly combined an appeal to democratic principles with a veiled threat of economic retaliation.[77]

In legislative halls, Duke's representatives sometimes bolstered the clarity of their arguments with the weight of the company's largesse. As an anonymous executive recalled later, "A bill would be introduced to a legislature to prohibit the manufacture or sale of cigarettes; it would be referred to a committee, and our people would have to get busy and pay somebody to see that it died." According to a report in the *New York Times*, the company dispatched a lobbyist armed with $20,000 "to compass the defeat" of a bill to ban cigarette sales in Washington State in 1893. He arrived too late, and the bill became law. However, the law was repealed at the next session of the legislature, two years later.[78]

On another occasion, Duke sent a functionary named George W. Turner to Chicago to defeat a proposed anti-cigarette ordinance, reportedly by offering $25,000 to a city alderman. Turner was the editor of the *New York City Recorder*, a short-lived newspaper in which Duke had invested heavily. According to the testimony of the seemingly offended alderman, Turner had come to see him in Chicago; claimed to have "the Mayor and most of the aldermen in his pocketbook"; and suggested the alderman contact Neil McCoull, the resident manager of the American Tobacco Company, if he wanted to get his share. Duke later admitted that Turner had gone to Chicago at his request, but insisted, "Mr. Turner went to Chicago simply as my friend to tell the newspapers of the injustice of the proposed ordinance." The credibility of this statement is weakened by a message Duke sent to Turner at a Chicago hotel, shortly before the alderman's honor was challenged: "Omitted to answer your question regarding McCoull. He is entitled to all confidence." Clearly, Turner's mission involved more than mere appeals to Chicago newspapermen.[79]

Eventually, the alderman and the company's agents each accused the other of attempted bribery. A grand jury investigated but returned no indictments, finding hints of culpability on both sides. The overall testimony, however, put the company "in a very unpleasant light," according to the *New York World*. The proposed ordinance, meanwhile, was tabled, although a similar measure was adopted two years later; it banned the sale of cigarettes containing "opium, morphine, jimpson [sic] weed, belladonna, glycerine or sugar" (the latter two ingredients were widely used as flavoring agents); imposed a $100 annual license fee on cigarette retailers; and outlawed cigarette sales within 200 feet of any school.[80]

Stung by the critical reports in New York newspapers (and no doubt concerned about their effect on the financial community), Duke enlisted the help of Levi P. Morton, Republican governor-elect of New York (and a former vice president of the United States). The *Recorder* had supported Morton's campaign for governor as a "reform" candidate; in turn, Morton had announced plans to appoint its editor, Turner, to his staff. In addition to backing Morton indirectly through the newspaper, it is likely that Duke also contributed directly to his campaign, given his consistent support of other Republican candidates. At any rate, he asked Morton to issue a statement—as a supposedly disinterested public official—to reiterate that "[e]very report of attempted bribery by Mr. Turner or anyone representing the Company of which I am President, is absolutely untrue."[81]

Notwithstanding the stout denials, the rumors about Duke's penchant for bribery continued to circulate. In 1898, a publicly outraged lawmaker in Tennessee contended that the company had tried to bribe him to work for the repeal of anti-cigarette legislation that he had sponsored the previous year. Representative Jesse Lafayette Rogers, a Republican, said Fuller had promised to pay him $500 if he would introduce a repeal measure that the lawyer had drafted. Rogers also said that a Republican National Committeeman had pressured him to support the repeal because the company was among the largest contributors to the Republican campaign fund. Both Fuller and the committeeman scoffed at the charges. "I know nothing whatever about the alleged bribery, and can say only that Mr. Rogers' remarks must be the ravings of a disappointed politician," Fuller said. The committeeman airily suggested that "[i]f Mr. Rogers was offered a bribe of $500 he must be a cheap man, or the smallness of the amount perhaps insulted him." The law remained on the books.[82]

Yet another alleged attempt at bribery virtually forced the Indiana legislature to prohibit cigarette sales and manufacturing in 1904. Right before a critical vote in the House, Representative Ananias Baker dramatically held aloft a sealed envelope and announced that it had been given to him by a lobbyist from the "tobacco trust," with instructions to vote against the bill. He opened it with a flourish: five $20 bills dropped out. It was widely assumed that similar envelopes had been distributed to other legislators. Baker left his colleagues little choice but to vote for the bill, lest their integrity be suspect.[83]

Duke's willingness to slide on the shady side of the law suggests something about the marginal position of cigarettes in American commerce. Executives of well-established enterprises have less need to protect their interests with illegal secret agents, envelopes stuffed with cash, and other dubious maneuverings.

Some of Duke's critics also accused him of trying to buy favor through philanthropy. He and his family gave huge sums to various good causes, particularly to Trinity College (now Duke University) and to the Methodist Episcopal Church South, which administered Trinity. Washington Duke had been converted to Methodism in childhood during one of the revivals that periodically swept through the antebellum South; the church was a major influence on his life from that point on. Between 1895 and 1900, he gave more than $300,000 to Trinity College; his sons James and Benjamin gave lesser but still sizeable amounts during that time. Emma Pegram, a member of a prominent North Carolina family, implied in a letter to her son George that the family's gifts were efforts to silence (or at least mute) the critics of the American Tobacco Company. "Somehow Buck Duke does not stand very high among the good people," she wrote. The college officials, she said in another letter, "don't care for the Dukes but they want all their money."[84]

The fact that the money came largely from the sale of cigarettes troubled some Methodists. Responding to one particularly "munificent" be-quest from Washington Duke in 1898, delegates to the Western North Carolina Annual Conference said they were "particularly gratified" that he had—under pressure—decided to make the gift in the form of cash instead of stock in the American Tobacco Company. They then resolved "that this and all other funds of the College shall be so invested as to prevent any just criticism of the Church, or pain to the conscience of its members." By this they meant the money should not be invested in the cigarette industry.[85]

If it was intended to quiet their critics in North Carolina, the Duke family's philanthropy did not succeed. The state's leading newspaper, the *Raleigh News and Observer*, continued to vilify "the tobacco trust" and its chief product. In one typical editorial, the paper declared that "[t]he Duke cigarettes not only destroy the mind and body and home but give this country a bad name abroad." To some degree, these claims were shaped by editor Daniels's political differences with the Dukes. The Dukes were staunch Republicans in a rabidly Democratic area, and Daniels—a militant white supremacist—thought they were soft on the color line. Daniels also sympathized with local tobacco growers, who felt abused by the cavalier methods of the American Tobacco Company's leaf buyers. In any case, the attacks distressed Washington Duke, so much so that he once told Daniels that he wished his son had never "put us into the [American Tobacco] Company and we could carry on our business like we used to do it. We were making lots of money and did not have any criticism." To a friend, he reportedly confided: "There are three things I never could understand: electricity; the Holy Ghost; and my son Buck." Meanwhile, a prominent North Carolina jurist suggested Trinity College's motto should be revised to read "Eruditio et Religio et Cherooto et Cigaretto."[86]

The North Carolina legislature, too, attacked cigarettes, making seven attempts to prohibit their sale between 1897 and 1917. The 1897 bill would have banned the manufacturing as well as the sale of cigarettes; among its supporters was a legislator who said that "any manufacturing interest whose existence depend[s] upon the making of idiots should go out of existence." Another said he had smoked cigarettes and they had nearly ruined him. Yet another presented testimony from a physician who swore "this terrible vice" was claiming the lives of 200 North Carolinians every year. The measure passed the House but died in the Senate.[87]

In this hostile climate, Duke bought insurance by diversifying. Under his direction, the American Tobacco Company aggressively expanded into other lines of tobacco, eventually dominating most of the industry. By 1910, Duke controlled 85 percent of the chewing tobacco trade, 80 percent of the smoking tobacco, 97 percent of the snuff, 91 percent of the so-called small cigars (all-tobacco cigarettes), and 14 percent of the regular cigars—in addition to 90 percent of the domestic cigarette market. Only cigar manufacturing remained outside his reach. "We wanted to have some-thing we could satisfy every taste with," Duke said later. In addition, the trust absorbed many related businesses, such as those involved in the production of licorice paste (used in making chewing tobacco), tin foil, cotton bags, and wooden boxes. As opposition to cigarettes increased in the United States, American Tobacco began aggressively selling cigarettes overseas, particularly in Japan and China. Duke and his family also invested in various enterprises outside the tobacco industry, from textiles to banking to mining to electric utilities.[88]

At the turn of the century, then, the cigarette industry appeared to be faltering. Sales were declining; the public remained resistant; the organized opposition was gaining momentum; and even Duke himself had concluded that the industry had a limited future. The manufacturers' efforts to defend their business against the advances of the reform-minded only seemed to inspire new fervor. For example, when the industry began promoting *The Truth About Cigarettes* (the pro-cigarette booklet that Duke sent to the president of the Chicago, Rock Island, and Pacific Railway), the WCTU took it as a sign of the desperation of the nearly defeated. "Before that time, we made our protest and conducted the fight on lines we considered best, without hearing from the cigarette manufacturers," Ingalls reported in 1898. "They evidently considered our efforts were not worth notice." Things had changed, she noted, with not a little satisfaction.[89]

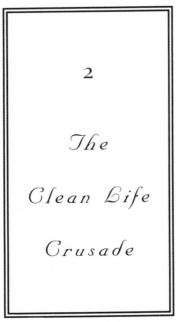

2

*The*

*Clean Life*

*Crusade*

It is little, my lad, but it's terribly bad,
The vile old Cigarette.
And without any joking, there's danger in smoking
The vile old Cigarette;
It adds to expenses and lessens the senses,
It only brings grief and regret;
Then let us endeavor to shun it forever,
The vile old Cigarette.
*Anti-Cigarette League (1912)*[1]

The campaign against cigarette smoking intensified in December 1899 when Lucy Page Gaston, an alumna of the WCTU, founded the Anti-Cigarette League of America. This group was to cigarettes what the Anti-Saloon League was to alcohol: a single-interest organization determined to eviscerate an industry it deemed harmful to the public welfare. By 1901, it claimed a membership of 300,000, with a paid staff overseeing chapters throughout the United States and Canada.[2]

Like Carry Nation—the hatchet-wielding prohibitionist—Gaston was a woman of fierce convictions, given to flamboyant tactics, nearly as likely to irritate her allies as her opponents. Both women had a knack for attracting public attention and influential support, although it is overstating the case to argue, as one writer does, that Gaston was second only to Nation as "the leading female reformer in America" during the early 1900s.[3]

Nation herself was among the prominent people who joined Gaston in the battle against cigarettes. Indeed, on at least one occasion, she demonstrated even more zeal for the cause than Gaston. During a visit to the Anti-Cigarette League headquarters in Chicago in 1904, Nation was aghast to see a picture of President Theodore Roosevelt on the wall. "My dear Miss Lucy," she reportedly said, "why do you have that picture in here? Don't you know he is a cigarette smoker? I have it from three eyewitnesses. Let me tear that picture up!" Gaston refused to believe such a slander, whereupon Nation promised, "If you will write to Mr. Roosevelt and get his statement that he does not nor ever did smoke cigarettes, I will give you fifty dollars for your work." Gaston promptly wrote to the president and received a reply from his secretary that Roosevelt had never used tobacco in any form. Nation entertained doubts about the veracity of "such chaff," but paid the bet anyway. The portrait remained on the wall.[4]

The Anti-Cigarette League was a manifestation of the reformist spirit that characterized the Progressive Era. This period—roughly bracketed by the Spanish American War of 1898 and the entry of the United States into World War I in 1917—was marked by intellectual excitement, political restlessness, and a vigorous and self-conscious desire to remake American society in almost every respect. The progressives sought to democratize the political system, regulate working conditions, restrict monopolies, protect consumers, conserve natural resources, diffuse the concentration of wealth, and professionalize medicine, education, social work, even child rearing. They also tried to repaint the nation's moral landscape, with crusades against alcohol, narcotics, prostitution, gambling—and cigarettes.

What follows is the story of how the cigarette fit into the progressive agenda. It focuses on Gaston and the coalition she put together to banish a habit that affronted the ideals of the new age in myriad ways. Gaston and her allies rode a wave of reform that threatened, for a while, to sweep the cigarette into the same cultural graveyard that was being prepared for alcohol.

Published photographs of Gaston depict a woman with a long, censorious face, thin of lip and prominent of nose, invariably dressed in somber clothing, making no concessions to vanity beyond a touch of lace at the neck. She favored the same type of round, rimless spectacles that Nation wore, and she tucked her hair into a similarly tidy bun. Taken as a whole, her image suggested a woman of serious purpose, not inclined to frivolity or small talk. (When a newspaper reporter commented on her lack of jewelry, she retorted, "Thousands of clear-eyed, finely developed, clean-lived young Americans are my priceless jewels.")[5]

Gaston could have been easily caricatured as a professional scold. Instead, she received consistently respectful treatment in both the mainstream and the reform press. Only after World War I did reports of her endeavors take on a decidedly mocking tone. The *New York Times*, for example, published dozens of straightforward accounts of Gaston's work in the early 1900s; but in 1922, it sneeringly described her as "this eminent woman of science." Sinclair Lewis included a thinly veiled reference to Gaston in his 1925 novel *Arrowsmith*. She was "the anti-nicotine lady from Chicago" who tried to demonstrate the hazards of smoking by injecting ground-up cigarette paper into laboratory mice at a midwestern health fair (thereby infuriating "an anti-vivisection lady, also from Chicago"). Whatever else might be said about Gaston, it is clear that she had the misfortune of outliving the popularity of her cause.[6]

Like her nemesis, James B. Duke, Gaston did not leave much of a written record. Many of the details about her early life come from a posthumous profile published in the *Outlook and Independent* in 1930. The writer noted that when Gaston first "consecrated her life" to banishing cigarettes, annual consumption was around two billion; by 1930—six years after her death—it was nearly two hundred billion. The article was titled "Lost Cause."[7]

Gaston was born May 19, 1860, in Delaware, Ohio, and reared in Lacon, Illinois, a comma of a town about one hundred miles southwest of Chicago. Her father, Alexander Hugh Gaston, was a non-smoking, teetotaling abolitionist who was said to bear an uncanny resemblance to Abraham Lincoln. He was an imposing man, six feet, six inches tall, with enormous feet and an ungainly gait. He gained local fame as a horticulturist, planting the prairies with mulberry, elm, and cottonwood trees. Her mother, Henrietta Page Gaston (described in her later years as a "lovely, old-fashioned woman"), was an early friend of WCTU president Frances Willard.[8]

Young Lucy grew up in a home that radiated the spirit of reform. She was teaching Sunday school at the age of thirteen; at sixteen, she was elected president of the Marshall County (Illinois) Sunday School Association. A younger brother, Edward Page Gaston, was lecturing on the evils of drink by the time he was sixteen; he later rose to prominence in prohibitionist circles in both the United States and Great Britain.[9]

As a student at the Illinois State Normal School in Bloomington in 1881, Gaston led raids on local saloons and gambling halls, smashing fixtures in a style that Carry Nation later made famous. The school—which had about 600 students at the time, 70 percent of whom were women—was a laboratory for new educational theories and for reformist ideas in general. This environment presumably encouraged the nascent inclination to improve society that Gaston had already picked up at home.[10]

Gaston taught school in several small towns in Illinois during the 1880s. Her interest in cigarettes as a social issue appears to date from this period. She was disturbed by the boys she saw sneaking behind the schoolhouse to smoke cigarettes; they developed "cigarette face," she said, and invariably failed their examinations.[11]

She also joined her mother in active work for the WCTU, writing for the *Union Signal* and serving as state superintendent of children's temperance work in Illinois. Her objective was to win new, young recruits to the cause. She began to regard cigarettes as a threat to this effort; their low cost and relative mildness made them easy to buy and to smoke and thus made them more attractive to young people than other forms of tobacco. She was certain that a youngster who smoked would be more likely to drink. In one pamphlet published by the WCTU, she warned that cigarettes were enticing youngsters into lives of fetid dissolution: "Thousands are leaving our Sunday schools, swearing like pirates, smoking like chimneys and headed straight for the saloon."[12]

Gaston soon became one of the "leading workers" of the WCTU, according to the *Union Signal*. Her "untiring efforts in behalf of the children cause her to be well known and loved all over the State." Increasingly, she focused her energies on cigarettes. By mid-1892, she had "thoroughly aroused" the WCTU, the Young Men's Christian Association (YMCA), and other groups about the dangers (physical and moral) of smoking. She apparently continued to work as a schoolteacher, but she was supplementing her income by lecturing for the WCTU on a part-time basis.[13]

Early in 1893, Gaston moved with her family to Harvey, Illinois, the so-called Teetotal Town then being developed on the outskirts of Chicago as a haven for the temperate and the devout. The town was the creation of Turlington W. Harvey, a wealthy lumberman, land speculator, and benefactor of Dwight Moody, a well-known evangelist. Harvey was a man who combined deep religious principles with the profit motive. He bought more than 700 acres of mostly unbroken prairie just south of Chicago, surveyed it, incorporated it as a town in 1891, and began aggressively selling lots. He opened a marketing office in Chicago, tapping into the crowds drawn to the city by the Columbian Exposition. Moody invested in the town and encouraged his followers to do likewise. By the time the Gastons arrived, Harvey's population had grown to about 5,000.[14]

Harvey and Moody worked together to create a town that would promote the values of Christian culture. Restrictive covenants were written into every sales contract, forbidding the use of the land for any "dangerous, vexatious or offensive purpose or establishment whatsoever," including drinking, gambling, and "lewd and immoral" practices. All businesses were required to close on Sundays. The town even made a halfhearted attempt to ban the delivery of Sunday newspapers. There were no theaters or picture shows. Public entertainment consisted largely of appearances by evangelists, gospel singers, suffrage speakers, and the like. High school students began each school day with a Bible reading and an inspirational talk from the principal. One of the principal's favorite "texts" was "He that controlleth his spirit is greater than he that taketh a city." Self-control was an important civic virtue in Harvey.[15]

The Gastons settled comfortably into this milieu, buying a house near the center of town and establishing themselves as one of the community's more notable families. Alexander Gaston opened a nursery. Lucy Gaston left the schoolhouse and moved into journalism. She worked first as the woman's editor of the *Harvey Headlight* and later as managing editor and copublisher of a rival paper, the *Harvey Citizen*. When a saloon opened for business in 1895, openly defying the town covenants, she led the attack through the pages of her newspaper. She condemned saloon operators as "hardened sinners" and recommended that their enterprises be subject to the "hatchet plan," as developed by her friend Carry Nation. She also used the legal system, in one case winning an injunction to overturn an ordinance that would have permitted the licensing of saloons in Harvey. Two years later, when the Cook County commissioners issued a saloon license despite the injunction, Gaston tried to have them arrested. She would show the same unflagging enterprise in battling cigarettes a few years later.[16]

Gaston's work soon attracted the notice of Willard, one of the most influential women in the country. In one editorial in the *Union Signal*, Willard applauded the "intellectual force and moral courage" that Gaston had demonstrated during her "great struggle with the powers of darkness" in Harvey. When Gaston's press was damaged, most likely by someone who took issue with her anti-saloon stand, Willard sent a personal check to help repair it. Later, she recommended Gaston for an important position as national superintendent of the WCTU's Department of Christian Citizenship.[17]

Gaston responded to this personal interest by becoming even more active in the WCTU. In addition to serving as an officer, she wrote articles for various WCTU publications and helped raise money to buy a new headquarters building for the organization in Chicago. At the same time, she took steps to claim as her own a target that the broader reform community had taken comparatively little notice of: the cigarette.[18]

In 1895, when Gaston made her first appearance before a legislative body (the Illinois General Assembly) and asked it to ban the manufacture and sale of cigarettes, she was thirty-five years old, unmarried, and living with her parents in Harvey. (An early romance ended when "I prayed it out," she once told a journalist.) She had some education, a gift for expression, an evangelical spirit, and enough leisure time to engage in serious efforts to uplift society. Her economic status can only be guessed at, but she at least had means enough to buy a building lot of her own in Harvey. The fact that both she and her brother received some higher education suggests that the family enjoyed a certain level of material comfort. In Gaston's case, that education consisted of one term at a normal school dedicated to training women to be schoolteachers. The family had not yet attained the degree of calm prosperity needed to provide her with a liberal education. On the other hand, few families had: by 1890, only about one in 400 American women had earned university degrees.[19]

The range of Gaston's activities—teaching, writing, lecturing—suggests that she had varied talents and abundant energy. It is easy to imagine that she felt frustrated by the limited options available to her in the small midwestern towns where she lived. An associate once described her as "quite unmanageable," and said that she "usually runs things to suit herself." As a young woman, she had close contact with the charismatic Willard, who exhorted women to change the world. With Willard as a model, teaching school in the hinterland may not have been enough to fulfill Gaston's sense of her own mission in life. She had already won a measure of public recognition through her temperance activities, first in Lacon and then in Harvey. Willard had held her up as an example of a woman who had developed "a municipal conscience." This sort of praise would no doubt have reinforced Gaston's interest in making her mark on the world.[20]

That she was a woman with ambition is indicated by some of her surviving correspondence, particularly with David Starr Jordan, the first president of Stanford University and one of her most important allies. Gaston persuaded Jordan to join the Anti-Cigarette League in 1904 and carefully cultivated his patronage for more than two decades thereafter. He served as an officer, donated cash, made personal appearances on behalf of the cause, and coined several quotable epigrams (such as "Cigarette-smoking boys are like wormy apples; they drop long before the harvest time") that he allowed to be used in fund-raising posters and cards. In one letter, Gaston asked Jordan to convince "others of influence and means" to accept positions on her advisory council, mentioning Luther Burbank and Thomas A. Edison as examples of "the kind of men we are aiming at securing." Such people, she explained later, could "command attention" and thereby encourage donations. "What we can do is measured only by what we have to do with, as is usual in reform movements," she pointed out. In this and other ways, she demonstrated a sense of history and a keen interest in securing a place in it for herself.[21]

Temperance work would have been a logical outlet for a woman with her background, interests, and ambitions. However, by the 1890s, that field was a crowded one, and already amply generaled. Compared to alcohol, cigarettes attracted relatively little attention from reformers. The opportunity presented by a largely unclaimed target seems to have been the deciding factor in calling Gaston to what would become her life's work.

In 1896, Gaston became managing editor of the *Christian Citizen*, published in Chicago by the National Christian Citizenship League. This was a nonpartisan group dedicated to applying "Christian principles" to public affairs. Her brother, Edward, was a member of the executive committee and probably had something to do with her selection as editor. Gaston made a number of important contacts in reform circles during the next few years. She met people such as Francis E. Clark and Wilbur F. Crafts, founders, respectively, of the Christian Endeavor Society and the International Reform Federation. She may have learned something about organizational techniques from these men.[22]

Gaston also began to shoulder her way into politics. She endorsed female suffrage, joined the Prohibition Party, and ran as the party's candidate for trustee of the University of Illinois. In one campaign speech, she said that women could be a "regenerating influence" in politics. She finished eighth out of a field of eighteen candidates for three positions on the board of trustees, collecting 14,506 votes in a statewide race. The three winning candidates each received more than 614,000 votes. After this perhaps chastening baptism, Gaston made no further forays into party politics until after World War I, when she attempted a quixotic run for the presidency.[23]

By the late 1890s, Gaston's attention had turned almost exclusively to the issue of cigarettes. She noticed boys loitering on street corners in Chicago, cigarettes lodged in surly mouths. It seemed as if they were "offering burnt incense to Satan." She read newspaper accounts of alleged cases of cigarette-induced insanity and crime. She once claimed to have seen a small boy collapse in convulsions on the street; according to her story, a policeman looked at the boy's fingers and said, "It's cigarets that's done it." Aided by her brother, she began haunting legislative halls, "buttonholing luckless and drowsy statesmen" (as one writer put it later), and demanding laws to ban cigarette sales not only to minors but to everyone.[24]

Legislators in many states were already prepared to believe the worst about cigarettes. The Illinois General Assembly, for example, defined them as "preparations of tobacco soaked in nicotine or impregnated with opium, stramonium, belladonna, alcoholic liquor, valerian, tonca bean, or any other deleterious or poisonous substance." That language was used in a total of six bills to ban cigarette sales and manufacturing in Illinois in the 1890s. None of the proposals passed, but their tone reflects the underlying suspicions about cigarettes.[25]

Like other expressions of progressivism, anti-cigarette sentiment was fed by a sometimes paradoxical blend of evangelical fervor, social pragmatism, and self-interest. Gaston represented the moral reform branch of the progressive movement; she acted out of the belief that cigarettes were launching pads to moral decay. Progressives who were interested in so-called structural reforms associated cigarettes with inefficiency. Both groups distrusted industrial Leviathans. Congress approved the Sherman Anti-Trust Act just a few months after James B. Duke organized the American Tobacco Company in 1890. From its inception until its court-ordered breakup in 1911, American Tobacco produced roughly 90 percent of the cigarettes made in the United States. Cigarettes provoked some antagonism simply because they were the products of a trust. The symbolism was powerful enough that anti-cigarette activists continued to attack the "Tobacco Trust" for years after it had actually ceased to exist.[26]

The coalition lined up against the cigarette also included tobacco farmers, manufacturers of cigars and chewing tobacco, and independent tobacco retailers. Some of the earliest and most persistent opposition came from North Carolina, where tobacco farmers resented the American Tobacco Company's high-handed tactics in controlling the market for cigarette tobacco. Cigar makers, alarmed by a steady erosion of their business throughout much of the 1890s, found it convenient to blame the cigarette. In fact, the major factor in the decline of the cigar was the decade's severe depression, not competition from cigarettes. Nonetheless, there is some evidence to suggest that cigar makers retaliated against their perceived enemy by spreading rumors that cigarettes were spiked with opium and mor-phine, wrapped in paper bleached with arsenic and white lead, and embellished with the remains of cigar butts picked out of gutters by tubercular tramps. Financier Bernard Baruch (who was involved in an attempted takeover of the American Tobacco Company in 1899) asserted that much of the "high-minded propaganda" against cigarettes was secretly financed by manufacturers of chewing tobacco and cigars, using "innocent crusaders as catspaws." (He added, wryly, that he hoped such information would not erode anyone's faith in human motives.) Tobacco retailers, meanwhile, complained about the low profit margin on cigarettes. "I am tired of getting off my stool 250 times a day to sell a five-cent package of cigarettes and then making only 10 cents on the whole lot," said one.[27]

In all, eight states considered anti-cigarette legislation during the first half of the 1890s. Most were in the South or the West, regions with strong traditions favoring either temperance or hostility to trusts, or both. The first success came in Washington State in 1893, when the legislature made it illegal to "manufacture, buy, sell, give or furnish to any one cigarettes, cigarette paper or cigarette wrapper." According to the *New York Times*, "Nine-tenths of the members who voted for the bill did not care a nickel about the reform of the cigarette fiend, but they were anxious to knock out the Tobacco Trust."[28]

The nation's first cigarette prohibition law excited little comment in Washington itself. The bill passed the state senate with no discussion and only one dissenting vote. The most prominent item in the Seattle papers on the day after the law went into effect was a wire service report about the electrocution of a young New York medical student on charges of poisoning his wife. He was said to be "the first man of any intelligence" to die in the then-new electric chair at Sing Sing. The article also noted that he smoked a large number of cigarettes on the night before his execution.[29]

Three months after the law was enacted, a federal court in Seattle declared it unconstitutional on the grounds that it improperly restrained interstate trade. This was an issue that would be debated time and again during the next two decades as other states enacted similar legislation and the industry fought back through the courts. The *New York Times* endorsed the court's decision in Washington, commenting, "The smoking of cigarettes may be objectionable, as are many other foolish practices, and it may be more injurious than other modes of smoking tobacco, but it is an evil which cannot be remedied by law." The next Washington legislature quietly repealed the law.[30]

The *Times* editorial struck at the heart of the early debate over cigarette smoking. The question was not whether cigarettes were harmful—the prevailing opinion was that they were—but whether it was possible or desirable to obliterate them by law. The *Times* concluded that cigarettes were not "a legitimate subject for legislative action." Gaston was among those who held firmly to the opposite opinion.

In this, she was part of a new impulse to push government beyond its traditionally narrow functions and into a more aggressive role in regulating the behavior of its citizens. Moral reformers such as Anthony Comstock demanded that the state promote "social purity" by stamping out vice in all its guises. Although there is no record indicating that Gaston had any direct contact with Comstock, she embraced his argument that private behavior could not be untangled from public welfare. In her view, the cigarette-smoking boy would become a weak, sickly, narcotized man, inclined to criminality, destined for pauperism, useless not only to himself but to society at large. The state had both the authority and the obligation to intervene. Since laws prohibiting the sale of cigarettes to minors had proven ineffective, broader measures were necessary.

In 1897, Gaston enlisted the aid of the Christian Citizenship League in petitioning the Illinois legislature to again consider prohibiting cigarette sales and manufacturing. More than fifty individual petitions were filed, each with about thirty signatures, calling on the legislature to ban cigarettes in the public interest. The petitions came from all over the state, including populous Cook County. Typical was one signed by forty public school teachers in Cairo, attacking the cigarette as "a deadly foe to the boys of our land; corrupting their morals, sapping their intellect, stunting their bodies and shortening their lives."[31]

Members of the Illinois House of Representatives responded to this pressure by unanimously passing a bill that would have made it illegal to sell, manufacture, or give away cigarettes, upon pain of a fine of $100 to $200 or thirty to sixty days in jail or both. The senate defeated the measure, whereupon its backers immediately submitted "A Bill Against the Evils Arising from the Sale of Cigarettes" by imposing an annual license fee of $2,000 on retailers. That bill, too, was defeated. Even so, Gaston and her allies were cheered by the generally favorable response to their proposals. In a letter to John R. Tanner, newly elected governor of Illinois, the president of the Christian Citizenship League pointed out that cigarette prohibition had received "large support," and said he hoped the governor would make it a priority in upcoming legislative sessions.[32]

Meanwhile, Gaston appeared before the Chicago City Council, lobbying for a proposal to ban the sale of cigarettes containing "opium, morphine, jimpson [sic] weed, belladonna, glycerine or sugar." Theoretically, this would have had the effect of prohibiting all cigarette sales, since glycerine and sugar were commonly used in the manufacturing process. As an added discouragement, the bill also required retailers to post a $500 bond and pay an annual license fee of $100, to sell a product that typically retailed for five cents a package. The city council, perhaps swayed by Gaston's eloquence, perhaps by the prospect of enhanced revenue from the sale of cigarette licenses, approved the ordinance.[33]

Gaston won support by linking the cigarette to other social problems, particularly to alcohol abuse. She claimed that certain elements in cigarette smoke irritated the nervous system to such a degree that the smoker would invariably seek relief through alcohol, morphine, or other drugs. From there, it was a short path to poverty, crime, and moral collapse. She told temperance workers that they could "do no greater service at this junction than to join hands enthusiastically in a great national movement against the cigaret." It was nothing less than "a fight for civilization." She promised that with victory, "Souls will be saved from eternal ruin, homes will be saved from untold sorrow, and our nation will be saved by its noble sons."[34]

She also promised that the victory would be swift and certain. This was an important factor in her early success as an organizer. Gaston pointed out that the cigarette was less ingrained than many other evils plaguing mankind and would therefore be easier to dislodge. She coupled this optimism with a warning: the habit was making inroads in American society, particularly among youth. Cigarettes were both dangerous and vulnerable. For these reasons, "the time is ripe for a sweeping movement" to eliminate them.[35]

The prospect of success against one foe, no matter how small, had considerable allure for people interested in moral reform. It might not be possible, as a supporter of an anti-cigarette bill in North Carolina put it, to "usher in the dawn of millennial peace and splendor" immediately, in "one full swoop," but a satisfying beginning could be made by stamping out cigarettes. Gaston offered the tonic of easy triumph to people who, for the most part, had been frustrated in their efforts to overhaul American society. She provided what the *Union Signal* called "new hope for freedom from at least this one evil."[36]

When Gaston founded the Anti-Cigarette League, she made it clear that the goal was to completely outlaw the manufacture and consumption of cigarettes. A former schoolteacher, she did not have much faith in the power of education as an agent of reform. She also wanted to take cigarettes away from everyone, not just children. So far as she could tell, cigarettes had no redeeming qualities. She sought a "war of extermination" against "this pest of modern society."[37]

The first recruits in Gaston's battle against cigarettes were temperance workers. Matilda Bradley Carse, president of the Chicago Central WCTU and founder of the Woman's Temperance Publishing Association, was a member of the league's original board of directors. Vandelia Varnum Thomas, a popular platform speaker for the WCTU, was vice president of the board. The league occupied offices in the Woman's Temple, a WCTU-owned building in Chicago. Its activities were publicized in the *Union Signal*.[38]

Like other reformist groups during the Progressive Era, the Anti-Cigarette League drew most of its strength from middle-class Protestants of Anglo-Saxon ethnicity, living in small to mid-sized cities, with access to printing presses, pulpits, speakers' platforms, legislatures, police departments, and courts. The founding officers included a banker, a lawyer, a wholesale seed dealer, a pension agent, and a professor at a homeopathic medical college. A group of Chicago businessmen provided the initial financing. However, at least a few supporters came from working-class backgrounds. For example, the legislator who sponsored a 1905 law that banned cigarette sales in Wisconsin was a blacksmith. Others, such as Henry Ford, were extremely wealthy.[39]

Virtually all those publicly identified with the group favored prohibition. Among the better known were Jordan; Harvey W. Wiley of the Food and Drug Administration; Benjamin B. Lindsey, a famous juvenile court judge; Irving Fisher, a leading economist; John Harvey Kellogg, the health reformer; Edison; and Ford, whose interests ranged far beyond the business of manufacturing automobiles. Of all the charges against cigarettes during the Progressive Era, the one that carried the most weight was the one that linked them to alcohol.

Anti-cigarette activists disagreed about exactly how smoking led to drinking. Gaston thought it had something to do with "furfural," a component of cigarette smoke that she believed had a "paralyzing influence" on the mucous membranes. The result was an intense thirst that could be relieved only by alcohol. Edison blamed "acrolein," which he thought was produced by the combustion of cigarette paper. The substance, he said, caused "permanent and uncontrollable" degeneration of the brain cells, leaving the brain-damaged smoker at the mercy of baser instincts. (Modern science recognizes acrolein as a by-product of the combustion of tobacco, rather than paper; it is considered a source of damage to lung cells.)[40]

William A. McKeever, professor of philosophy at the Kansas State Agricultural College and, later, a director of the Presbyterian Board of Temperance and Moral Welfare, argued that smokers were inclined to drink and otherwise "yield to the evil suggestions of others" because of the effect of cigarettes on the heart. He used the sphygmograph—a device for recording the pulse rate—to demonstrate this effect. When attached to the radial artery, with an appendage much like a blood pressure sleeve, the machine created dramatically jagged white lines on a strip of dark paper, easily reproduced in newspapers and magazines. McKeever maintained that the lines showed the physiologic changes associated with smoking, beginning with an increase in heartbeat, followed by a period of "prostration," during which the smoker was particularly susceptible to the lure of alcohol.[41]

Much attention was focused on nicotine, which had been recognized in crude form as an element in tobacco as early as 1571. According to Wiley, nicotine induced "Lethean passivity" in smokers, making them more inclined to use alcohol, cocaine, opium, and other drugs. Jordan characterized nicotine as a "nerve irritant." As he explained it, "It is one of the peculiarities of nerve-disturbing drugs that when taken, they seem to quiet the pain they have caused. But when the effect passes, the pain reappears.

The system calls for more and thus the drug habit begins." A weakened nervous system would make an individual more susceptible to the use of alcohol and other drugs. This kind of argument had powerful appeal during the early 1900s, when the public was becoming increasingly aware of the social problems created by drug use.[42]

Lindsey, whose work as a juvenile court judge in Denver, Colorado, brought him international attention, was among many progressives who contended that cigarette smoking led not only to alcohol and drugs but to crime. A dependable speaker for the Anti-Cigarette League in the early 1900s, he told audiences that most criminals started out as cigarette smokers. "One bad habit led to another," he said. "The nicotine and poison in the cigaret created an appetite for alcoholic drink. The cigaret . . . invited all the other demons of habit to come in and add to the degradation that the cigaret had begun." Lindsey often required that the juveniles who appeared before him stop smoking as a condition of probation. (In the 1920s, Lindsey espoused the principles of what he called "companionate marriage," which many took to mean free love. This made him something of a pariah among other reformers. Although he had lost interest in the Anti-Cigarette League by that point, his assistance probably would have been unwelcome, even if he had offered it.)[43]

Some of Gaston's supporters went beyond cigarettes to condemn tobacco in all its forms. In a popular handbook titled *How To Live*, Fisher ranked tobacco as second only to alcohol as a risk to "healthful living." (He also scorned it as a waste of money.) At the National Conference of Social Work in 1918, he predicted that science would eventually prove that smoking was just as harmful as drinking. Fisher's stature as an economist was eroded by his misplaced confidence in the stock market in 1929 (shortly before the market crashed he announced that "[s]tock prices have reached what looks like a permanently high plateau"), but he remained influential in reform circles until his death in 1947. By then, *How To Live* had gone through 21 editions and sold more than half a million copies.[44]

Kellogg wrote one full-length book, published dozens of pamphlets, produced a film and a lantern slide show, and delivered hundreds of lectures on the theme "How Tobacco Kills." As head of the Battle Creek Sanitarium and also as a director of the Michigan Board of Health, he refused to hire anyone who used any kind of tobacco. One young doctor, being interviewed for a position with the Board of Health in 1915, recalled that Kellogg asked him only two questions: Did he drink liquor? Did he use tobacco? In Kellogg's mind, tobacco was an ally of alcohol, and it was equally harmful whether snuffed, chewed, or smoked in pipes, cigars, or cigarettes.[45]

Gaston herself rarely spoke out against any other kind of tobacco. She was a nominal sponsor of a 1913 petition to Congress to prohibit the production, manufacture, sale, and importation of tobacco, but for the most part, she confined her activities to cigarettes. "I am no defender of tobacco in any form," she said. "But the cigarette is in a class by itself." Most of her backers agreed.[46]

Gaston's support came not only from prohibitionists, but also from religious leaders, the medical profession, educators, and the business community. There was, of course, considerable overlap. People who gave time or money, or both, to the Anti-Cigarette League tended to be evangelical Protestants who favored prohibition and were engaged in (or had fathers or husbands who were engaged in) either medicine, education, business, or the ministry. Baptists, Presbyterians, and Methodists were much more likely to join the cause than Catholics or Jews. The Columbia Association of Baptist Churches, the General Assembly of the Presbyterian Church, and the Methodist General Conference all voted, in 1909, to condemn smoking; the Catholics, meanwhile, were hosting monthly "smokers" (where smoking was not only permitted but encouraged) in their parish halls and guild rooms. Twenty-four of the 143 people listed as officers on letterheads of the Anti-Cigarette League before World War I were ordained Protestant ministers, and two others were nonordained Protestant leaders; only one was a Catholic priest.[47]

Among the more prominent Protestants who joined the league were Clarence True Wilson, general secretary of the Methodist Episcopal Board of Temperance, Prohibition, and Public Morals; Francis E. Clark, founder of the Society of Christian Endeavor, a movement to promote Protestant values, including abstinence from alcohol; and Daniel A. Poling, Clark's successor as head of the Christian Endeavor movement, and editor of the *Christian Herald*, an important Protestant journal. In the glowing tip and smoky effluent of a cigarette, these religious leaders found a compelling analogy to fire and brimstone.

The league also was sanctioned by Protestant service organizations, such as the Salvation Army and the YMCA. William Booth, founder of the Salvation Army, condemned all smoking as unclean, injurious to health, wasteful, disagreeable to others, unnatural, and self-indulgent. He once set forth "Fifty-Four Objections to Tobacco," writing that it has "an injurious influence on the brain, and nervous system generally," including the heart; "arrests the growth of the young"; "tends to insanity"; "is expensive"; is a "great waste of time"; "is a great promoter of drinking"; "tends to lead its victims into bad associations"; and "is powerful in leading to forgetfulness of God." All eight of the Booth children were taught to shun tobacco as if it represented the devil himself. Booth's son Ballington, director of Salvation Army activities in the United States until he established his own religious and social welfare organization in 1896, served as a member of the advisory board of the Anti-Cigarette League in 1912 and as vice president in 1914 and 1915. During the years 1904 to 1917, the Army used the pages of its national magazine, the *War Cry*, to conduct increasingly vigorous attacks on tobacco. The most lurid of these were aimed at cigarettes. A few local chapters of the Salvation Army organized their own anti-cigarette leagues.[48]

The YMCA was even more aggressive in condemning the use of cigarettes. The organization's founder, Sir George Williams, denounced them
as a "growing evil" in 1896; he reiterated his opposition several times
before his death in 1905. Articles on the dangers of cigarettes appeared
frequently in YMCA publications. Typical was one titled "Is Smoking Injurious?" by Dr. George J. Fisher, medical director of the YMCA. The answer was yes. Among the sources cited was Charles B. Towns, a well-
known anti-drug crusader (and an officer of the Anti-Cigarette League)
who included tobacco on his list of "habits that handicap." An article titled
"Effects of Cigaret Smoking on Young Men" was illustrated with a drawing
depicting the progress of a smoker, from upright young man to slouching
derelict. Yet another concluded that cigarettes were a cause of crime. As
further inducement to probity, a YMCA magazine published a letter from
Connie Mack, legendary baseball player and manager, saying cigarette
smokers would never amount to much. The YMCA also provided a forum
for Gaston and other anti-cigarette activists, publishing their writings, pub-
licizing their activities, and inviting them to lecture in YMCA facilities.[49]

The involvement of these various religious leaders and groups reflects
the importance given to questions of morality in the early anti-cigarette
movement. Even discussions about the effects of cigarette smoking on
health tended to have moral overtones. In part, this was a consequence of
the limits of contemporary medical science. With only a narrow understanding of the process of disease, physicians themselves often attributed
ill health to immoral habits; if you were moral, you were healthy. Furthermore, the people who dominated public discourse in general tended to
be more interested in public morality than in personal health. They advocated temperance, spirituality, sexual restraint, and self-sacrifice instead
of self-indulgence. "Healthism"—the pursuit of a sort of supercharged
health, far beyond the mere absence of disease—had not yet become a
national faith.

Most of the doctors who attacked cigarettes during the Progressive Era
regarded health as a secondary issue in the debate over smoking. For example, Dr. Daniel H. Kress, an officer of the Anti-Cigarette League, theorized that cigarettes were more dangerous than other kinds of tobacco
because the smoke was more likely to be inhaled and thus to come into
contact with an extensive area of the lungs, where it could cause more
damage than if confined to the mucous membranes of the mouth. Nonetheless, he thought the effects of cigarettes on "character" were far more
serious than those on health. In 1913, Kress—a neurologist who first
gained public notice by advocating improved waste disposal and other sanitary reforms—temporarily left a private practice in Washington, D.C., to
establish several stop-smoking clinics for the league. He said later that
America would not be able to maintain its "greatness" with a cigarette-
smoking populace. Dr. John N. Hurty, Indiana state health commissioner
(and a close friend of Kellogg), claimed that cigarettes caused insanity, led
people to crime, contributed to "race deterioration," and encouraged the

use of alcohol, morphine, and patent medicines. Almost as an afterthought, he said they also caused heart disease.[50]

In emphasizing morality over health, these physicians were looking back to the late sixteenth century, when reports about the consequences of smoking first began to circulate in Europe. The author of a 1601 "Warning for Tobacconists" surveyed the existing literature and concluded that tobacco caused "infinit maladies." In his famous *Counterblaste to Tobacco*, King James I of England excoriated his subjects for using a substance that was "harmefull to the braine" and "dangerous to the Lungs," among other things. Benjamin Rush reported in 1798 that tobacco caused certain diseases of the mouth, throat, stomach, and nervous system and was generally detrimental to health. None of these writers, however, believed that smoking was dangerous primarily because it was unhealthy. Likewise, the authors of several nineteenth-century American medical school theses condemned smoking as more of a moral issue than a health risk.[51]

Nonetheless, a few state legislatures took steps to regulate cigarettes on the grounds of health during the early 1900s. In 1907, Illinois made it illegal to manufacture, sell, or give away "any cigarette containing any substance deleterious to health, including tobacco." The Missouri legislature approved (although the governor refused to sign) a 1913 bill "to conserve the public health" by prohibiting the sale or possession of cigarettes. However, the organized medical community had no public presence in the debate over these measures, or any others involving cigarettes. Only about 10 percent of the people who served on the board of the Anti-Cigarette League held medical degrees. Of these, the majority were homeopaths: practitioners of a therapy that the American Medical Association disdained as quackery.[52]

Doctors had little interest in cigarettes as a health issue partly because they were preoccupied with other problems. Although the profession had made advances in preventive medicine and the control of some infections, doctors were still limited in their ability to cure disease once it developed. Medical research was directed toward the search for curative agents. Meanwhile, doctors were fighting to gain respectability, by imposing new standards for medical education, licensing, and regulation. Questions about tobacco and health were left largely to those involved in the health reform, eugenics, and temperance movements. It is tempting to speculate that orthodox, or "regular," physicians were slow to recognize the hazards of smoking because so many of the early warnings came from people they regarded as "faddists" (and competitors). Even if physicians had become involved, their opinions might not have had much influence; in pre–World War I America, the medical community had relatively little prescriptive authority over social behavior.[53]

In any case, many doctors discounted the claims of the anti-tobacconists as unfounded; some even defended smoking as a useful anodyne for the stresses of modern life. For example, a Johns Hopkins–trained physician, writing in *Harper's Weekly* in 1913, described tobacco as a "solace," one that most people could enjoy "without the slightest qualm or fear." He said he had searched the medical literature in vain for any evidence condemning tobacco in any form when used by "normal men." As late as 1948, the *Journal of the American Medical Association* was arguing that "more can be said in behalf of smoking as a form of escape from tension than against it . . . there does not seem to be any preponderance of evidence that would indicate the abolition of the use of tobacco as a substance contrary to the public health."[54]

In contrast, health reformers and medical "irregulars" painted ghastly pictures of the fate awaiting every smoker, with particular horrors reserved for those who indulged in cigarettes. Some of this rhetoric was extreme, as in a report about a cigarette smoker whose veins had burst upon his untimely death at age twenty-five, revealing blood "black as ink"; but some was remarkably prescient, given present-day understanding.[55]

The list of ailments attributed to cigarettes in the reform literature included cancer, emphysema, heart disease, and most of the other problems now associated with smoking. The major exception was lung cancer, which was very rare until the 1930s, and not even formally recognized as a disease until 1923. However, Charles A. Greene, the self-described "father of omnipathy," warned that cigarettes could impair lung function, as well as cause heart attacks. Kellogg (a conventionally trained physician) insisted that smoking caused both heart disease and certain cancers, and he predicted that science would eventually prove it. An unidentified homeopathic physician, quoted in an anti-tobacco tract in 1882, declared that cigarette smoking would shorten a life by ten years. The medical establishment did not begin to accept such arguments until the middle of the next century.[56]

Far more significant than doctors in the early anti-smoking movement were businessmen, many of whom regarded cigarettes as impediments to efficiency. Cigarette smokers seemed either nervous or stupefied, in either case lacking the steadiness needed for modern industry and business. Financial backing for the Anti-Cigarette League came largely from businessmen, such as Julius Rosenwald, president of Sears, Roebuck, and Company; Andrew Carnegie, who once donated $1,000 in response to a challenge from Rosenwald; and William C. Thorne, president of Montgomery, Ward, and Company. Thorne promised that his firm would contribute $100 a year to the league; the Chicago-based Heath and Milligan Manufacturing Company pledged the same amount.[57]

Elbert Hubbard, the so-called "Sage of East Aurora" (New York)—a former soap salesman who helped revive the Arts and Crafts movement in America by preaching positive thinking, perseverance, and enterprise to entrepreneurs—said cigarette smokers simply could not be trusted. Hands that hold cigarettes, he said, "are the hands that forge your name and close over other people's money." Dozens of major employers agreed with him. The Chicago, Burlington, and Quincy Railroad, the Rock Island Railroad, the New Haven Road, and the Atchison, Topeka, and Santa Fe Rail-

road were among the public transportation companies that fired any workers caught smoking cigarettes on or off the job. The president of the
Colorado Fuel and Iron Company notified all his employees that those who
were unwilling to give up cigarettes should seek employment elsewhere.
Their prospects were scarcely more promising in government jobs. For
example, the civil service commission of Duluth, Minnesota, barred cigarette smokers from all jobs with the city, including the police and fire
departments.[58]

John Wanamaker, arguably the most influential merchant in America
in the early twentieth century, rejected all job applicants who admitted (or
showed any evidence of) cigarette smoking. Wanamaker did not like smokers in his department stores even when they were simply depicted in art-
work. He gave the postimpressionist painters who designed posters for his
stores a free hand except for two subjects: they could not paint nudes or
people smoking.[59]

Like Wanamaker, most employers discriminated only against the use of
cigarettes, not other forms of tobacco, and the stated reasons had more to
do with efficiency than with morality. The vice president of a large manufacturing company in Buffalo, New York, used the word "efficiency"
seven times in a one-page letter explaining why he had no use for cigarette
smokers. The general superintendent of the Pittsburgh Railways Company
(which operated all the streetcar lines in Pittsburgh) said he would not
hire such people because they were careless and prone to accidents.
Although these executives shared the view that cigarette smokers were
morally suspect, they rejected them as employees in the name of productivity.[60]

Henry Ford, who swore that no cigarette smoker would ever work for
the Ford Motor Company, explained why in *The Case Against the Little
White Slaver*, which he published in four volumes between 1914 and 1916.
The book consists of statements from employers about the undesirability
of cigarette smokers as employees, interspersed with testimonials from ath-
letes and other celebrities as to the virtues of clean living, and cautionary
tales about smokers who came to bad ends. According to Ford, the attitudes of businessmen were "not a matter of sentiment," but "a plain business proposition." Cigarette smokers simply could not be trusted.[61]

Both the courts and editorial writers generally accepted the rights of
employers to restrict the use of cigarettes by their workers. For example,
a Washington district court ruled in favor of a Tacoma manufacturing
company when an employee protested his dismissal for smoking cigarettes
on the job. The *Yakima Herald*, in an editorial supporting the decision,
commented, "A man has a right to smoke, but he has no right to smoke
where and when his employers forbid it."[62]

The rules had little practical effect, since only a small proportion of the
population smoked cigarettes, but they helped reinforce anti-cigarette attitudes among legislators. In a lengthy report on "The War Against the
Cigarette" in 1909, the *New York Times* attributed the enactment of pro-

hibitory laws in eight midwestern states to the influence of business. "Business didn't preach—it practiced," the paper commented. "It didn't say: 'For the sake of your immortal soul, cut out the smoke.' It said: 'If you smoke, skiddoo—no job for you.' " The Times concluded that "the best reformer is not a reformer."[63]

Even some reformers came to recognize that appeals to utility carried more weight in the modern world than fevered warnings about moral dangers. Consider the case of Herbert F. Fisk, a professor of education at Northwestern University and principal of the Northwestern Academy, a preparatory school, in Evanston, Illinois (home of the WCTU). Fisk joined the anti-cigarette crusade under the banner of temperance. A meticulous record keeper, he maintained a thick file of pamphlets and clippings on the relationship between smoking and drinking. He marked as particularly important a report that the Keeley Institute—which offered "cures" for alcoholism and drug addiction—refused to accept patients who smoked cigarettes. Cigarette smokers were not only more likely to start using alcohol and other drugs, they were less likely to give them up as long as they continued to smoke. Fisk also saved an editorial from the *Michigan Advocate* (a Methodist paper) describing cigarettes as a "modern Moloch of selfishness and uncleanness," leading to "world-wide degradation." As a member of the Anti-Cigarette League, he worked with Gaston to develop public presentations based on such themes.[64]

Later, he tried a less heated approach, stressing the effects of smoking on scholarship and employment opportunities. He found it noteworthy that many "great businessmen" believed cigarette smokers were "far less useful" than nonsmokers. He conducted surveys at the Northwestern Academy that he said proved smokers were poor scholars. He announced that smokers would no longer be admitted to the academy and any who were currently enrolled would be expelled if they did not quit. "Boys who smoke are no good to the school, learn nothing themselves, and set a bad example to the other students," he said. His remarks struck many newspaper editors as reasoned and praiseworthy.[65]

On the eve of World War I, the forces arrayed against the cigarette seemed formidable. Reformers had succeeded in outlawing the sale—and in some cases, the manufacture, advertising, possession, and use—of cigarettes in thirteen states; although three of those states had subsequently repealed their laws, prohibitory bills were pending in six others. The United States Supreme Court had upheld the constitutionality of such laws in an important decision involving cigarette prohibition in Tennessee in 1900. Cigarettes were subject to a number of other restrictions, varying with the locale. Two states had outlawed their use on school property, and many school districts refused to hire teachers who smoked them at any time, anywhere. Virtually every state banned the sale of cigarettes to minors. Florida had made it illegal not only to sell them to minors but to "persuade, advise, counsel or compel" a minor to smoke. In Nevada, smoking was prima facie evidence of delinquency.[66]

In the minds of many citizens, cigarettes remained a mark of deviancy. As an early settler of Casper, Wyoming, remembered it, the sale of "ready-mades" was "limited to women of the underworld and their hangers-on. The average citizen would have been embarrassed if seen smoking one." More than thirty years later, he could still recall the shock it gave him when one of the town's most prominent pioneers returned from serving two years in Congress, unconcernedly puffing away at a cigarette. The congressman was not reelected, his display of "degradation" having figured heavily in his defeat. In many parts of the country, a cigarette-smoking politician simply did not project qualities that appealed to middle-class voters. This was demonstrated in Memphis, Tennessee, in 1917. One of the charges brought against an unpopular mayor was that he smoked cigarettes. He was forced to resign.[67]

Meanwhile, the number of anti-smoking groups proliferated. The Anti-Cigarette League, which once had little competition, was now joined by a Non-Smokers' Protective League, founded by Dr. Charles G. Pease, a dentist and homeopathic physician, in New York City in 1911; a No-Tobacco League, based in Indiana but expanding westward; an Anti-Cigarette Smoking League, aimed at school children in the East; and a reinvigorated Anti-Narcotics Department in the WCTU. (There was some overlap of membership. For example, five of the eleven original directors of the Non-Smokers' Protective League were also active in the Anti-Cigarette League.) In the South, the WCTU was organizing a "colored Anti-cigaret League." A field that had once received only desultory attention from a few temperance workers had been redefined as a viable and important area of reform.[68]

Although the groups had differing objectives—some seeking to extinguish tobacco in all its forms, others concentrating only on cigarettes—they united in demanding curbs on public smoking. Jordan, an active member of both the Anti-Cigarette League and the Non-Smokers' Protective League, complained that smoke from pipes, cigars, and cigarettes "is intensely irritating to the eyes, nostrils and lungs of those who have not become case-hardened to it." Wiley, one of the incorporators of the Non-Smokers' Protective League, called for a virtual end to any smoking in public, saying, "A man has not the shadow of right to inflict unwholesome smoke and his vile breath on the community at large." Kress was confident that "[t]he time is not far distant when . . . protection will be afforded on our street cars and other public places to those who are liberal enough to permit others to smoke, but do not wish to inhale the smoke at second hand." However, in campaigning against "second hand" smoke, Kress and others gave only passing attention to the health of nonsmokers, concentrating instead on their comfort and safety.[69]

In an important victory in New York in 1913, the Non-Smokers' Protective League convinced the state's Public Service Commission to outlaw smoking on the railroads, streetcars, ferries, and waiting rooms within its jurisdiction. The decision came after a public hearing during which the sins of smokers were catalogued at length. One woman testified that her hat had been set afire by a cigarette flung from a subway platform; fortunately, it was a sturdy winter hat and not a filmy and more combustible summer model. A few smokers tried to speak in their own defense, but "they had no arguments to back them up in their opposition but ridicule," according to a report in the *New York Times*. One smoker asked for pity. "Spare a little of our vices," he said. "We shall be a long time dead. They have a constitutional right to breathe fresh air; haven't we got a constitutional right to the pursuit of happiness?" The Non-Smokers' Protective League insisted, and the commission agreed, that the rights of nonsmokers should prevail.[70]

In another case, also in 1913, the victory went to the smokers. The United States Senate rejected a resolution, introduced by the reform-minded Senator Benjamin ("Pitchfork Ben") Tillman of South Carolina, that would have banned smoking in the Senate chamber by anyone at any time. Senator Charles E. Townsend, a distinguished progressive, refused to support the proposal despite a plaintive letter from Tillman about the effects of tobacco smoke on the old and the sick. It was said that the smoke in the Senate was so thick that the solons could scarcely be distinguished from the mahogany chairs on which they sat. But it was produced mostly by cigars, tokens of power, and consequently subjected to few restrictions.[71]

The Anti-Cigarette League, meanwhile, was sending recruiters around the country; distributing pledge cards to school children; and soliciting donations from church, temperance, and business groups. The field secretary for Michigan reported that he had lectured in eighty-five churches during one four-month period in 1912; an organizer in sparsely populated northern Nevada set up four chapters with a combined membership of 1,000 that year. These efforts brought in little money, but they succeeded in keeping the league's name and its cause before the public.[72]

The league attracted even more attention after Kress opened a stop-smoking clinic in its Chicago headquarters in 1913. The clinic offered a "cure" that involved painting the smoker's throat with silver nitrate. The chemical reacted with elements in cigarette smoke to produce extreme nausea. Penitents who might be tempted to backslide were supplied with gentian root, which supposedly had tonic qualities when chewed. Messenger boys, chorus girls, housewives, an occasional businessman, and the idly curious trooped in to the clinic—along with reporters looking for feature stories. The clinic was so successful that the league soon established a second one in Chicago, for women only, followed by others in Detroit, Cincinnati, and elsewhere in the Midwest. Gaston took to carrying a supply of gentian root with her at all times, to be thrust upon any unwary smokers she chanced to encounter.[73]

Other anti-smoking activists opened similar clinics in New Jersey, California, and Washington State. Several were administered by juvenile court judges, who offered young offenders a choice between taking the cure or going to detention, on the theory that cigarettes encouraged lawlessness. The silver nitrate treatment was more humane if not more effective than that favored by the superintendent of the Boys' and Girls' Aid Society in Seattle in the early 1900s: he used ankle chains to break young "cigarette fiends" of the habit.[74]

Gaston remained tireless in her efforts to banish what she invariably called "the evil" or "the curse" of cigarettes. "There has never been anything to equal our present effort, over which I have burned the midnight oil," she wrote to one supporter. After the Illinois Supreme Court ruled that the 1907 state law prohibiting cigarette sales was unconstitutional, she initiated a campaign to recall the judges. According to one account, she nearly succeeded. Failing that, she tried to revive the law. Between 1908 and 1917, the Illinois legislature considered twelve bills that would have banned the manufacture, use, sale, keeping for sale, owning, or giving away of cigarettes, each one promoted by Gaston and the Anti-Cigarette League.[75]

She also made her presence known at the Chicago City Council. She convinced one of the city aldermen to introduce a bill to prohibit cigarette sales in 1911. The measure was tabled after the city attorney ruled that the council did not have the authority to take such an action. Three years later, Gaston helped draft a bill making it illegal not only to sell but to give away cigarettes within the city limits. The latter provision was an attempt to close an often-used loophole: in areas where only sales were banned, dealers would give away cigarettes—with the purchase of matches for fifteen or twenty cents. Gaston submitted a legal brief, prepared by a Chicago law firm, defending the constitutionality of cigarette prohibition. In addition, she provided each alderman with literature printed by the league, including "Why the Cigarette Is Deadly" and copies of its monthly magazine, *The Boy*. The aldermen also heard from lobbyists for the tobacco industry and from the city attorney, who took a dimmer view of the proposal than Gaston's attorneys. The proposed ordinance was tabled.[76]

Gaston, defeated but unbowed, was soon circulating petitions for other laws, including one compelling cigarette smokers to walk in the middle of the streets. She also took on as a personal mission the task of enforcing the existing city ordinance outlawing sales to minors. After convincing the city police chief to deputize her, she reportedly filed more than 1,000 complaints against Chicago tobacco dealers whom she accused of violating the law.[77]

Outside Chicago, it was more of the same: lobbying for legislation, promoting the "cure," passing out gentian root, seeking converts and contributions. She traveled throughout the East and Midwest whenever funds permitted, giving speeches and attending conferences. Gaston financed much of this travel herself, but she gratefully acknowledged a $500 donation from Rosenwald that made it possible for her to attend the Cleveland Conference of Charities in 1912. She rarely missed the annual convention of the WCTU and often had a place on the program. At the 1911

convention in Milwaukee, for example, she exhorted the convention delegates to escalate the battle against cigarettes. "Eleven states have outlawed the cigaret," she said. "Is your state among them?"[78]

She found receptive audiences in places such as Topeka and Cleveland
and even Washington, D.C., where cigarettes were still socially marginal.
In Detroit, the prestigious Twentieth Century Women's Club sponsored a
stop-smoking clinic. At Battle Creek, Kellogg invited her to develop an
exhibit on the evils of cigarettes, to be financed by Ford and displayed
permanently at the sanitarium. The influential Woman's Club of Chicago
endorsed the Anti-Cigarette League; the *Institution Quarterly* included it on
its list of worthy agencies engaged in "philanthropy, charity and social
betterment."[79]

In New York City, however, she had less success. She sought an invitation to speak at the Colony Club, which drew its membership from the
women of the city's wealthiest families; the club declined. She asked the
members to sign pledges of abstention; few did. The cigarette had already
begun to poke its nose into the parlors of the urban upper class. Mrs. Jacob
H. Vanderbilt herself had gone so far as to open a "tea and cigarette room"
as a refuge for women of the New York Four Hundred. In programs for
the 1910–11 season at the Metropolitan Opera House and several Broadway theaters, patrons of genteel culture could read ads for Egyptian Deities,
Philip Morris, and half a dozen other brands of cigarettes.[80]

There were other problems. Despite all the speeches, the meetings, the
lobbying; the pamphlets, articles, and books; despite the earnest pledges
signed by boys who promised never to smoke and the girls who promised
never to speak to boys who did; despite all the people who took the "cure"
and all the state laws, the city ordinances, and the petitions to Congress:
despite all this, Americans were smoking more cigarettes than ever before.
More than 16 billion cigarettes were manufactured and sold in the United
States during 1914, an increase of 2 billion over the previous year. These
were cigarettes that were taxed. Several billion more were rolled by their
consumers and were thus tax exempt. Cigarettes still accounted for only
about 7 percent of the total tobacco consumption in the U.S.—far behind
pipes (34 percent), chewing tobacco (29 percent), and cigars (25 percent)—
but they were gaining both market share and respectability.[81]

The rebuff from the Colony Club underscored another problem for Gaston and her supporters: enmity toward cigarettes was most pronounced in
areas where they were least popular. This is reflected in the legislative
record. Cigarette smoking was relatively uncommon in the states that outlawed it. As the *New York Times* observed in a 1909 report, "Cigarettes
were doing a hundred times as much harm on the east side of New York
as they were doing in Wisconsin and Indiana but New York hadn't much
to say. New York, serene in its smoke, remarked only that children less
than 16 years old should not smoke cigarettes and that dealers should not
sell children cigarettes." To the urbane easterner, "[p]assing an anti-

cigarette law seemed almost as ridiculous as it would [be] to pass a law prohibiting a woman from wearing more than three pounds of false hair." In contrast, the governor of Minnesota, rather than scorning the cigarette prohibition bill that came to his desk as a product of the silly season, signed it "as seriously as he would have signed a measure to supply funds for the public schools."[82]

Once enacted, the laws were rarely enforced. Occasionally, police departments would experience little spasms of virtue (or perhaps develop a thirst for payoff money) and make a few arrests; but by and large, they were not overly zealous about chasing down cigarette smokers. Any enforcement efforts tended to be brief and concentrated in small towns rather than cities. This was demonstrated in Washington State in 1909, when the legislature amended an existing law to ban the possession as well as the manufacture and sale of cigarettes. According to newspaper reports, police in small towns around the state made about sixty arrests altogether during the first month the law was in effect, but only six more during the next three months, and none thereafter. No arrests were reported in Seattle, which was hosting the Alaska-Yukon-Pacific Exposition at the time.[83]

Among the few who ran afoul of the law was William D. "Big Bill" Haywood, the legendary labor organizer. As head of the radical Industrial Workers of the World during the most turbulent years in American labor history, Haywood was accustomed to legal difficulties. He had faced strike-breakers, Pinkertons, sheriffs, hostile grand juries, and numerous indictments, for everything from murder to sedition. His only convictions, however, came in June 1909, when he was found guilty of possessing "the makings" in the hamlets of North Yakima and Davenport. Similar charges in a third town, Ellensburg, were dropped at the direction of the county prosecutor, who thought the law was unconstitutional. Years later, in his autobiography, Haywood claimed, "My persecution and the publicity that followed it caused the repeal of the anti-cigarette law." In fact, opposition to the law had been building for some time among legislators who regarded it as unenforceable. "When you pass a law you know is going to be violated, as the gentlemen opposing (repeal) admit the present law is violated, you are merely bringing all law into contempt," said Senator Josiah Collins, a member of the judiciary committee, who led the effort to legalize cigarettes. The legislature repealed the law at its next session, two years later.[84]

A study of cigarette prohibition in Wisconsin in 1912 showed that "the law is flagrantly and openly violated," primarily because "there is a great demand for cigarettes and local officials will not enforce a law in the face of a popular demand." The researcher found no record of any prosecutions. He reported there had been virtually no change in the number of retailers selling cigarettes since the law was enacted, in 1905. He concluded the statute was "useless" and recommended that it be repealed. The legislature did so three years later, in 1915; Oklahoma also repealed its anti-cigarette law that year.[85]

In addition to these problems, the anti-cigarette movement was being undermined by internal dissension. Ironically, this discord was an outgrowth of its early success. As more people were attracted to the cause, there was more disagreement about goals and tactics. Several key figures changed their minds about the effectiveness of coercive measures, especially those aimed at adults as well as children. For instance, Wiley once said he supported all efforts to "curtail or restrict, obliterate or destroy the pernicious habit of cigarette smoking." Later, he argued that legislation should be a last resort, and then applied only to people under age twenty-one. He was willing to grant adults the right to smoke, so long as they did so in a way that did not offend abstainers.[86]

Gaston made no such concession. Long after most other anti-cigarette activists had acknowledged the impossibility of legislating the industry out of existence, she remained a self-described "extremist of extremists." She made her position clear with the blunt signature she put on letters to supporters: "Yours for the extermination of the cigarette." To doubters, she offered a pamphlet titled "Why the Manufacture and Sale of Cigarettes Should Be Prohibited by Law." She adopted a new slogan: "A Smokeless America by 1925."[87]

Conflict over this issue resulted in two efforts to unseat Gaston as superintendent of the Anti-Cigarette League. The first came three years after the league was organized, when the then-president, Frank V. Irish, a retired professor from Ohio State University in Columbus, summarily demoted her. In a letter to Fisk, one of Gaston's admirers at Northwestern University in Evanston, Irish hinted at problems created by Gaston's "visionary schemes." He described her as "erratic, and very reckless in her business methods," and said she "causes us a great deal of trouble." Gaston, for her part, complained about being "misunderstood and misrepresented." One year later, the Anti-Cigarette League had a new president and Gaston was back in business as superintendent. She tweaked her opponents by commenting, in *The Boy*, that "An effort was made to shift the national work to other hands, but unsuccessfully, and . . . the 'old original' League continues to be the recognized power." The official objective remained the elimination of the cigarette industry by law.[88]

However, the tension persisted, waxing and waning over the years, until the entry of the United States into World War I brought it to a head. Gaston was appalled by the widespread enthusiasm for supplying American soldiers with cigarettes. "People seem to be entirely swept off their feet," she wrote to no less a personage than Secretary of War Newton D. Baker, "and the general impression prevails that as soon as a man puts on the uniform he must begin to dope up preparatory to a possible trench experience. This, of course, is the greatest folly." She enclosed several pamphlets, an application for membership in the Clean Life Club, and a flyer

("War Bulletin No. 1") that claimed "a cruel injustice is being done in encouraging indulgence in cigarettes." If soldiers had to die, she added, they should "go into the presence of Almighty God clean"—free from "an enslaving habit" whose effects "closely resemble the use of opium."[89]

This intemperate tone was a source of embarrassment for the directors of the Anti-Cigarette League. It seemed unpatriotic, and it was certainly impolitic, to attack a commodity military leaders said was necessary to the victory of good over evil. Gaston became an object of ridicule; where once she had commanded respect in the pages of newspapers and magazines, now she was openly mocked. Still, she had sufficient support within the league to hold onto her position until the end of the war. Less than two months after the armistice, however, she was forced to resign.[90]

Gaston's critics also challenged her business methods, which she herself described as "somewhat confusing." The writer Frances Warfield put it this way: "She was incapable of arranging papers, or keeping records or files. Money flowed loosely through her fingers; the cause kept her almost constantly in debt, since her vision was always a jump ahead of her bank balance." Illinois State Senator Henry Evans of Aurora, tired of being badgered by Gaston to move her anti-cigarette bills out of his committee, once accused her of "making a mighty good thing" out of her crusade—implying that she was personally profiting from it. Gaston angrily pointed out that her salary often went unpaid.[91]

In contrast to the Anti-Saloon League and, to a lesser degree, the WCTU, the Anti-Cigarette League rarely enjoyed a financial cushion. The monthly budget ran to about $1,250, and expenses typically exceeded income. Gaston's surviving correspondence indicates that she struggled constantly to find money to pay her bills. "We have always felt the 'cramps' that are common to work of reform," she wrote to Jordan. "People who are generous hearted toward other causes rarely respond in generous fashion to a work like ours and enthusiastic workers are allowed to grow discouraged and give up the fight." To Rosenwald, she complained, "So much of our time and strength is being spent in the effort to make the work possible instead of being able to go straight to the task." She appealed to one supporter for a donation of $100, pointing out that the costs of "[h]eadquarters, an abundance of printed matter and a force of active workers in the field make a considerable sum imperative." He sent her $5. She told a reporter for the *Chicago News* that she had often called upon her brother Edward to finance her activities. Even that did not always pay the bills, as indicated by the intermittent publication of *The Boy*. At least one employee filed a lawsuit against her, seeking payment of back wages.[92]

Her disdain for compromise and her shortcomings as a fund-raiser cost Gaston the leadership of the movement she had helped ignite. She never regained the influence she had had in the years before the war. For much of the last decade of her life, her fellow reformers merely tolerated her, at best. However, the movement itself persisted. Indeed, as cigarettes made further inroads in American society, they inspired even greater opposition. The apotheosis of the anti-cigarette campaign was yet to come, in a world that would be reordered by an assassin's bullet, fired in Sarajevo on June 28, 1914.

# The Little White Slaver Goes to War

The war maimed, killed, and devastated;
but the worst thing the war did was entrench the cigarette.
*Lawrence Leslie*[1]

*C*igarettes began to move into the mainstream of American culture during World War I. By 1920, they accounted for 20 percent of the total tobacco consumption in the United States, compared to less than 7 percent in 1914. The war did not initiate this change, but it accelerated it. Millions of American soldiers smoked cigarettes given to them during the war as a gesture of support by their government, by civic organizations, and by ordinary citizens. This helped transform what was once a manifestation of moral weakness into a jaunty emblem of freedom and democracy. By wrapping cigarettes in the protective cloak of patriotism, the war undercut the campaign against their use. The opposition briefly revived in the postwar years, in response to increased smoking by women, but the milieu had changed and the cigarette was no longer the easy target it had once been.[2]

When the United States entered the war in April 1917, the sale of cigarettes was illegal in eight states, and anti-cigarette bills were pending in at least twenty-two other states. The sheer volume of legislation, proposed and enacted, suggests the degree to which cigarette smoking affronted the nation's values in the pre-war era. Most Americans would have agreed with Rev. William "Billy" Sunday, the popular evangelist, who once said "[t]here is nothing manly about smoking cigarettes. For God's sake, if you must smoke, get a pipe."[3]

The war helped legitimate cigarettes by linking them to an icon of manliness and civic virtue: the American soldier. Benedict Crowell, assistant secretary of war, estimated that 95 percent of the American Expeditionary Forces used tobacco in some form. Cigarettes were by far their smoke of choice. The War Department attributed this in part to the fact that the troops were younger, on the average, than those in earlier years, and young men preferred cigarettes to other forms of tobacco. Cigarettes also had certain practical advantages: they fit easily into a uniform pocket; were more portable than pipes or cigars; could be smoked quickly; and required no special equipment to use, beyond a light. Furthermore, cigarette butts could easily be recycled into new smokes—an important consideration during wartime, when supplies were uncertain. The various relief agencies that helped provide the troops with tobacco and other sundries also preferred cigarettes: cigars were more likely to spoil during damp weather, and pipes were easily broken. Chewing tobacco was both portable and durable, but it offended the sensibilities of many relief workers; they resolutely passed out cigarettes instead.[4]

The use of cigarettes by servicemen was sanctioned by both official edict and public consensus. Congress ordered the War Department to include them in the rations issued to soldiers overseas, and it subsidized their sale to soldiers at post exchange stores and canteens at home and abroad. As a result, the American government soon became the largest single purchaser of cigarettes in the world. The War Industries Board encouraged domestic production by designating cigarette manufacturing as an essential industry, giving it access to raw materials and transportation networks (and protecting it from any troublesome labor disputes.) Newspapers, business groups, women's clubs, and many other organizations established private funds to augment government supplies. Even some groups that had once been hostile toward cigarettes—including the YMCA and the Salvation Army—helped supply them to servicemen.

Much of this was done in the interest of diverting the soldiers from other, more objectionable sins, particularly those involving what one contemporary called "bad liquor and worse women." The United States had marched off to war under the banner of moral reform. Its leaders were determined to extend the purifying impulse to the armed forces. Congress banned the sale of alcohol to men in uniform; it also stipulated that prostitution-free zones be established around military camps. Having been denied access to wine and women, the men were encouraged to comfort themselves with song and smoke.[5]

In addition, the war indirectly promoted the cigarette habit by quickening the pace of urbanization and industrialization. Pipes and cigars need constant attention from the smoker; chewing tobacco requires frequent spitting (a challenge to sanitation if not to aesthetics). The cigarette, in contrast, is fast, convenient, and less offensive to nonsmokers in close quarters than other forms of tobacco. It can be smoked in brief intervals, while the user is operating machinery or engaged in some other task. These are important advantages in an urban, industrial world.

The war also stimulated various social changes that favored increased cigarette smoking: it smudged the lines separating the roles of men and women; opened up a generational divide; and unleashed a quest for liberation in all areas of human endeavor. Postwar America valued that which was "up to date" and "wide awake." The cigarette, relatively uncommon until after the turn of the century, enjoyed the benefits of novelty. Moreover, since the modern cigarette industry had been launched in the United States, it had an aura of Americanism, at least when compared to the foreign-dominated brewing industry. This served it well during the xenophobic era of World War I. All these influences worked together to redefine what Henry Ford had called "the little white slaver," investing cigarettes with new cultural meaning and flattening the barriers that had limited their acceptability.[6]

In this and other ways, the war siphoned support from the anti-cigarette movement. Much of the financial backing, as well as a good deal of the ideology, for the organized opposition to smoking had come from prohibitionists. The war provided them with a powerful new rationale for national prohibition: that the production of alcohol wasted grain and other food needed to feed the allied armies. Having appealed to patriotism in arguing for prohibition, they were in a poor position to deflect pro-smoking arguments that were likewise grounded in patriotism. Additionally, with the prospect of a long-awaited victory against alcohol, many prohibitionists figuratively cleared their plates, retreating from other issues in order to concentrate on what they regarded as the primary foe.

Their very success further subverted the anti-cigarette campaign, by planting the seeds for a postwar backlash against the reform impulse in general. Thus, a few weeks after his famous transatlantic flight in 1927, Charles A. Lindbergh deliberately lit a cigarette during a dinner in his honor, repudiating an anti-smoking group's effort to use him as a role model. "I won't be played for a tin saint," he said. (Lindbergh continued to smoke in public despite a critic's threat to "communicate with Colonel Lindbergh's mother on the matter.")[7]

Where there's war, the saying goes, there's smoke. Tobacco can calm the frightened, sedate the wounded, energize the weary, and distract the bored. For centuries, military commanders have regarded it as essential to the fighting man. "You stink of brandy and tobacco, most soldier-like," one character said to another in the British playwright William Congreve's comedy *The Old Bachelor*, written in 1693. General Antoine Charles Lasalle, hero of the Napoleonic wars, reportedly went so far as to insist, "A hussard must smoke; a cavalryman who does not smoke is a bad soldier." From the Civil War through the Vietnam War, the American government defined tobacco as a military necessity by including it in the basic rations issued to troops on the front lines. (Both the Union and the Confederate troops received a tobacco ration during the Civil War.) Beginning with the Thirty Years' War of the early seventeenth century, every major war has been associated with an increase in overall tobacco consumption in the nations involved, initiated by the use of tobacco by soldiers.[8]

Wars also have influenced the ways in which tobacco is used. Soldiers gathered in camps far from home invariably experiment with local products. Americans who fought in Mexico in 1848 came back smoking cigars. Consequently, the cigar industry flourished, at the expense of the "quid" (chewing tobacco). The Crimean War of 1854–56 helped popularize cigarette smoking in Britain and France, Anglo-French troops having picked up the habit from their Turkish allies and Russian enemies. The returning soldiers, fresh from an ennobling adventure in a distant land, were imitated by admiring civilians. At the end of the American Civil War, Union soldiers stationed near Durham, North Carolina, acquired a taste for the local "bright leaf" tobacco. Orders for more of that distinctive tobacco came back from points all around the country, creating a demand that profited local manufacturers, including Washington Duke.[9]

Many American soldiers smoked their first cigarettes while stationed in territories acquired during the Spanish-American War of 1898. Initially, their officers viewed the new habit with deep suspicion. Both the army and navy tried to discourage it, particularly among young recruits, on the grounds that it impaired health and decreased efficiency; the officers recommended either pipes or chewing tobacco instead. The United States Military Academy at West Point banned the sale and possession of cigarettes in 1903; the quartermaster and commissary were ordered to supply pipes and mild smoking tobacco to cadets in an effort to blunt the appeal of cigarettes. President Theodore Roosevelt himself approved the dismissal of two cadets who were court-martialed on charges stemming from the possession of cigarettes (in one case, a package had slipped from the cadet's sleeve during French class; he claimed he had not known it was in his sleeve and was dismissed for lying).[10]

Emulating West Point, cadets and faculty members at the Rhodes Military Institute in Kinston, North Carolina, organized a chapter of the Anti-Cigarette League in 1905; its goal was to "create and maintain a wholesome public sentiment against cigarette smoking." West Point itself reiterated its ban on cigarettes in 1911. Cadets were warned that they faced dismissal for violating the policy, and they were also given anti-cigarette literature, including *The Cigarette Smoking Boy* by William McKeever.[11]

The navy attempted to prohibit the use of cigarettes by sailors under age twenty-one in 1907, but gave it up as unenforceable, despite testimony from the surgeon general that the habit was "a serious impediment to robust health in the Navy." Young sailors ("bluejackets" or "jackies") insisted life at sea would be impossible without cigarettes. As one of them put it:

It's all right to talk about your cigars and your pipes, but cigarettes are cigarettes, and when you once get to liking the little sticks there's nothing that can take their place. Then don't forget that life on the ocean, with none of your women folks or girl friends around to break the monotony, is a lot different from life ashore, and I tell you those dreamsticks help you to pass away many a dreary and home-sick hour.[12]

Even so, two years later, Rear Admiral Seaton Schroeder, commander in chief of the Atlantic battleship fleet, recommended that all enlisted men be forbidden to smoke cigarettes. "The habit injures the men physically and does not benefit them mentally," he said. At the least, he added, the navy should not sell cigarettes in its ships' stores. The *New York Times* endorsed Schroeder's proposal, saying, "[T]he excessive use of cigarettes is not conducive to good shooting or clear thinking." Secretary of the Navy George von L. Meyer apparently agreed, up to a point. He issued an order prohibiting the sale of manufactured cigarettes in naval canteens; however, the order did not apply to cigarette tobacco and papers, which continued to be sold.[13]

By the time the United States entered World War I, cigarettes no longer attracted official censure in military life. West Point had all but given up trying to enforce its ban, after a report from the academy's chief medical officer that "a large percentage" of cadets were "habitual cigarette smokers," most of them having acquired the habit at the academy. The commander of cadets recommended that upperclassmen, at least, be permitted to smoke whatever they wanted. "No distinction should be made between cigarettes and other forms of tobacco," he said, adding, "Cadets constantly see officers smoking cigarettes and it is doubtful if it is much more injurious than other forms of tobacco unless continually inhaled well into the lungs."[14]

In a series of thirty articles written for daily newspapers and intended to help recruits and draftees prepare for military training, the War Department made only two references to tobacco, in each case simply advising "immoderate" smokers to cut down. Raymond B. Fosdick, chairman of the Commission on Training Camp Activities, personally approved a health booklet—distributed at the training camps—that claimed, "If you will save your smoke till after luncheon, you'll never have smoker's heart."[15]

Writing to a New York medical journal, a military judge advocate dismissed as "ridiculous" the argument that cigarette smoking was deleterious to health, at least for adults who smoked a "reasonable quantity." As proof, he pointed to Admiral George Dewey, hero of the Spanish-American War, "who was an inveterate cigarette smoker throughout his life and retained the most remarkable health and vitality." Dewey died in 1917 at the age of 80. Later that year, his widow helped organize a fund to buy cigarettes for sailors.[16]

Military physicians sometimes advised servicemen to avoid "excessive" use of cigarettes, but they rarely defined the point at which "moderate" smoking veered into "excessive." The author of a popular military hygiene book concluded that "[m]oderate smoking, indulged in after meals and in periods of relaxation, cannot be said to be very harmful, if at all so." He cautioned that excessive smoking could cause "irritation of the vocal organs and the bronchial tubes," but properly indulged, the cigarette habit "should not be interfered with." This theme was repeated in a 1917 handbook approved by Surgeon General William C. Gorgas. Early the next year, an article in the journal *Military Surgeon* cleared cigarettes as a source of pulmonary tuberculosis and suggested they had less effect on the heart than pipes or cigars.[17]

Some physicians not only tolerated but even encouraged cigarette smoking, at least during times of stress. A navy doctor, summing up his observations at the end of the war, argued that the use of cigarettes and other forms of tobacco was "a means of diversion which, far from interfering with a man's performance of duty, attaches him to it and renders it less burdensome." He noted that other investigators had discovered that smoking increased the pulse rate and blood pressure, but in his view, those physiological effects were insignificant compared to the overall benefits of the habit. A physician assigned to the Army Medical Corps cautioned against the dangers of inhalation for certain "susceptible" individuals, but he also said he himself had never seen any deleterious effects from smoking cigarettes nor had any of his colleagues.[18]

There were dissenting opinions. In a 1914 handbook on military hygiene, an officer in the United States Medical Corps wrote that "even the moderate use of tobacco is not without possibilities of evil, and cannot be indulged in habitually except at some risk." Cigarette smoking, he added, "is perhaps most likely to be prejudicial to health." After the war began, several physicians attached to allied troops expressed concern about the use of cigarettes by servicemen. For example, a member of the Canadian Expeditionary Force's medical staff, speaking in Minneapolis in August 1917, said that soldiers who smoked were more likely to get bronchial infections. The *Scientific American* published a report from the British *Lancet* warning that "tobacco-smoking is a species of drug habit, although perhaps a mild one if we leave out the question of excess, and the continual drawing of tobacco smoke into the mouth or, worse, deeper into the respiratory tract, introduces toxic risks." A report in another medical journal blamed cigarettes for an increase in the incidence of "tobacco heart" among British soldiers. Meanwhile, surgeons in a London military hospital complained that well-meaning people were impeding the recovery of wounded soldiers by showering them with cigarettes. "Nobody objects to an invalid smoking three or four cigarettes a day, but there is grave danger in fifteen or twenty," the hospital superintendent said.[19]

For the most part, however, physicians expressed little concern about the increasing use of cigarettes by servicemen. When a group of clergymen objected to the distribution of cigarettes by the Red Cross, a New York medical journal insisted, "The intense nervous strain imposed by the conditions at the front in the present war requires that everything possible should be done to allay nervous irritation. It would be the height of folly, both from a medical and a military standpoint, to deny tobacco to men at the front." An army doctor told the *New York Times* that cigarettes were indispensable as an anodyne for wounded soldiers and men just out of the trenches. Others testified that smoking helped calm patients before, after, and sometimes even during surgical operations. In his memoir of the war, Lawrence Stallings claimed that cigarettes were often used to ease withdrawal from morphine in military hospitals. "You could tell who was quitting the drug by watching the cigarettes glowing among the night lights," he wrote.[20]

Even after reports surfaced about the high number of draftees who could not comply with minimum standards of fitness, military officials made little effort to discourage cigarette smoking on grounds of health. In the early months of the war, up to 70 percent of the men who reported to local draft boards failed to pass their physical examinations. The War Department subsequently pressured doctors to be less "exacting" in examining men for military service, but even so, at least one-quarter of those who were examined were rejected.[21]

A few civilian doctors argued that smoking was a factor in the high rejection rate, but both military authorities and the general public ignored them. Among the most forceful critics was John Harvey Kellogg, who regarded tobacco as no less a threat to health than alcohol, red meat, and infrequent excretion. "The cigarette is known to be an enemy of scholarship, of culture, of morals, of health and vigor, and yet it is tolerated, even encouraged," he wrote. "The millions of cigarettes now being fired at our soldiers will every one hit its mark and do its mischief. More American soldiers will be damaged by the cigarette than by German bullets." A Cleveland physician, offering unsolicited advice to the army through the pages of a New York newspaper, suggested "excessive" smoking accounted for 90 percent of the men rejected for problems involving the heart, eyes, ears, and nervous system. In Red Bluff, California, Dr. Sarah E. Wise told an audience that "[o]ne of the glaring causes of failure to qualify for the army on the part of thousands of Americans is the use of tobacco." This prompted the *Sacramento Bee* to point out that the majority of those who qualified also used tobacco.[22]

Meanwhile, military authorities were issuing urgent calls for cigarettes and other tobacco products to be distributed to the troops. General John J. "Black Jack" Pershing, commander of the American Expeditionary Forces, reportedly said tobacco was as vital to the war effort as food or bullets. He singled out cigarettes, pleading that production be increased to meet military needs. His position was reiterated by other high-ranking officers. "A cigarette may make the difference between a hero and a shirker," said Major Grayson M. P. Murphy, one of Pershing's top aides. "In an hour of stress a smoke will uplift a man to prodigies of valor; the lack of it will sap his spirit." General George W. Goethals declared tobacco was no less important than food. Even the commander in chief, President Woodrow Wilson (a nonsmoker himself), condoned tobacco for military purposes, as demonstrated by his support of the *New York Sun*'s "smokes for soldiers" fund.[23]

In government communications during the war, the phrase most often used in connection with cigarettes was "necessary comfort." The underlying message was that soldiers who were sedated ("comforted") by smoke would be less likely to succumb to other temptations. The war had not dissipated the reformist impulses of the Progressive Era, but merely narrowed them. The new priority was to "make the world safe for democracy," and to do so with an army that was clear-eyed and undebauched—the first military force in history to be swept clean of alcohol and prostitutes. As H. L. Mencken commented in a typically caustic column in the *New York Evening Mail*:

> Disappointment now devours the vitals of those optimists who hoped and believed that the entrance of the United States into the war would throw a wet blanket over the uplift. Far from being retired to the rear, there to eat out their great throbbing hearts, the uplifters are more noisily to the front than ever before. The only difference is that they now concentrate the stupendous power of their rectitude upon the boys in khaki.[24]

One month after the United States entered the war, Secretary of War Newton D. Baker sent a letter to the governors of all the states and to the chairmen of all the state councils of national defense, seeking their cooperation in guarding the morality of the troops. It was, he said, "a military necessity, to do everything in our power to . . . conserve the vitality of the men in the training camps." To ensure that the camps, and the neighborhoods surrounding them, would be free of "temptation and peril," Baker appointed a Commission on Training Camp Activities, headed by Fosdick, a tireless moral crusader. The YMCA was assigned the task of protecting the morals of soldiers overseas. The goal of both organizations was to divert the men from drink, drugs, lust, and gambling by providing "substitute attractions," such as athletics, group singing, inspirational movies and books—and tobacco, including cigarettes.[25]

Tobacco was an approved mood-altering substance that could mitigate what Fosdick called "free time problems." It was both a distraction from and a compensation for the various deprivations of military life. One YMCA report quoted a soldier as saying that the troops could "keep sober a long time" if they but had enough to smoke. In addition, by providing ample smoking supplies in military canteens, the government could encourage soldiers to stay on the bases instead of going to nearby sinful cities to buy what they wanted. Secretary of the Navy Josephus Daniels (a determined prohibitionist and at one time an unrelenting foe of the American Tobacco Company) personally endorsed a proposal to establish a tobacco stand at the training camp at Annapolis Junction, Maryland. It was in the best interests of the service, he said, to have cigarettes and other tobacco products readily at hand.[26]

The surviving records of the Commission on Training Camp Activities clearly reflect the priorities of Fosdick and his fellow self-described "moral engineers." The files contain hundreds of reports from various vice vigilantes—groups appointed by Fosdick to monitor social conditions in and around the camps. Their members diligently counted the number of soldiers and sailors seen drinking, entering houses of prostitution, gambling, or otherwise misbehaving in their communities. They occasionally noted other problems, including profanity, blasphemy, and lax observance of the Sabbath. For example, the League of Christian Reformed Churches for the Spiritual Care of Our Soldiers detected an increase in cursing, and asked President Wilson to forbid all members of the army, navy, militia, and marines to use the name of God in vain. The Columbia Avenue Methodist Episcopal Church in Philadelphia discovered that theatrical performances were being held on Sundays at the Plattsburg, New York, training camp. But the primary emphasis was on "intoxicating liquors and lewd women" (or, as another writer put it, "drink and lust"). The moralists in the American government believed these were more deadly to the average soldier than the dangers of the trench itself.[27]

Cigarettes had once been included in the matrix of vice: people who smoked them were said to be more likely to drink, take drugs, gamble, swear, and frequent houses of ill repute (either as clients or staff). Under the peculiar conditions of the war, they were redefined as palliatives that could help men resist such temptations. A retired medical officer, commenting on the increased use of cigarettes in the military, expressed a common point of view when he said the soldiers "have got to do something, and smoking, in my opinion, injures them less than any other 'vice' they could acquire." A confidential report to Fosdick ranked the "special social problems" facing the troops as follows: drinking, gambling, prostitution, child marriage, rape, and illegitimacy. Cigarettes had no standing in this new hierarchy of sin.[28]

Congress considered but firmly rejected a proposal that would have categorized cigarettes and other forms of tobacco as threats to the welfare of the troops. In the last frenzied weeks before the United States entered the war, Senator George E. Chamberlain of Oregon, chairman of the Senate Military Affairs Committee, introduced a bill to outlaw tobacco along with alcohol and prostitution in and around military or naval cantonments, camps, forts, posts, officers or enlisted men's clubs, navy yards, and ships. The bill passed the House and was pending in the Senate when Congress adjourned in March of 1917.[29]

The origins of the proposed anti-tobacco clause are not clear. It might have been inserted by an aide; Chamberlain, a Democrat, had not previously been associated with the opposition to either alcohol or tobacco. Nonetheless, when he reintroduced the bill a week later—during a special session called by President Wilson to consider war-related legislation—he again proposed that tobacco be banned from training facilities. Chamberlain subsequently combined his training bill with a conscription bill prepared by the War Department. Again, the anti-tobacco clause survived.[30]

Within days of the House vote on the original proposal, the Tobacco Merchants Association, the National Cigar Leaf Tobacco Association, and other trade organizations had organized a letter-writing campaign, asking their members to send personal protests to Congress. Industry executives held press conferences and dispatched news releases, all oriented to the theme that tobacco was "an absolute necessity" to men at war; to withhold it would be "indefensible," if not "barbarous" or at least "criminally wrong."[31]

Many newspaper editorialists agreed. To the *Chicago News*, the anti-tobacco clause was the work of a "small souled zealot more eager to ride his own hobby than to serve his country." The *Sacramento Bee* considered it part of a "sinister" effort by "the prohibitionist who would, by legislative enactments and the confiscation of property, force others to think as he thinks . . . and do without what he proscribes." The *Cincinnati Enquirer* thought it reflected a "perverse and hateful puritanism," produced by a "hysterical horde." The *Cleveland Leader* blamed "some Congressional jester, insensible to the full idiocy of his act. Even a fanatic could hardly have proposed such a thing seriously." The *New York Times*, on the other hand, said it was "probably deliberate and done with the purpose of discouraging enlistments." The *Los Angeles Times* cast one of the few editorial votes in favor of the proposal, suggesting, "It would be quite a feather in Uncle Sam's cap if he would break the tobacco habit in camp so that the boys might go abroad free men, as far at least as their appetites are concerned."[32]

Meanwhile, in Congress, legislators were elbowing each other in the rush to defend tobacco. Senator Warren G. Harding of Ohio scolded his colleagues for "loading the army conscription bill with the theoretic plans of vagrant philosophers, cranks and puritanical reformers." Harding had both personal and political reasons for denouncing the proposal. A cigarette smoker himself, he also had a strong constituency among the cigar leaf growers of Ohio.[33]

Chamberlain quickly retreated in the face of this overwhelming opposition. The very day that he reintroduced the bill, he wrote a conciliatory letter to Charles Dushkind, secretary of the Tobacco Merchants Association. As approved by Congress one month later, the Conscription Bill instituted a draft of men between the ages of twenty-one and thirty; established thirty-two training camps; banned the sale and possession of alcohol in the vicinity of the camps; made it illegal to sell alcohol to any man in uniform anyplace at any time; and required that a cordon sanitaire be established around each camp to ensure that it be free of "houses of ill fame, brothels, or bawdy houses" within a radius to be determined by the secretary of war. The bill made no mention of either cigarettes or tobacco.[34]

Congress was less willing to include tobacco in the rations issued to the troops, rejecting a measure introduced in July 1917 by a New York congressman to provide servicemen with sixteen ounces of tobacco a month. The bill attracted little opposition (the WCTU being one of the few protesters on record); it was strongly supported by the tobacco industry; and it had precedence, tobacco having been given to soldiers on the front lines in every major war since the Civil War. Its cost was apparently the deciding factor in its defeat. In March 1918, a Massachusetts congressman introduced another bill to add tobacco to the rations, but it was superseded by an order issued by the War Department—at the request of General Pershing—providing that every member of the American Expeditionary Forces be given a daily supply of either cigarettes, smoking tobacco, or chewing tobacco. To Benedict Crowell, assistant secretary of war, the action served as "the official recognition of tobacco as a necessity for men in active service." It also acknowledged the new popularity of cigarettes: previous wartime rations had included only pipe or chewing tobacco.[35]

The daily ration consisted of a choice between four manufactured cigarettes, enough tobacco and cigarette paper to roll ten cigarettes, or four-tenths of an ounce of chewing tobacco. Few men chose the latter, Crowell noted. The War Department offered only cigarettes, "the makings," or chewing tobacco in the rations because they were less expensive and easier to transport than cigars or pipes, but it provided unlimited supplies of all kinds of tobacco for sale, at subsidized prices, in military post exchanges, both at home and overseas. However, even when they could buy cigars at prices below wholesale, the men preferred cigarettes. At the end of the war, the government held a large stock of surplus cigars in its warehouses in France, but relatively few cigarettes.[36]

As the single greatest tobacco buyer in the world, the American government shipped an average of 425 million cigarettes a month to France alone, along with an even greater quantity of loose tobacco for hand-rolled cigarettes. During the last nine months of the war, the entire production of Bull Durham—the most popular roll-your-own brand—was consigned to the Subsistence Division of the War Department. Altogether, the government sent about 5.5 billion manufactured cigarettes overseas, along with enough tobacco to roll another 11 billion; in contrast, it shipped only about 200 million cigars. Of nearly $80 million in federal spending on tobacco products between April 7, 1917, and May 1, 1919 (the end of the demobilization period), more than 80 percent was used to buy cigarettes and cigarette tobacco.[37]

The War Industries Board—the agency created by Wilson to regulate the American economy during the war—considered rationing the amount of tobacco available to the civilian population in order to ensure that the demands of the military could be met. Instead, Bernard Baruch, head of the board, designated tobacco an essential industry, giving it access to vital raw materials, fuel, and transportation networks. Baruch believed tobacco was important to both military and civilian morale. People would sacrifice more freely if they were not demoralized by resentment over being deprived of their favorite smokes. Accordingly, he asked James B. Duke (still an important figure in the cigarette industry despite the court-ordered breakup of the American Tobacco Company in 1911) to direct efforts to expand production to meet both civilian and military needs. As Baruch told the story in his autobiography, "I called in the man in charge of the tobacco section and said, 'Mr. Duke is running things now.' When Duke demurred, I said, 'You don't like how we're doing things. Show us what we must do.' " Duke's "valuable suggestions" helped triple cigarette production during the war.[38]

Several reform groups called upon the government to restrict the cultivation of all kinds of tobacco and order the land planted with food crops instead. Among them was the WCTU, which noted with approval that some planters had voluntarily reduced their tobacco acreage after the United States entered the war. In a petition to President Wilson and United States Food Commissioner Herbert Hoover, the WCTU said, "What the few have done voluntarily the rest should be required to do." The *No-Tobacco Journal* (published in Butler, Indiana) claimed that food production could be increased to the point that conservation would not be necessary if all the tobacco acreage were given over to food crops. On the other hand, the tobacco trade press urged farmers to plant more tobacco, arguing that people would eat less and thus conserve food if they could smoke more. This position was reinforced by news reports quoting Lord Rhondda, food controller in Great Britain, as saying, "Men would eat a great deal more if they did not have tobacco." According to the industry, tobacco could alleviate critical food shortages both at home and abroad, it being easier to transport than other perishables. Neither Baruch nor Hoover appears to have been influenced by any of these arguments. There was no mention of tobacco in any context during the Congressional debate on the food bill, passed in Aug. 10, 1917, which, among other things, instituted national prohibition of alcohol as a wartime food conservation measure.[39]

The government was only one source of tobacco products for servicemen. Thousands of tons were provided by civic groups and service organizations, including some that had been involved in the anti-smoking movement before the war. One of the most remarkable demonstrations of a change in attitude came from the YMCA, which accepted a commission from the War Department to operate all military post exchanges and canteens overseas. Chief among the list of products sold at these facilities was tobacco. By the end of the war, the YMCA had shipped 820 tons of cigarettes, 187 tons of smoking tobacco, 176 tons of chewing tobacco, and 34 tons of cigars to France. Shipments continued during the demobilization period. Altogether—including tobacco the agency purchased from European suppliers—YMCA workers distributed more than 2 billion cigarettes to soldiers in France, along with 50 million cigars and 18 million cans of smoking tobacco. Cigarettes were the most popular item in the YMCA canteens: more than 70 million were sold during a single month late in the war.[40]

Some of those cigarettes were passed out by YMCA officials who had spent years warning young men of the dangers of smoking. Among them was Daniel A. Poling, head of the United Society of Christian Endeavor and chairman of the United Committee on War Temperance Activities in the Army and Navy. Poling had been an active supporter of the Anti-Cigarette League. He had often lectured about the "fine fiendishness" of "nicotine bondage," particularly in the form of cigarettes. He defected from the crusade against smoking after working as a volunteer in a YMCA canteen near the front lines, where he sold $800 worth of cigarettes in three days. His experiences convinced him that cigarettes were an important source of comfort for men who might otherwise be tempted by "worse things." In his words:

> There are hundreds of thousands of men in the trenches who would go mad, or at least become so nervously inefficient as to be useless, if to-bacco were denied them. Without it they would surely turn to worse things. Many a sorely wounded lad has died with a cigarette in his mouth, whose dying was less bitter because of the "poison pill." The argument that tobacco may shorten the life five or ten years, and that it dulls the brain in the meantime, seems a little out of place in a trench where men stand in frozen blood and water and wait for death.[41]

Before the war, the YMCA had been a reliable source of support for Lucy Page Gaston and other anti-cigarette activists. YMCA publications repeatedly warned their readers about the harmful effects of cigarette smoking, linking it to such problems as "lack of robustness, anemic appearance, imperfect development, brazen attitudes, listless actions." Although the organization was primarily concerned about the effects of cigarettes on young people, it also attacked as "a falsehood" the argument that cigarettes were harmless to adults. Of 133 individual associations surveyed in 1915, most did not permit cigarette smoking in their facilities. Even those that allowed the use of other types of tobacco banned cigarettes. "Most cigarette smokers have more vicious habits," one YMCA official said, explaining the reasons for the policy. But once the United States entered the war, the YMCA not only abandoned the battle against cigarettes, it went over to the other side.[42]

In very short order, the YMCA found itself among the largest distributors of tobacco in the world. It was selling cigarettes and other tobacco products in each of its 1,507 canteens in France, and giving away millions of cigarettes to soldiers on the front lines and in hospitals. According to one account, the haze from the smoke in a typical YMCA canteen was so thick, "the lanterns were the merest glimmer through the smoke." In canteens where smoking was not permitted, because of local fire regulations, YMCA representatives took pains to distance themselves from the rules; they feared they would lose favor with the soldiers if they were too closely associated with any restrictions on smoking.[43]

In YMCA magazines, articles about the assorted evils of the demon weed were shoved aside by stories and photographs celebrating the agency's efforts to supply soldiers with cigarettes. One photograph, of a female YMCA volunteer handing a package of cigarettes to a smiling soldier, was captioned "Just What the Doctor Ordered." An accompanying article, headlined "Safeguard Your Health," emphasized fresh air, cleanliness, and regulation of the bowels; it did not mention the effect of smoking on health. Another photograph showed a heavily bandaged soldier, lying on a stretcher laid on the ground, arms at his sides, a cigarette in his mouth, a YMCA worker kneeling beside him to help him smoke it. Every issue of *Association Men* (the YMCA's national monthly magazine) published in 1918 included at least one article with favorable references to cigarettes; and nearly every issue was illustrated with at least one photograph or drawing depicting soldiers enjoying cigarettes provided by the YMCA.[44]

This astonishing conversion was not free of controversy within the agency. Some YMCA personnel worried about the propriety of peddling a substance previously condemned as a conduit to the devil. Many of those who accepted the distribution of cigarettes to soldiers as a wartime necessity held the line at their use by employees of the YMCA itself. "No man can suck cigarettes, wear the YMCA uniform and maintain the respect and confidence of the men," *Association Men* editorialized. The employees could provide the cigarettes, but not smoke them.[45]

The issue of whether the YMCA should sell cigarettes at all was overshadowed at one point by controversy over the prices at which they were sold. Many soldiers complained that they had to pay more for cigarettes in overseas canteens operated by the YMCA than they did in government commissaries. Typically, the YMCA charged thirteen cents for a package that cost eight or nine cents in the commissaries—and ten cents at retail in the United States. Reports in a number of newspapers and magazines accused the agency of profiteering.[46]

The charges were extremely embarrassing to YMCA officials, particularly those who had been reluctant to go into the cigarette business in the first place. They defended themselves by pointing out that the War Department was subsidizing the commissaries by underwriting the costs of transportation, insurance, and storage; while the YMCA was required to pay those expenses itself. Also, because the government had taken over so much of the production of American manufacturers, the YMCA was often required to buy cigarettes on the European market, at inflated prices. Eventually, the War Department agreed to sell supplies to the YMCA at cost. In addition, the agency's War Work Council decided to absorb any difference between operating expenses and income, reversing an earlier decision to make the canteens pay for themselves. Canteen prices subsequently were reduced, although they remained slightly above those charged in the commissaries.[47]

Even more troublesome for the YMCA were several instances in which canteens sold cigarettes that had been provided by newspaper "smoke funds" and were intended for free distribution to the troops. The cigarettes had been shipped to France in care of the quartermaster; some were inadvertently sold to the YMCA, which, in turn, sold them to soldiers. When the soldiers opened the packages, they found gift cards inside, with the names and addresses of donors who had contributed to the fund. John R. Mott, executive director of the War Work Council of the YMCA, and other officials described this as an unfortunate blunder, due partly to the fact that the cigarettes had been packed in cases that were not clearly marked as gifts; and partly to the difficulties of trying to provide a commodity for which demand far outstripped supply.[48]

On the front lines and in hospitals, the YMCA gave away cigarettes, distributing more than one million to soldiers in one army division alone. The agency often experienced great difficulty in getting such supplies to the front, but persevered because, as one official put it, "it is generally recognized that tobacco in one form or another is necessary to the comfort of the soldier." One intrepid volunteer, Maude Radford Warren of Chicago, once walked nine miles on the Alsatian front carrying forty pounds of cigarettes on her back; she was hit by shrapnel twice but did not turn back until she had delivered her supplies. Another worker stood beside the entrance to a regimental dressing station giving hot drinks and lighted cigarettes to every wounded man, holding his post through shelling and gas attacks for twenty-two consecutive hours. The YMCA made particular efforts to provide free cigarettes to men who were about to go "over the top." At least one four-legged assistant was pressed into that service: a dog named Dobut, of indeterminate breed, who was equipped with a special backpack and trained to carry cartons of cigarettes directly to soldiers in the trenches.[49]

At one meeting of the Commission on Training Camp Activities, Mott was asked why the YMCA did not give free cigarettes to all soldiers, not just those on the front lines or in hospitals. He replied that the agency would quickly exhaust its budget if it did that. With more than 2 million men overseas, if each one smoked just one package of cigarettes daily, more than $300,000 would go up in smoke every day. By using its resources to pay for shipping and other expenses, the YMCA could make more cigarettes available to more soldiers for a longer period of time. A dollar that might buy one free carton for one soldier could stretch to stock a canteen with enough for ten or more cartons for sale. Although the men might grouse about the canteen prices, they would be even more disgruntled if the shelves were empty.[50]

Like the YMCA, the Salvation Army had long been opposed to the use of tobacco. The *War Cry*, the Salvation Army's national magazine, published numerous articles about the hazards of smoking in the early 1900s. The cover of one issue showed a cigarette smoker progressing from wife beating to drunkenness to the gutter, in a sort of reverse, nicotinized "Pilgrim's Progress." An article in another issue exhorted readers to "labor continuously to save those about you from this great evil." Yet by the end

of the war, the Salvation Army was sending an estimated 15 tons of cigarettes and smoking tobacco to France every month. It preferred cigarettes
over other forms of tobacco because they were easier to transport, but at
least one worker helped "the dear boys" celebrate Christmas of 1918 with
cigars. Captain Margaret Sheldon reported in her diary that she traveled
more than one hundred miles to a supply center in order to obtain cigars
and other treats for a Christmas party at a garrison near the Argonne
Forest.[51]

The Salvation Army avoided any controversy over price by giving away
its tobacco. This was largely a logistical decision. At the behest of the War
Department, the Salvation Army concentrated on providing services to
men on the front lines, following troop movements rather than establishing
permanent canteens in the rear. It had fewer personnel in the war zone
than the YMCA (only about 120 as of November 1918, compared to the
YMCA's 6,300); and it operated fewer canteens (about twenty-five compared to 1,507). The small staff and increased mobility made it simpler to
give away the tobacco rather than sell it.[52]

In any case, soldiers often commented on the Salvation Army's liberality
in letters to their families. "[While] still within range of shell-fire we were
met by two Salvation Army lassies with hot chocolate and cigarettes," one
soldier wrote, adding that no other organization was as valued by servicemen. Another, complaining about the prices charged in the YMCA canteens, said, "The Red Cross and the Salvation Army are the only ones that
do any real good at the front," because they provided free smokes.[53]

The American Red Cross was even more liberal in supplying free cigarettes. It gave away more than 1 billion that it purchased directly from
manufacturers, along with several billion more provided by newspaper and
other private funds. Only the United States government and the YMCA
distributed more cigarettes to soldiers in France. Red Cross volunteers in
the United States also worked to ensure that servicemen in training camps
and domestic military bases were not forgotten in the rush of enthusiasm
for soldiers Over There. For example, in Richmond, Virginia, the local Red
Cross committee placed donation boxes around the city and collected more
than 5,000 packages of cigarettes, handing them out to soldiers on sentry
duty at nearby Camp Lee. At the end of the war, the Red Cross welcomed
returning servicemen with gifts of more cigarettes.[54]

The Red Cross avoided the taint of commercialism by insisting that none
of its employees or volunteers sell any tobacco, anytime, anywhere. In one
case, it rejected a proposal from a Connecticut contractor who wanted the
agency to open booths selling cigarettes and other "harmless trifles" at
military construction sites—despite the contractor's assurance that such
booths "would do a large and profitable business," providing an opportunity "to turn many an honest penny."[55]

Initially, the Red Cross had planned to give one free carton of cigarettes
to every soldier on the front lines every month. This proved impractical,
however, because of limited supplies. The agency consequently rationed its

stock, giving priority to the wounded. When there were shortages, the able-bodied received Bull Durham, Duke's Mixture, and other "roll-your-own" tobaccos; the "ready-mades" were reserved for the hospitals and the medical evacuation trains.[56]

Red Cross personnel regarded manufactured cigarettes as useful seda-tives for sick or wounded men, particularly for those who could not roll their own or manage a pipe or cigar. Colonel Harvey D. Gibson, director of the agency's activities in France, said cigarettes were as important to the wounded as surgical dressings. A soldier on a stretcher might be too feeble to move a hand, "but put a cigarette to his lips and light it and he'll get some comfort," he said. According to the commanding officer of a field hospital serving the 81st Division, "[T]he very first thing the wounded man wants to quiet his nerves is a smoke." He added, "[T]he American Red Cross came to our rescue in passing those God-sent smokes to the boys on the operating table or in the evacuation wards."[57]

Military photographers recorded many instances of uniformed Red Cross workers—wearing armbands emblazoned with the distinctive cross on a white background—offering cigarettes to soldiers on stretchers, in hospital beds, and on evacuation trains. These photographs were distributed by the Committee on Public Information and widely published in American news-papers and magazines. In one typical photo, a Red Cross worker looked on with approval while a YMCA secretary helped a bandage-swathed man on a stretcher smoke a cigarette. Another showed a female volunteer, holding a large basket of cigarette packages, handing one to a broadly grinning soldier in a hospital bed, while nearby patients looked on hope-fully. This photograph was captioned "When Red Cross Hospital Visitors Bring Cigarettes the Wounded Men Smile." Yet another photo showed a Red Cross nurse lighting a cigarette for a thickly bandaged man on a medical evacuation train. Soldiers often expressed gratitude for such ser-vices. According to one, Red Cross nurses were "one of the greatest bless-ings on earth," because they not only provided cigarettes, they lit them, too, on request.[58]

By freely dispensing cigarettes to soldiers, the YMCA, Salvation Army, and Red Cross transferred some of their own respectability to a once-disreputable product. This was particularly true of the Red Cross, which enjoyed tremendous prestige during World War I. The agency's stature was reflected not only in the hundreds of millions of dollars it collected in wartime fund-raising drives, but in the countless volunteers who rolled bandages and packed soldiers' "comfort kits" (often tucking cigarettes into them) for the Red Cross. The agency also carried the imprimatur of the federal government, functioning as a quasi-governmental entity under the terms of a charter issued by Congress in 1900. This status was reinforced in 1911 when President William Howard Taft designated the Red Cross as "the only volunteer society now authorized by this government to render aid to its land and naval forces in war." Woodrow Wilson served as the agency's titular head during World War I; Taft was chairman of its central

committee. When the Red Cross handed out cigarettes to soldiers, it acted
with the moral authority of an agency unsullied by any charges of profiteering or sectarianism, serving as an arm of the government during a
time of national crisis.[59]

The civilian campaign to provide "smokes for soldiers" began shortly
after the first American troops reached France, in June 1917. It was pre-
cipitated by newspaper stories with headlines such as "OUR ARMY IN
FRANCE IS SHORT OF TOBACCO" and "BOYS AT FRONT NEED TO-
BACCO." The message was amplified by letters from servicemen to their
families and friends, complaining about the scarcity and costliness of tobacco, especially American cigarettes. Many such letters were published
in hometown newspapers. Even the *Hastings (Michigan) Banner*, whose
publisher detested cigarettes, printed letters from soldiers asking for them.
It soon became difficult to pick up a newspaper or magazine without reading about cigarettes and soldiers in some context; to walk into a department store, hotel, theater, or restaurant without passing a red, white, and
blue collection box for a tobacco fund of some sort; or to stroll down a
street without seeing a poster about the importance of keeping "Johnny"
in smokes.[60]

People from all layers of American society responded to these appeals:
the wealthy, the foreign-born, the celebrated, the ordinary, even the imprisoned. The Consolidated Stock Exchange canceled its annual Christmas
party and sponsored a benefit to raise cigarette money instead. The New
York Stock Exchange, the New York Boat Owners' Association, and J. P.
Morgan helped support a smoke fund operated by the *New York Sun*. Society women in New York and Chicago established a National Cigarette
Service Committee to supply the friendless and the orphaned. During a
fancy dress ball in Palm Beach, Florida, some of the nation's wealthiest
citizens—including Mr. and Mrs. Edward T. Stotesbury, Mrs. Alfred G. Vanderbilt, William Randolph Hearst, and Pierre du Pont—donated more than
$30,000 to a fund to buy cigarettes for sailors. Meanwhile, inmates at San
Quentin and several other prisons gave up their tobacco rations in the
interest of beating the Hun.[61]

By the fall of 1917, private smoke funds were multiplying like amens
at a revival. Their sponsors ranged from the American Forestry Association to the U.S. Transport Service to the Pennsylvania Railroad to Ambulance Company No. 2 of Meriden, Connecticut. The *New York Sun* organized one of the first (established June 29, 1917) and most successful
(collecting roughly $430,000). More than 440 newspapers, along with 100
magazines, supported the "Our Boys in France Tobacco Fund," which sent
about $400,000 worth of tobacco—mostly cigarettes—overseas. Many
other papers conducted independent campaigns. Among them was the
*Butte (Montana) Miner*, which melded self-interest with patriotic duty by
promising to send one dollar's worth of tobacco overseas in return for a
one-year subscription ($7), or fifty cents' worth for a six-month subscrip-
tion ($3.74). "Do your bit," the paper urged. "Help swell the tobacco fund

and at the same time get the best paper published in the state of Montana."[62]

The New Jersey State Committee on Public Safety created a "big brother club" to provide cigarettes and other "necessities" to soldiers from New Jersey. High school girls in New York organized a "squad sisters club" to do the same for servicemen from their state. Children staying with their families at a Catskills resort asked that the traditional Fourth of July fireworks display be canceled and the money donated to a smoke fund. Those who protested the distribution of cigarettes to soldiers did so at the risk of having their patriotism questioned. There was even some talk that they might be prosecuted under the Espionage Act of 1917, on the assumption that only an "alien enemy" would object to such a worthy enterprise.[63]

The Mutual Film Corporation made a one-reel film titled *My Lady Nicotine*, starring the popular actress Billie Rhodes, which dramatized the need for tobacco overseas. Theaters around the country set up boxes in their lobbies to collect pennies from children and cigarettes from smokers. Movie stars, headliners from vaudeville and Broadway, and other celebrities helped raise money for the cause. Ethel Barrymore, Eddie Cantor, Fannie Brice, Will Rogers, W. C. Fields, Lillian Russell, Pauline Frederick, and the opera singer Ernestine Schumann-Heink were among the stars who performed at benefits for various tobacco funds (Fields did a "comedy juggling act"). The stars of stage and screen continued to express support for servicemen by giving them cigarettes after the war. Mary Pickford, for example, photogenically handed cartons to men on the battleship *Texas* in early 1920. Sophie Tucker appeared at so many benefits that she was called "the Smoke Angel."[64]

Men in training camps and those preparing to embark or en route to Europe received special attention, since the government provided a free tobacco ration only to men on active duty overseas. Troop trains in the United States were met at almost every stop by well-wishers bearing gifts of candy and cigarettes. The Red Cross conducted a special campaign to provide a Christmas carton of cigarettes to all military men in each of the nation's thirty-two military cantonments and training camps, including those in states that had outlawed cigarettes. A group of officers' daughters organized an Army Girls' Transport Fund to ensure that servicemen had enough to smoke while traveling to Europe. "An army girl 'smokes up' the transports, while other funds 'take the trenches,' " the group explained in a poster. During a parade down Fifth Avenue for 25,000 departing national guardsmen in New York City, enthusiastic citizens bombarded soldiers with boxes of cigarettes, gum, and candy, to the point, according to one observer, "that it is fair to say that many a soldier lad . . . fervently wished that the Government would deal out trench helmets on this side of the Atlantic instead of the other." No serious injuries were reported, although some blood was spilled by errant bayonets, lowered too hastily as soldiers bent to scoop up their prizes.[65]

The volume of cigarettes and other tobacco products being sent to France created serious problems of congestion both at the shipping points in the United States and the receiving ports in Europe. Orders from the various newspaper funds alone reached such a level that the five leading manufacturers established a special factory to package them; and employees of the Internal Revenue Service worked overtime in order to process them for shipment to France. (The federal government waived the collection of excise taxes on institutional consignments of tobacco to members of the American Expeditionary Forces; but it required that the tobacco carry special revenue department stamps.) Finally, in the spring of 1918, the War Department cut off shipments from private citizens to individual soldiers, saying their needs were being well met by the service organizations, the newspapers, and the government itself.[66]

Meanwhile, the role of cigarettes in military life was being celebrated in American popular culture, from songs ("While you've a lucifer to light your fag, smile boys smile"); to books (including *Over the Top* and *First Call*, by Arthur Guy Empey); to censor-approved photographs of soldiers smoking in newspaper Sunday supplements; to films (such as Charlie Chaplin's 1918 *Shoulder Arms*, in which Chaplin chose a rifle, a gas mask, and a cigarette as essential props for his portrayal of a doughboy); to poetry, as in this opening stanza from an ode titled "No Longer 'Coffin Nails' ":

> "Coffin nails" was what we said
> But the war has changed the name.
> The cigarette is now first aid
> In this hellish, killing game.[67]

Gaston and her remaining allies in the anti-cigarette movement looked upon all this with a mixture of disgust and dismay. In a letter to Secretary of War Baker, Gaston said it was "the greatest folly" to "dope up" soldiers with cigarettes. A Boston woman, writing to Secretary of the Navy Daniels, more gently suggested that "unlimited cigaretts" [sic] were a "mistaken indulgence" and "not what experience would dictate as a suitable background for future strenuous endeavors." These letters were duly passed on to Fosdick, who filed them and apparently gave them no further thought.[68]

The protesters were particularly galled that religious groups would countenance the distribution of tobacco in any form, let alone the pernicious cigarette. Marshall L. Cook, publisher of the *Hastings Banner* and a prominent supporter of the YMCA, at first insisted that it was simply not true; reports that the YMCA was selling cigarettes were "a slander," probably spread by "a secret enemy of the United States." Later, he conceded that "just now the 'coffin nails' have such a hold upon the American people that it is almost useless to oppose the habit." As if to prove his point, one town in Texas raised money for a new YMCA building by asking residents to "put a nail in the Kaiser's Coffin" with their donations. The

Texans had recycled an old pejorative and turned it into a friendly ally in a righteous cause.[69]

The Reverend Stanley H. Roberts, an army chaplain, complained that servicemen were "literally being deluged" by cigarettes provided by "their Christian friends." Roberts said the men should be given only "legitimate comforts." L. H. Higley of Butler, Indiana, editor and publisher of the *No-Tobacco Journal*, deplored the fact that "the YMCA, the Red Cross and even the Salvation Army have all fallen victims to a wild, intemperate popular enthusiasm" for cigarettes. He sent a copy of the journal to John Mott, general secretary of the YMCA, but Mott took no more notice of the criticism than had Baker, Daniels, and Fosdick.[70]

Roberts and many other critics claimed that the entire "smokes for soldiers" campaign had been orchestrated by the "tobacco trust," with the intent of fastening an addictive habit on millions of young soldiers. The author of a booklet titled *Kaiser Nicotine* singled out the American Tobacco Company as the fabricator of an alleged demand for cigarettes by the military. The WCTU, the Non-Smokers' Protective League of America, the Kansas State Teachers' Association, and the General Assembly of the Presbyterian Church issued similar statements. Clarence True Wilson, head of the Methodist Episcopal Board of Temperance, Prohibition and Public Morals, said the industry had not only "duped" the Red Cross and other organizations into passing out cigarettes, it had put enough "dope" in its products to turn the unsuspecting doughboys into hopeless addicts. Residents of Hammond, Indiana, took these charges seriously enough that they decided to send Bibles to soldiers instead of cigarettes.[71]

Frederick W. Roman, an economics professor at Syracuse University, argued that manufacturers had manipulated the government, the service organizations, and the press into promoting cigarettes in a calculating effort to get rid of surpluses created by the outbreak of war in 1914. In *Nicotine Next*, a booklet published by the WCTU, he said the war had greatly curtailed American exports to Europe, leaving the manufacturers with goods for which they had no market. In his view, they were foisting their products on the armed forces in a desperate attempt to create new markets.[72]

In fact, the American cigarette industry was characterized by shortages rather than surpluses after 1914. Factories in Virginia and North Carolina operated day and night in a largely futile effort to keep up with new orders. Overall exports quadrupled, from roughly 2.5 billion cigarettes in fiscal 1914 to 9.1 billion in 1918. This was largely the result of increased demand from Asia, which dominated the American export market; exports to Europe accounted for less than 3 percent of the overall market before the war. Domestic sales also increased, jumping by 40 percent between 1915 and 1916 alone. By 1917, the American Tobacco Company (maker of Lucky Strikes, Pall Malls, and several other brands) was receiving orders for an average of 50 million cigarettes a day, more than double the com-

pany's production capacity at the time. The war gave American manufacturers a tremendous advantage by disrupting the operations of their European competitors, in both foreign and domestic markets. Instead of being
saddled with surpluses, they struggled to supply the growing demand for
their products.[73]

This is not to say that the manufacturers did not fully exploit the marketing opportunities provided by the war. Information published in trade
journals and other periodicals indicates that they clearly recognized the
value of being associated with the war effort. One journal pointed out that
no other form of advertising was quite as effective as handing a package
of cigarettes to a soldier who needed some sort of distraction. Manufacturers also expected that brands favored by members of the American
Expeditionary Forces would influence the civilian market—that civilians
would emulate the soldiers by smoking what they smoked. Beyond that,
patriotism could serve as an amulet against the reformers. "Demonstrate
that you're doing your damndest to help lick Germany, and when your
case comes up again you'll have several points in your favor," another
journal advised its readers.[74]

The tobacco industry as a whole took this advice to heart. Some cigar
stores provided receptacles for the collection of peach and apricot stones,
said to be needed for the manufacture of charcoal for gas masks. The stones
were of negligible value from a military standpoint, but they helped demonstrate the merchants' public spirit. Many retailers papered their display
windows with patriotic posters. They placed flag-draped barrels by their
cash registers to collect donations of money, tobacco, and tinfoil for the
war effort. Some decorated their windows with maps showing the location
of key battles, artfully arranging packages of cigarettes around the maps.[75]

The American Tobacco Company itself claimed credit for the proliferation of newspaper smoke funds, although it insisted its motive was patriotism, not profit. "We were the first to establish the 'Smokes for Soldiers'
funds throughout the country—an enterprise that aroused people everywhere to the solders' need for tobacco and turned hundreds of thousands
of willing dollars into smoke ammunition for our boys at the front," the
company boasted. Sales agents offered to sell cigarettes to newspapers at
a discount, in return for free advertising: a situation that "helps Peter as
well as Paul!" Typically, the newspapers paid twenty-five cents for a quantity of tobacco costing thirty-five cents wholesale and forty-five cents retail.
In return, they agreed to promote American Tobacco brands with a daily
front-page display box, along with occasional three-or four-column articles
or displays at the top of an inside page. Other cigarette manufacturers
made similar arrangements with newspapers, as did major tobacco retailers.[76]

Some critics smelled the odor of kickbacks and bribery in this, but the
truth seems to be both less nefarious and more complex. The tobacco
interests, no less than newspapers and other businesses, wanted to prove
their patriotism. It was not merely good business, but mandated by the

mood of a country that had convinced itself that "[t]his war is being fought on a higher plane than any war that ever preceded it, and from higher motives." It was almost a moral imperative to be associated with such a cause. The very openness of the discourse in the trade journals suggests that the tobacco industry took pride in its conduct during the war and believed it would be rewarded with customer loyalty in the future.[77]

Manufacturers of all kinds of tobacco incorporated military themes into their advertising and gave free samples of their products to servicemen. Cigarette makers, however, were more aggressive in efforts to "capitalize the present wartime interest" than their more established competitors. For example, in August 1917, Liggett and Myers Tobacco Company announced that it was giving 1.5 million cigarettes (Fatimas, Piedmonts, and Chesterfields) and 20,000 bags of smoking tobacco to the Red Cross. In contrast, the makers of Tuxedo pipe tobacco did little more than hand out small paper envelopes containing a scant pipeful each to men at training camps.[78]

Cigarette companies and their executives paraded their patriotism by being conspicuously involved in campaigns to sell Liberty Bonds and raise money for the Red Cross, YMCA, and Salvation Army. American Tobacco bought $6.2 million worth of Liberty Bonds, followed by Liggett and Myers ($3 million), the P. Lorillard Company ($2.5 million), and the R. J. Reynolds Tobacco Company ($1 million). Percival S. Hill, president of American Tobacco, headed a committee that collected more than $300,000 for the YMCA, Salvation Army, and several other groups that provided cigarettes to soldiers. Hill also served on the Red Cross War Council, which directed various fund drives for the Red Cross; his colleagues on the council included the presidents of P. Lorillard (makers of Helmar, Murad, and Egyptian Deities cigarettes), the Tobacco Products Corporation (Melachrino, Nestor, and Tareyton), and the United Cigar Stores Company (which operated more than 400 retail tobacco stores nationwide). Hill's son, George W. Hill, vice president of the company, worked for the Red Cross in France. Other cigarette executives made well-publicized individual donations of cash to the YMCA and Salvation Army.[79]

A cynic might suspect that such contributions were intended to help the recipients see cigarettes in a new light. On the other hand, General Pershing and other military commanders had pronounced tobacco a necessity for the fighting man, and few organizations were inclined to challenge the authority of the military, at least during the war. The Red Cross and the YMCA both said they distributed cigarettes and other tobacco products because General Pershing asked them to. The enthusiasm for cigarettes as an expression of support for soldiers was too spontaneous and too widespread to have been produced solely by the machinations of manufacturers. It came, instead, from particular developments associated with the war itself, and the degree to which cigarettes suited the various needs of military commanders, relief workers, the public at large, and the soldiers themselves.

Officers in all branches of the military accepted cigarettes as valuable adjuncts to discipline and morale. Troops who had plenty to smoke were considered easier to control, a belief reinforced by reports that lack of tobacco had contributed to widespread mutinies by French soldiers in 1917. A veteran from Wyoming remembered being given unlimited quantities of cigarettes in the trenches and urged to smoke them for their "sedative effect." A tobacco industry executive marveled that "cigarettes have almost been forced on the soldiers." A naval commander said cigarettes were invaluable both in keeping the men alert and helping them to relax. French and British officers gave their men a measure of rum or brandy before they were ordered to attack; American officers passed out cigarettes instead.[80]

General Leonard Wood summed up the military's position when he said that "[n]othing gives a soldier in the field more pleasure and contentment than a cool, refreshing smoke after a hard day's fighting or while awaiting call to the firing line." The Army's chief medical officer—Surgeon General William Gorgas—concurred. According to Gorgas, the military advantages of tobacco as a way of promoting "contentment and morale" among the troops outweighed its medical disadvantages. Gorgas (who had gained fame for his success in controlling yellow fever during the building of the Panama Canal) had strongly opposed smoking before the war. However, he told an anti-smoking group that it was "inadvisable" to object to the use of any kind of tobacco by soldiers during wartime.[81]

The direct experience of relief workers in the field convinced them that cigarettes were an important "comfort" to the men they served. Elizabeth Parks Hutchinson, a YMCA volunteer in a field hospital in France, carried a supply with her at all times; a single smoke, she said, could "smooth away the lines of pain and weariness" in a soldier's face. Clarence B. Kelland, a YMCA supervisor in France, describing the effect of a cigarette on a wounded soldier, wrote: "The expression on his dirty face was such a reward as few men ever earn." According to another YMCA worker, cigarettes were particularly valuable in helping men recover from attacks of poison gas.[82]

Time and again, in their private writings as well as in their official reports, relief workers made positive comments about cigarettes. One YMCA volunteer, writing in his diary, reported encountering a weary battalion returning from the front, their "brains dulled and exhausted by misery." He and three colleagues stood on both sides of the line of march, lighting cigarettes and handing them to the soldiers. "Each man, when he got his cigarette, seemed to forget his troubles," he wrote. "He straightened up and became a man again instead of a wearied drudge." The YMCA's national magazine carried numerous other anecdotes in a similar vein, including this one:

> One of our fine secretaries (a preacher) who felt the smoking of a cigarette to be almost an unpardonable sin, found himself in the trenches with the men wounded and dying about him. In their pain and suffering they asked for cigarettes. There were no matches to be had. This man

who had never smoked obtained a light, lighted a cigarette, put it in his mouth and for hours went about among the men placing cigarettes in their mouths and lighting them from the one he kept burning between his own lips.[83]

The soldiers battled mud, vermin, tedium, and fear in the trenches; conditions were not much better behind the lines, where the barracks had walls so thin, it was said, people next door could be heard changing their minds. The severe cold of the winter of 1917–18 was followed by an epidemic of influenza, which ultimately spread around the world and killed more soldiers than the war itself. Under the circumstances, a cigarette did not seem such a bad thing. "Stop this talk against tobacco," Rev. Perry Atkins, president of the YMCA's War Work Council, told an audience in Ann Arbor, Michigan. "God knows what a comfort it is to men in the trenches. Let them have it." (Some people suggested that if nothing else, cigarettes could serve as a prophylactic against influenza.)[84]

Relief workers used cigarettes as a way of establishing rapport with soldiers, hopefully as a prelude to spiritual guidance and moral uplift. *Association Men* published several versions of the following scenario: A YMCA secretary comes to an army outpost to open a canteen. The soldiers shun him, saying they don't want any "parson" in their midst. He opens the canteen anyway, cheerfully selling "Sweet Caps" (Sweet Caporals, a popular cigarette, made by American Tobacco), "Bull" (Bull Durham, another American Tobacco product), and other brands. His willingness to sell cigarettes and the "makings" without censure converts the men; he has proven himself to be a "regular fellow," one worthy of respect. That being the case, they will be more receptive to his attempts to steer them away from the temptations presented to men "with nothing to do in the evenings but drink French wines and follow their own impulses." Such tales dramatized the transformation of cigarettes from sinful indulgence to ally of virtue.[85]

For the people at home, the smoke funds—like the Liberty Bond drives—helped create a sense of shared purpose in a nation that had been badly divided before the war. Some of the largest contributions to the *New York Sun*'s smoke fund came from ethnic neighborhoods, including Italian, German, Russian, and Bohemian. Merchants in Chinatown raised thousands of dollars for the fund. The Young Men's Hebrew Association in Mount Vernon, New York, held a "tobacco shower and dance" to collect boxes of cigarettes to send to soldiers and sailors overseas; the Young Women's Hebrew Association of Brooklyn sponsored a "revue and dance." In another expression of national cohesion, fifty foreign language newspapers joined forces to send $10,000 worth of gift tobacco (21,000 cartons of cigarettes) overseas in time for Christmas.[86]

Like the Liberty Bonds, the smoke funds provided a litmus test for public demonstrations of patriotism. Most newspapers published a daily list of contributors and the amounts donated. The *New York Sun* encouraged readers to solicit donations as a way of "proving your patriotism and testing that of your friends." Margarete Matzenauer, a Metropolitan Opera star, defended herself against charges of being pro-German by citing her efforts to raise money for tobacco funds. She noted that she had performed at one benefit with the Red Triangle Symphony Orchestra, sponsored by the Central Branch of the Brooklyn YMCA. There was no further questioning of her loyalty.[87]

Cigarettes also served as emblems of solidarity between the people Back Here and the soldiers Over There. The United States had never been involved in a crusade like the one to make the world safe for democracy; its warriors inspired the adoration due mythic figures (at least for the duration). Cigarettes were used in the same way as votive offerings. General Pershing encouraged this by saying that more important than the actual tobacco was "the thought to the soldier that those providing the solace are behind him." New York Governor Charles S. Whitman sent a check to the *Sun*'s smoke fund along with a note reading, "There is so little, after all, we can do for the men who are doing so much." One soldier, a nonsmoker, recalled that he promptly took up the habit in order to show his gratitude to the well-meaning people who thrust packages into his hands at every station as his troop train traveled to its destination.[88]

For soldiers—many of whom were away from home for the first time—cigarettes were an important medium of social exchange. The offer of a cigarette or the sharing of a light eased the awkwardness of an introduction, sealed the bonds of friendship, relieved homesickness, and drew men into common fellowship. A shared smoke was a way of connecting in a disconnected world. The P. Lorillard Company recognized this function in an advertisement for Helmar cigarettes, showing two soldiers, one lighting his cigarette from the tip of the other's, the fusion of the two men represented by their mingled cigarette smoke. "Face to Face," said the caption, "We All Like Helmar." The cigarette had brought the men together, allowing them to transcend their differences and find common ground.[89]

The very qualities that made cigarettes attractive to the purchasing agents for the War Department, YMCA, Red Cross, and other agencies enhanced their utility as a social solvent: they were inexpensive, portable, and easy to use. The relative mildness of cigarette tobacco gave it a more universal appeal than pipes, cigars, or chewing tobacco. Soldiers of all nations accepted cigarettes as tokens of brotherhood. Americans arriving in France broke the ice with French sailors by tossing them cigarettes. In more than half a dozen scenes in Erich Maria Remarque's classic World War I novel, *All Quiet on the Western Front*, smoking is intertwined with fellowship. When soldiers shared cigarettes with both their allies and their enemies, they were proving that the fraternity of smoke could surmount even the artificial barriers of war.[90]

The presence of an addicting element (nicotine) certainly added to the appeal of cigarettes, but it is important to distinguish between their physiological effects and their cultural role. When soldiers recorded their own thoughts about cigarettes, they emphasized the social context: smoking as a display of camaraderie, a remedy for boredom, a solace to the dispirited. In letters acknowledging the receipt of newspaper gift tobacco, servicemen invariably mentioned the value of the tobacco as a reminder "that the folks at home are thinking of us boys." Robert M. Hutchins, president of Chicago University in the 1940s, said that learning to smoke was as much a part of his initiation into military life as learning to swear; both served as badges of fraternity. William K. Dingledine—who volunteered for the Ambulance Corps after graduating from the University of Virginia—thought servicemen smoked primarily because they were bored. "Contrary to popular opinion, war is not a state of perpetual activity, not even for soldiers at the front," he wrote to his mother. "For every hour of activity there are many more when there is nothing to do but wait at one's post— and these hours of waiting are unspeakably gummy. Here is the chief explanation of why soldiers smoke so much."[91]

Cigarette smoking also increased among the civilian population. Bernard Baruch believed this was due partly to wartime prohibition: people were smoking more because they were drinking less. Another factor was the war-related prosperity, which allowed many tobacco users to upgrade from pipe or chewing tobacco to manufactured cigarettes. But Baruch and many other contemporary observers also concluded that the various "smokes for soldiers" campaigns had promoted cigarettes by breaking down the remaining prejudices against them.[92]

A business magazine, commenting on the cigarette's elevation in "the world's esteem," attributed it to the approval of military authorities and relief organizations. Percival Hill agreed, concluding, "The war is largely responsible for this great increase in cigarette smoking." A tobacco trade journal pointed out that "[s]tate after state has adopted statutes prohibiting the use of cigarettes, yet there are now but few persons who have not contributed something toward a fund for supplying these same cigarettes to the soldiers." Two organizations that had previously opposed the use of cigarettes (the YMCA and Salvation Army) cheerfully dispensed them during the war. Another, associated with health (the Red Cross), gave them to the sick or wounded. Temperance workers handed them out as aids to sobriety. These activities helped make cigarettes more acceptable to respectable Americans. (The trade press believed that the YMCA's turnaround on tobacco was particularly significant. A decade earlier, no one could have imagined that the YMCA would end up distributing hundreds of millions of cigarettes; the fact that it had "has more significance now than a book full of anti-tobacco arguments.")[93]

At the least, the cigarette had a higher profile at the end of the war than it had at the beginning. The *New York Sun*, for example, published a front-page promotional box and a lengthy inside story focused on cigarettes every single day from June 1917 until January 1919. It also carried appreciably more cigarette advertising at the end of the war than it had at the beginning. Cigarettes also edged into advertisements for other products, as in one for Victrola that showed several cigarette-smoking soldiers listening appreciatively to music played on one of the company's machines. The makers of White Rock mineral water used a lighted cigarette and a pair of white gloves as props in an advertisement linking their product with other symbols of the good life. Gimbel Brothers Department Store in New York City promoted a men's clothing sale with a drawing of an overcoated man in a bowler hat holding a cigarette. The combination of news coverage and advertising meant that Americans were seeing more positive images of cigarettes and cigarette smokers in their periodicals.[94]

As reflected in the pages of magazines and newspapers, the most visible cigarette smokers were no longer dudes or degenerates, but wounded heroes. The Committee on Public Information commissioned a widely reproduced painting by S. J. Woolf that showed an injured soldier inhaling deeply on a cigarette while waiting for treatment at a first aid station in France. Sunday supplements printed photographs with captions such as "Nicotine Solace of the Wounded" and "Cigarettes Console the Convalescent Blind." The photographs often featured women or children helping soldiers smoke. In one typical example, a moppet of about age five, dressed in a frilly frock, with ribbons in her curly blond hair, held a match to a cigarette for a soldier whose right arm had been amputated.[95]

One measure of the cigarette's increasing respectability was the fact that the ship which carried President Wilson to France for the Paris Peace Conference was stocked with a generous supply of a popular brand (Fatimas) for members of the (nonsmoking) president's party. Two months after the armistice, civic officials in New York City were considering taking down the "No Smoking" signs in train stations so as not to inconvenience the returning servicemen. Dr. George Fisher, physical training director of the National War Work Council of the YMCA (and author of a 1917 report concluding that cigarette smoking was unhealthy), said that while he personally deplored the habit, he thought it would be "inadvisable" to ban smoking in YMCA facilities. The War Department eventually decided that troops on active duty in any future conflict should be given not just four but sixteen cigarettes in their daily rations.[96]

The war, a California newspaper editorialized, might not have made the world safe for democracy, but it had made cigarette smoking safe for democrats.[97]

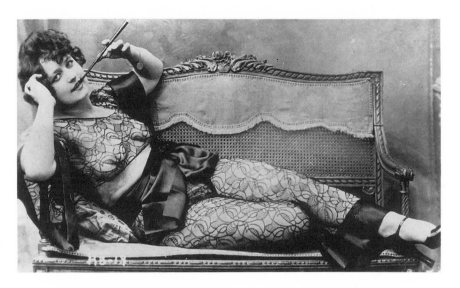

A Gay Nineties belle strikes a seductive pose with a cigarette. (Corbis-Bettman)

James B. Duke at about age 14, when he was put in charge of production in his family's tobacco business. (Special Collections Library, Duke University)

Newsboys smoking at Skeeter's Branch, St. Louis, Missouri, in 1910. (Library of Congress)

Anti-cigarette cartoon published in the *Union Signal*, national magazine of the Woman's Christian Temperance Union, 1912. (Courtesy of National Woman's Christian Temperance Union)

Lucy Page Gaston in front
of the Chicago First District
Court, 1904. (Chicago
Historical Society)

Henry Ford and Thomas A. Edison both objected to cigarettes, and
refused to hire anyone who smoked them, on or off the job. (National
Archives)

An "Anti-tobacco crank" jumps through smoke rings blown by the devil in this illustration from *Life*, May 1917. (Library of Congress)

Military authorities released many photos like this one, showing a Red Cross volunteer giving cigarettes to American soldiers on a troop train in France during World War I. (National Archives)

Winifred Bryce was one of thousands of Red Cross volunteers who distributed free cigarettes to injured men in France during World War I. (National Archives)

Exterior of a YMCA canteen in France. (YMCA of the USA Archives, University of Minnesota)

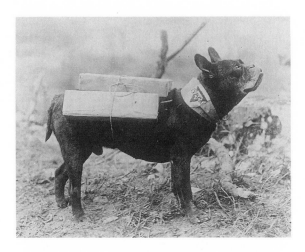

The YMCA went to great lengths to deliver free cigarettes to soldiers on the front lines, even pressing this dog ("Dobut") into service. (YMCA of the USA Archives, University of Minnesota)

A California newspaper cartoonist illustrated the theme that tobacco would be next on the reform agenda. (*Sacramento Star*, April 19, 1919)

## SMOKING AFFECTS MARKSMANSHIP

IN careful tests made of a group of men, both smokers and non-smokers, in shooting on a regular rifle range, they lost 4.8 per cent. in their score after smoking one cigar, and 6 per cent. after smoking two cigars. The men *gained* 13.2 per cent. in their score when they did not smoke.

**YMCA**

Anti-smoking poster distributed by the YMCA in 1919 fails to mention the agency's role in distributing cigarettes and other tobacco products to soldiers during World War I. (YMCA of the USA Archives, University of Minnesota)

Franklin D. Roosevelt's cigarette was as much a part of his persona as his confident grin. (Corbis-Bettman)

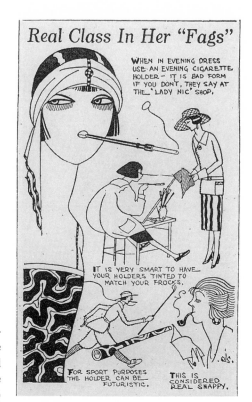

Women were the fastest-growing segment of the cigarette market after World War I. (*Sacramento Star,* June 21, 1922)

The photographer dared the viewers to separate the boys from the girls in this 1926 photo (three of the swimmers are male). (Corbis-Bettman)

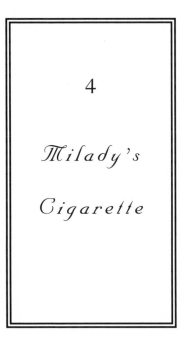

4

*Milady's*

*Cigarette*

Tea houses are springing up where women can
purchase a cup of tea, but also enjoy a cigarette.
How far will it go? What is the end?
*Anti-Cigarette League (1920)*[1]

The anti-cigarette movement appeared to be moribund at the end of
World War I. It had lost important allies and was gaining new opposition, particularly from veterans' groups. The movement might have
sputtered out entirely (at least until 1964 and the first Surgeon General's
Report on Smoking and Health) but for two developments: the ratification
of the Eighteenth Amendment and the growth of the cigarette habit among
women. The success of the campaign for national prohibition inspired the
demoralized anti-smoking forces to new efforts; the female smoker provided
a new target.

Paradoxically, cigarettes ceased to be a mark of effeminacy for men at
the same time more and more women began to smoke them. Although
concrete data about the percentage of women who smoked are not available for the years before 1935, contemporary observers agreed that women
constituted the fastest growing segment of the cigarette market after the
war. "Women are smoking like—well, like men," an industry analyst reported in 1919. In the ten years between 1918 and 1928, American cigarette sales quadrupled. The increase could never have been so large, Frederick Lewis Allen argued in *Only Yesterday*, "had it not been for the women

who now strewed the dinner table with their ashes, snatched a puff between [theater] acts, invaded the masculine sanctity of the club car, and forced department stores to place ornamental ash-trays between the chairs in their women's shoe departments."[2]

Tobacco trade journals quoted surprised executives who said women who had once bought cigarettes for soldiers were now buying them for themselves. A clerk at a Fifth Avenue tobacco shop told a reporter for the *New York Times* in 1920 that half the store's patrons were women. A tobacconist at another shop said he was serving seventy-five to one hundred female customers a day, compared to perhaps ten to twelve before the war. The tobacco industry as a whole avoided the recession that affected much of the economy in the immediate postwar period. According to James B. Duke, who remained a major stockholder of the American Tobacco Company although no longer involved in its daily operations, the industry owed much of its health to greater use of cigarettes by women. In recommending that investors buy tobacco securities in 1919, the *Magazine of Wall Street* predicted that the industry would profit from women even more in the future.[3]

An oft-quoted report in an advertising journal estimated that women smoked 5 percent of the cigarettes sold in 1923 and 12 percent of those sold in 1929. Since the average female smoker consumed fewer cigarettes per day than her male counterpart, the percentage of women who smoked at all presumably would be higher. In a retrospective study conducted in 1985, only about 5 percent of women who were in their twenties in 1925 admitted having smoked then. However, the number of women interviewed was small, and their memories subject to the vagaries of time. When Michael Vincent O'Shea, a Wisconsin educator, asked a group of sixty women who were prominent in art and literature about their use of tobacco in 1923, most said they smoked. At the end of the decade, a major tobacco retailer guessed that about half the women in New York City smoked. Insurance underwriters blamed increased smoking by women for a substantial rise in the number of cigarette-related fires around the country, saying women were less practiced and thus more careless than male smokers.[4]

Whatever their actual numbers, female smokers became far more visible in the 1920s, as reflected in newspapers, magazines, billboards, novels, and, increasingly, in the new medium of motion pictures. Women were seen smoking in hotels, restaurants, trains, and other public facilities, especially in larger cities. (An anti-cigarette activist claimed that some of these were "cappers" who were paid by cigarette manufacturers to light up in public, but this cannot be proven.) Late in the decade, manufacturers began—tentatively at first, then more boldly—to advertise directly to women. Other advertisers, too, appealed to female smokers. For example, a campaign for a brand of toothpaste asked "Can a Girl Smoke and Still Be Lovely?" The answer was yes, if only she kept her teeth stainless by frequent brushing with the advertiser's product. All this helped legitimate smoking by women, encouraging even more to smoke in public. It also brought new recruits into the battle against cigarettes.[5]

The sight of a woman wreathed in smoke was still profoundly offensive to many Americans, even those who had liberally given cigarettes to soldiers during the war. The cigarette may have been a symbol of democracy when smoked in the trenches by the boys Over There; it was something else entirely in the lips of the girls Back Home. The Board of Temperance, Prohibition, and Morals of the Methodist Episcopal Church was one of several reformist groups that issued a new call to arms, warning that "[n]o nation can maintain the vigor which has been characteristic of the American people after its women begin the use of cigarettes."[6]

The controversy over female smoking was embedded in a larger debate about the position of women in American society. Women began to smoke more openly at the same time they began demanding greater economic and political equity with men. Tobacco was one of the markers that had differentiated the roles and conduct of the sexes. By smoking, women undermined traditional standards for proper female behavior. If they could smoke, they could do anything. "By such argument," an anti-smoking activist wrote, "even bobbed hair would be excused."[7]

Although this debate intensified in the years after World War I, its roots can be traced back to the colonial era. As discussed in chapter I, it was not uncommon for women to smoke pipes or use snuff in colonial and frontier America, when gender roles were more fluid and women worked in economic partnership with men to produce needed goods and services. Not until the early nineteenth century did tobacco begin to acquire gender-specific qualities. This change coincided with the expansion of industrial capitalism and the concomitant movement of women to the margins of the producing economy. After the Civil War, nonagricultural women of the middle and upper classes participated in the economy primarily as consumers, not producers. Instead of making bread, they bought it, from large baking companies; their meat and produce came from the market, not from kitchen gardens and adjacent pastures; their clothing came from mail-order houses or department stores rather than from their own needles. In place of earlier economic roles, these women had accepted new social responsibilities, including the guardianship of morality.[8]

The new moral code consigned tobacco to the male realm. Its use was thought to appeal to physical—that is to say, baser—instincts. Women who smoked seemed to abdicate their position as morally superior to men. In addition, the odors and detritus of tobacco conflicted with new standards of hygiene for women; they did not suit the image of milady as the embodiment of purity. A "true woman" would not only not use tobacco herself, she would not condone its use in her presence. In Victorian America, respectable men repaired to the drawing room for postprandial cigars and brandy while respectable women gathered in the smoke-free parlor.[9]

Male and female spheres began to converge again in the early twentieth century. More and more women entered the work force; graduated from colleges; participated in politics. The percentage of women working for wages increased from 10 percent in 1860 to nearly 25 percent in 1910; by 1920, women were represented in all but thirty-five of the 572 occupational classifications listed by the Bureau of the Census. In 1890, only about 25 percent of American college graduates were women; by 1900, the figure was 40 percent. As women began to participate more directly in the economy and in other aspects of civic life, more and more of them smoked, generally favoring the modern cigarette over the old-fashioned pipe or snuff. For these women, the cigarette was a convenient emblem of their new place in the world. The symbolism was reflected in a turn-of-the-century photograph of an aproned man and a trousered woman in a role-reversal situation; he was shown serving a meal while she prepared to light a cigarette.[10]

This is not to suggest that women had achieved full equality with men. Although they had breached many male dominions, they remained at the lower levels; and there was a great deal of resistance to any further integration. Opposition to smoking by women was one sign of this resistance. In taking up a habit long associated with men, female smokers challenged deeply held notions about the proper relationship between the sexes; they provoked reactions that went beyond the long-standing debate about tobacco itself.

As with most historical changes, the boundaries around this one are indistinct. American women did not entirely abandon tobacco during the Victorian era. Nathaniel Currier, half of the famous team of Currier and Ives, made a lithograph in 1847 that showed a young woman reclining on a couch and smoking a cigarette. (The artist demonstrated his disapproval by putting a cigarette container in the form of a devil on the table beside her.) One of the first published references to cigarettes in the United States—in an 1854 anti-tobacco tract by Russell T. Trall, a temperance and health reformer—linked them to women. Trall said he had seen some "ladies" smoking cigarettes in New York City. Such reports, however, were rare until the late nineteenth century. The *New York Times* published only three articles with any reference to women and tobacco between 1851 and 1880 (the second of which, in 1877, dismissed as a "gross exaggeration" a tract writer's claim that women were "fast becoming slaves" to cigarettes); in the next two decades, it printed more than a dozen. The volume of prescriptive literature condemning tobacco use by women also expanded, which suggests that more women were using tobacco: there is little need to denounce that which rarely occurs.[11]

Although most of the denunciations assumed that only the most dissolute and degraded women would have anything to do with tobacco, there were hints that smoke was creeping into more respectable venues. For example, a group of twelve well-bred students at the Wilson Female Seminary in Redfield, Massachusetts, were caught smoking cigarettes late one night in 1880; news of their disgrace was published in the *New York Times*. Mrs. John A. Logan, an early anti-cigarette activist and widow of a notable Civil War hero, testified that she had personally seen women "who claimed leadership in society" sink to the level of "the degenerate and depraved" by smoking cigarettes, "holding the poisoned paper tubes between their dainty fingers while the curling smoke from nostrils and mouth ascended above their aristocratic heads." She also reported that it had become customary in certain sets for women to exchange jewel-encrusted cigarette cases and costly holders as gifts. According to the WCTU, "ladies' smoking clubs" were operating in several cities in 1885. Further, "A graduate of one of our best ladies' seminaries has so fearfully retrograded that she indulges in a daily after-dinner cigarette."[12]

Cigarettes were often introduced into upper-class parlors by women freshly returned from grand tours abroad, where smoking was well established in "smart" circles, especially on "the Continent." Madame Dudevant, better known by her sobriquet George Sand, helped popularize smoking among her female counterparts in the French intelligentsia in the mid-nineteenth century. Americans often commented on the prevalence of smoking among upper-class women in England. Some American women who sojourned in these settings adopted the practice as proof of their worldliness.[13]

A series of lithographs published in New York in the 1880s depicted fashionable women smoking in various public situations, including while traveling by train and while horseback riding. By the 1890s, at least one New York hotel had opened a smoking room for women, responding to a "smoking craze" among its well-heeled clientele. Novelists, too, attested to the fact that cigarettes were not unknown in "society" circles. Ellen Olenska, heroine of Edith Wharton's *Age of Innocence*, was a practiced smoker who kept her cigarettes in a small gold case dangling from a bracelet. Lily Bart, Wharton's heroine in *The House of Mirth*, attached her gold cigarette case to a string of pearls. The title character of F. Marion Crawford's 1893 novel *Marion Darche* regularly offered cigarettes to all her guests, male and female alike, insisting, "You must all smoke and make yourselves happy."[14]

Because the use of tobacco by women remained deeply stigmatized in middle-class culture, its extent in the decades before World War I is difficult to document. By the early teens, however, there was enough of a market to lead small manufacturers to introduce a few brands aimed at women. Most had floral themes, such as Rose Tips and Milo Violets. Within just a few years, millions of such cigarettes were being sold, presumably to a mostly female clientele. A report at the end of the fiscal year 1917 showed a 15 percent increase over the previous year in federal tax revenue from the sale of tobacco products; government officials concluded that much of it came from the growing popularity of cigarettes among women.[15]

Despite these encroachments, widespread public acceptance of cigarette-smoking women was still many years in the future. Even fictional smokers provoked reproof. The (male) editor of the *Southern Tobacco Journal* was so incensed by *Marion Darche* that he called for a boycott of all novels in which women smoked or even contemplated smoking. A writer for the *New York Times* complained that heroines who smoked besmirched both womanhood and literature. A character in the 1898 musical *The Runaway Girl* shocked even sophisticated New Yorkers by smoking onstage while singing "Sly Cigarette" ("Why did you teach me to love you so / When I have to pretend that I don't you know").[16]

James B. Duke himself, once the leading cigarette manufacturer in the world, was appalled by women who used his product. When a newspaper reporter, in a rare interview with Duke, asked his opinion of female smokers, he exploded: "Why, if any woman in my family ever smoked one of those darned things, I'd, I'd. . . ." Before he could elaborate, an alert secretary intervened: "Isn't that one subject you never discuss, Mr. Duke?" Duke, properly cued, said "Yep," and then told the reporter, "Just leave that out, young man. Leave it out." His wife, according to a close friend, smoked anyway, albeit secretly.[17]

Women who smoked despite such disapproval tended to defy other conventional mores, particularly in the realm of sexuality and politics. Smoking both symbolized and reinforced their separation from mainstream culture. The fictional Ellen Olenska, after all, was involved with a married man; she also had lived in Europe, in a "Bohemian" quarter given over to "people who wrote" and others on the fringes of proper society. There was something "perverse and provocative" about her. Lily Bart was involved in a scandal and came to an unfortunate end. Marion Darche entertained several potential suitors while still married to her ne'er-do-well husband (a nonsmoker).[18]

As Richard Klein has pointed out, the first women to be publicly identified with cigarettes were those who were paid to stage their sexuality: prostitutes, actresses, dancers. The act of lighting a cigarette signaled a certain sexual openness; women who did so violated traditional roles by actively giving themselves pleasure instead of either avoiding it or passively receiving it. After about 1890 or so, when a woman dangled a cigarette it did not necessarily mean she was a prostitute, but it did suggest that she might be available—although on her own terms. It was this association with hubris that led Frances Benjamin Johnston, an avant-garde photographer, to choose a lighted cigarette and a tankard of ale as props for an intentionally shocking self-portrait in 1896.[19]

For Emma Goldman—who advocated birth control, free love, free speech, and political violence (not necessarily in that order)—smoking was just another expression of disdain for bourgeois morality as a whole. Goldman was imprisoned several times and eventually deported from the United States for her activities as an anarchist. Describing her experiences in Blackwell's Island Penitentiary in New York in 1893, she said that having to give up smoking was one of the greatest hardships of life in prison for her (female inmates were permitted snuff but not cigarettes). The deprivation produced "torture almost beyond endurance." By that time, Goldman was going through forty cigarettes a day; her habit had escalated with her commitment to radical politics.[20]

Smoking was far more common among feminists than among more conservative women. Janitors at a hall used by suffragists in Reno, Nevada, in 1908 complained that the women left the premises littered with piles of ashes and cigarette butts after every meeting. Some years later, a janitor at the Ventnor, New Jersey, City Hall threatened to go on strike unless he received higher wages to compensate for the added work he said was necessary to sweep up the cigarette debris deposited during the weekly meetings of the League of Women Voters. In 1912, the Women's Political Union in New York City raised money for the suffrage campaign by selling cigarettes embossed with the motto "Votes for Women." A contributor to the *Atlantic Monthly* theorized that feminists tended to smoke because the act was freighted with political significance. Each cigarette served as a "symbol of emancipation," and as a "temporary substitute for the ballot." The writer added that such women sometimes forced their hapless male companions into "an unholy competition of numberless cigarettes," with the men struggling to keep up for fear of being reduced to "mollycoddledom."[21]

Alice Roosevelt Longworth, daughter of Theodore Roosevelt, was typical of young women from respectable families who flirted with unconventionality by smoking in the pre-war years. Chastised for smoking in the White House after her father became president, in 1901, she said she would smoke on the roof. She smoked even though "some of the women I know who smoke look peculiarly leathery" ("though perhaps they would look leathery anyway," she added, rationalizing). She kept her cigarettes in a gold vanity case, which she sometimes flourished in what she later described as a deliberate effort to "stir up" her elders.[22]

President Roosevelt (a teetotaling nonsmoker himself) remonstrated with her privately, but voiced no public opinion about his daughter's habit. Others were less reticent. Delegates to the national convention of the Prohibition Party in 1908 rescinded an invitation to Mrs. Longworth, holding that a cigarette-smoking woman would be "out of place" at a gathering of prohibitionists. (Rumors that she attended horse races further tarnished her reputation.) Two years later, the Anti-Cigarette League, the WCTU, the four Christian Endeavor societies of Fairbury, Nebraska (a town with a population of 5,294), and the Susan B. Anthony Suffrage Club of Cincinnati, Ohio, all petitioned her to stop smoking. The *New York Times* condemned the petitions as misguided, if well intentioned. Since "a considerable majority of the better people in this country view the practice with disfavor," all that was needed to maintain order was "silent pressure."[23]

Reports about "Princess Alice" and her cigarettes stimulated lively discussions all around the country. The *Sacramento Bee* thought it was bad enough for men to smoke, but "a thousand times more offensive when a woman is the offender." Smoking by women was not nice at any time; it

was nasty, degrading, and unwomanly in the extreme when done in public; "absolutely not one word can be said in its extenuation"; and Mrs.
Longworth should heed the "earnest mothers who have begged her to
refrain from setting such a bad example." On the other hand, at a meeting
of the Daughters of the American Revolution in Pittsburgh, Pennsylvania,
a prominent member rose to say: "We needn't all get up our feathers
simply because Mrs. Longworth smokes cigarettes. Why, a hundred years
ago our great-grandmothers sat with their husbands and smoked corncob
pipes." In the 1930s, an unrepentant Alice appeared in magazine ads endorsing Lucky Strike cigarettes.[24]

Society smokers such as Longworth received attention disproportionate
to their numbers. For example, the *New York Times* made a news story out
of the fact that Mrs. Edward T. Stotesbury once offered cigarettes (stamped
with her monogram in gold) to each of her 150 guests, male and female
alike, at a dinner dance at the Philadelphia Ritz-Carlton. Meanwhile, perhaps the largest single group of women who smoked indulged their habit
quietly, attracting virtually no notice. These were immigrants from southern and eastern Europe. For immigrant women, as for men, a cigarette
would have been an inexpensive, familiar comfort; possibly it helped dull
the pangs of hunger. The voices of such women are difficult to hear, partly
because they smoked in private, in keeping with Old World traditions. In
one case, however, an immigrant woman's private habit became a public
issue, opening a small window into the nexus of sentiment around female
smokers, pro and con.

Elizabeth Dudka, a twenty-six-year-old Russian émigré, lived with her
husband Edmund, a machinist, and their two children (ages four and two)
in a tenement in Elizabeth, New Jersey. She smoked several Russian-made
cigarettes a day. Her husband disapproved. One evening, trying to knock
a lighted cigarette from her mouth, he hit her on the cheek; she shrieked,
the police came, and the resulting quarrel was brought before Police Court
Judge Owen P. Mahon. According to press accounts, the judge dismissed
the case against the husband and said the wife ought to be spanked for
smoking. The New York papers, in the words of a trade journal, "got all
riled up about it," and sought out Mrs. Dudka's side of the story.[25]

Reporters writing about Mrs. Dudka emphasized her domesticity: her
"spotless gingham apron," her "shining" stove, with its "singing kettle"
and "steaming pot," her baby in a cradle with a "snow white covering."
In the eyes of the reporters, at least, she was a model of neatness, order-
liness, and maternity. Interviewed in her kitchen, she began by insisting
she was not addicted to cigarettes and went on to argue that smoking
them made her a better mother:

> I could stop now, this minute; but why should I? Where is the harm?
> Who will deny a mother that small comfort? In your fashionable New
> York hotels and restaurants women pull out their gold and silver cases,
> take out a cigarette, monogrammed, perhaps, and smoke in public. But

they do not, they cannot, know the restfulness, the mental relaxation that comes from inhaling a Russian cigarette in one's own kitchen, alone, removed from the too critical eye of the public. You may say that if more young mothers stayed at home with their children and smoked a cigarette in their kitchen, instead of going off to cabarets and dances, there would be more real happiness and home life in the world.[26]

Women who smoked in public attracted both attention and censure; they often ended up on the front pages of the newspapers, if not in jail. They were noticed partly because they were still unusual; and partly because, fearing disapproval if they smoked outdoors, they tended to smoke indoors in places where it was not customary for even men to smoke, including railroad dining cars, retail stores, florist shops, and art galleries. Frances Perkins (the first woman to hold a cabinet position, as Franklin Roosevelt's secretary of labor) once complained that women did not smoke like "gentlemen." Major hotels usually provided smoking rooms for men but not for women; women consequently smoked in the hotel dining rooms, lobbies, and other public spaces, where they invariably caused a stir.[27]

Two socially prominent women stunned San Francisco in 1908 by lighting up in a popular cafe, engaging in what a newspaper reporter called the "Continental custom" of smoking, puffing away "as if there had not been anything to disapprove in their action." When a woman lit an after-dinner cigarette in the dining room of the then-new Ritz-Carlton in New York in 1910, her waiter rushed to tell the head waiter, who rushed to tell the hotel manager, who rushed to tell the hotel's vice president that a woman was smoking in the dining room. She was left undisturbed, however, after the vice president ruled that the matter was best governed by the dictates of society. "American women know best what is the correct thing to do in a public restaurant, and I would never dream of posing as an arbiter of etiquette," he said. A few years later, the hotel opened a tobacco shop for women, called the Ladies' Humidor.[28]

James B. Martin, owner of the popular Cafe Martin in New York City, announced at one point that women would be permitted to smoke publicly on his premises. He revoked the dispensation after ten days of social pressure. The Cafe Martin would provide a private lounge for women smokers, but they would not be allowed to puff away in the public dining rooms. "I believe now that the bulk of the American public is averse to this innovation," said the chastened proprietor.[29]

Reports about women smoking in restaurants and other public places provoked the New York City aldermen into several efforts to outlaw the practice. The first came in 1908, when they approved an ordinance sponsored by Alderman Timothy Sullivan, who said the sight of a woman smoking tended to weaken the respect men ought to have for her. A twenty-nine-year-old woman was arrested on charges of violating the law; she was jailed for a day in lieu of a $5 fine after she told the magistrate, "I've got as much right to smoke as you have." As it developed, a court clerk had mistakenly posted the ordinance as approved when in fact it had been vetoed by the mayor. Still, it was clear that women could not yet smoke with impunity, even in cosmopolitan New York.[30]

Three years later, the aldermen, led by majority leader Frank Dowling, tried once again to prohibit women from lighting up in public. However, corporation counsel Archibald R. Watson advised them that any ordinance aimed only at women would be set aside by the courts. Watson said the aldermen were proposing to control personal behavior that might be vulgar or indelicate, but was not necessarily a threat to health, morality, or public safety. The aldermen reluctantly abandoned the effort, prompting the *New York Times* to suggest that having wasted their time on one "silly . . . obviously futile" ordinance, they ought to try another: prohibiting the wearing of murderous hatpins.[31]

These were only two of many attempts to use the force of law to curb smoking by women in New York. State Assemblyman Joseph Sullivan of Corona asked the legislature to ban the sale of cigarettes altogether in 1905, saying it was necessary to save "foolish" and "lightheaded" women from themselves. "Women in society have taken to smoking cigarettes, and persons who are on the ragged edge of society think that they have as much right," he said. "All roads to ruin are open when they begin to smoke." The legislature rejected the proposal. Notwithstanding the absence of a law, policemen in New York City and elsewhere in the state occasionally arrested women for smoking anyway, categorizing them as public nuisances. Most were released immediately, but one woman, Jennie Lasher, was sentenced to thirty days in the county jail in Binghamton, New York, on a charge of smoking in front of her children and thereby endangering their morals. She was arrested on the basis of a complaint filed by her husband, William, a baker, who objected to her smoking. The *New York Times*, in a front-page story headlined "JAIL FOR SMOKING MOTHER," reported that Mrs. Lasher swooned in court when the sentence was announced, then bade goodbye to her seven-year-old son and five-year-old daughter and was escorted to her cell.[32]

In most parts of the country, female smokers had not yet become conspicuous enough to attract special legislative attention. A city ordinance enacted in Wenatchee, Washington, made it a misdemeanor for boys under age twenty-one to smoke cigarettes, but did not mention girls, on the assumption that only boys would be tempted to smoke. When a New Hampshire legislator introduced a bill in 1913 to prohibit the sale of tobacco in any form to women, a House committee promptly tabled it, concluding there were not enough cigarette-smoking women to bother about in New Hampshire.[33]

For the most part, social sanctions still functioned to restrict female smoking outside metropolitan areas. Sinclair Lewis illustrated this in his novel *Main Street*. His heroine, Carol Kennicott, moved as a young bride to the fictional Gopher Prairie in 1912. While hosting the party that introduced her to the small town's social elite, she briefly contemplated light-

ing a cigarette, in an effort to shake her new neighbors from their ener-
vating complacency; but she "dismissed the obscene thought before it was
quite formed." Women of "society" might be seen smoking in New York,
San Francisco, and other urban centers, but not in the Gopher Prairies of
America. The author of a popular etiquette book made this clear by insisting that a proper young woman could have nothing more to do with
cigarettes beyond consenting to permit male friends to smoke them in her
presence. "To go beyond this point," the author explained, "is to overstep
the borders of wise convention and pass into bohemia, with which, in these
pages, we have no concern or authority.[34]

During the 1912 presidential campaign, Ellen Axson Wilson, wife of
candidate Woodrow Wilson, took the extraordinary step of calling a press
conference to deny rumors that she tolerated smoking by women. Mrs.
Wilson was not suspected of smoking herself; she stood accused only of
not objecting to women who did. It was also said that she intended to
keep the White House supplied with cigarettes for the convenience of female visitors. A cigarette-toting First Lady was such a potential political
liability that Mrs. Wilson, presumably at the urging of her husband's campaign advisers, appeared at a press conference to insist that no woman in
her household had smoked or would ever smoke. Not until Eleanor Roosevelt in the 1930s did a First Lady smoke publicly (Mrs. Calvin Coolidge
reportedly smoked, but only in private).[35]

Even as cigarettes gained acceptance when smoked by men around the
time of World War I, resistance to their use by women hardened. The
YMCA, which distributed billions of cigarettes to soldiers during the war,
warned those same soldiers to stay away from "loud speaking, cigarette-
smoking women—so-called 'flappers.' " Women were encouraged to give
cigarettes to soldiers (and Red Cross nurses sometimes lit them for
wounded men), but they were not supposed to smoke them themselves, at
least in public.[36]

The Ladies' Walking Club of New York City, the Young Women's Hebrew Association of Brooklyn, the Needlework Guild of America, and
countless other women's groups supported "smokes for soldiers" funds
with block parties, rummage sales, revues, and dances. Even the WCTU
tacitly accepted the distribution of tobacco to soldiers. But when the Army
and Navy Field Comfort Committee was asked to include cigarettes in
"comfort kits" given to Red Cross nurses and other women in military
support positions, women's groups were horrified. Advocates of the proposal said smoking would help soothe jangled nerves and neutralize unpleasant hospital odors. The committee, mindful of the outcry, decided to
distribute cigarettes to men only; the women would get hairpins, face powder, and sewing needles instead.[37]

Daniel A. Poling was convinced by his service with the YMCA overseas
that cigarettes were a useful antidote to sin for soldiers. On the other hand,
he thought the idea of women smoking under any circumstances was
"very disquieting, to say the least." Poling shuddered to see women en-

gaged in "a wild nicotine debauch" while he was on assignment for the YMCA in England and France. In the dining room of his hotel in London, "I found literally scores of women, perhaps as many as three hundred, smoking. The young, the middle-aged, and the old, were all at it." To Poling, women who smoked violated the social contract between the sexes. Women were supposed to serve as a restraining, uplifting influence on men; without that influence, males would sink into moral depravity.[38]

By the time the United States entered the war, then, two contradictory trends were evident: more women were smoking, and they were encountering greater and greater resistance. The war intensified both trends. "Girls are doing things / They've never done before," one poet wrote; "All the world is topsy-turvy / Since the war began." The boyish profile of the flapper replaced the exaggerated curves of the Victorian matron as a fashion ideal. Women cut their hair, rouged their cheeks and lips, adopted less restrictive clothing. They moved into the workplace in ever-growing numbers. They demanded the vote. Increasingly, they smoked. The more they smoked, the more heated the opposition.[39]

Smaller manufacturers—who were quicker to respond to the female market than the major companies—experimented with new brands aimed at women, such as Haidee, made by Chalkadia and Company of New York, and Pera, from the Strand Cigarette Company of Philadelphia. Strand also produced made-to-order "lady's size" cigarettes, with monograms and tips covered with silk or silver or gold paper. Several companies manufactured cigarettes with red tips, to match the lip rouge that more and more women were wearing. An importer brought in Parisian cigarettes rolled in rose, blue, green, or orange paper, for stylish women who wanted to smoke something dyed to match their gowns.[40]

Chic accoutrements appeared in fashionable stores: smoking jackets for women; handbags designed to accommodate cigarette packages; cigarette holders made of jade, amber, mother-of-pearl, or tortoiseshell, carried in dainty perfumed boxes; collapsible "cigaret tubes" made of gold, which folded into tiny cases to be dangled from neck chains when not in use; and jewel-encrusted cigarette cases. A Chicago company began marketing a combination vanity/cigarette case, with a mirror attached to the inside cover. According to one report, cigarette holders accounted for less than 10 percent of the overall market for smokers' novelties before 1914; in 1920, the figure was 60 percent, with most of them being sold to women.[41]

By the early twenties, the use of cigarettes by women was established enough to have inspired certain codes of behavior. For example, it was bad form to smoke without a holder while wearing evening attire. The preferred holder for evening use was long, slender, and black, with a tiny ring of rhinestones precisely one inch from the end. Second in favor were models in amber, ornamented with jewels, ebony, or tortoiseshell. Women could also order holders tinted to match their frocks. For sports use, there were holders with camouflage designs.[42]

It is tempting to attribute the dramatic increase in female smoking to the blandishments of advertisers. Many writers, from Josephus Daniels, writing his autobiography in the 1940s, to anti-smoking activists in recent years, have made that assertion. Edward Bernays, renowned public relations and advertising adviser to the American Tobacco Company, claimed to have single-handedly popularized smoking for women by convincing several prominent debutantes to hold cigarettes as "torches of freedom" in the 1929 Easter Day parade in New York City. As Bernays told it, this single stunt, reinforced with clever new advertising campaigns, induced women to smoke virtually overnight. The problem with this assessment is that women were smoking in significant numbers long before the industry began directing messages to them. Advertisers made virtually no direct overtures to the female trade until after that trade was already so large and so widely accepted that it was safe to do so.[43]

Throughout most of the twenties, trade journals warned their readers to avoid any hint, in advertising or in store displays, that women should smoke, out of fear of unleashing "the busybody element." Although "as every one knows, there are a great many women in this country who do smoke," one journal noted, "any suggestion in the advertising or the conduct of a store that women are being encouraged to smoke is likely to be used by the Anti-Tobacco League as evidence that the use of tobacco should be prohibited." In his address to the annual meeting of the Tobacco Merchants Association in 1920, President Charles J. Eisenlohr urged advertisers "to include nothing that may be subject to criticism and to exclude everything that may prejudice the public." The recent enactment of national prohibition, he added, should be taken as a warning to tread lightly lest Lady Nicotine follow King Alcohol into oblivion.[44]

Although cigarette manufacturers had long used women's images in promoting their products, beginning with the trading cards used as package stiffeners in the 1880s and 1890s, they rarely suggested women themselves should smoke. In one exception, in the early 1880s, the Duke family tobacco company produced a poster that implied smoking could improve a woman's disposition. The poster, titled "My Mother-in-Law," showed a contented woman sitting next to a baby cradle; while she was not actually smoking, the cradle held two packages of "Duke of Durham" tobacco. In 1897, Cameron and Cameron Tobacco Company of Richmond advertised in the *Southern Tobacco Journal*'s Christmas issue with a drawing of a woman smoking a cigarette. The Soter Company of New York did not go quite that far in promoting its La Turka cigarettes in 1916; its advertisements showed a woman, in harem silks, only holding a cigarette.[45]

The P. Lorillard Tobacco Company sometimes featured women in advertising for its various Turkish brands (Murad, Helmar, Egyptian Deities). The company used stylized drawings of models who were clearly occidental (women who looked as though they had never been east of Brooklyn Borough Hall, as one observer put it) and placed them in oriental settings (often lounging on divans, dressed in harem pants, with pyramid-like structures in the background). One fanciful advertisement for Murad in 1917 showed three women sitting on the smoke that was artfully curling from the tip of a giant cigarette. In a more daring advertisement for Helmar two years later, a turbaned woman held a cigarette between her lips. These examples are noteworthy because of their rarity. Prior to the mid-1920s, women seldom appeared in cigarette advertisements and when they did, they were usually positioned well in the background, far from any actual smoke.[46]

Social scientist Michael Schudson examined two urban newspapers and a general circulation magazine and found no advertisements picturing women smoking or obviously appealing to women smokers before 1926. That was the year when Liggett and Meyers showed a man and a woman seated on a moonlit riverbank, the man smoking a Chesterfield and the woman coaxing him to "Blow Some My Way." It still took some time before women moved from secondhand to direct smoke in cigarette advertisements. In 1927, Philip Morris promoted its new brand, Marlboro ("Mild as May"), with an ad showing a woman smoking; this appeared on the back cover of *Le Bon Ton*, a women's fashion and travel magazine. Other Marlboro promotions asserted that "[w]omen—when they smoke at all— quickly develop discriminating taste." The Marlboro ads were illustrated by a feminine hand in silhouette holding a lit cigarette, but women still did not hold or smoke cigarettes in advertisements for more established brands. When opera star Ernestine Schumann-Heink and actress Florence Reed recommended Lucky Strike as soothing to the throat in 1927, they were not pictured with cigarettes. That same year, P. Lorillard advertised Old Gold ("Not a Cough in a Carload") with a series of cartoons showing women smoking, but apparently published them only in college newspapers. More typically, advertisements for the major brands showed women merely looking on as men smoked.[47]

The breakthrough came in 1928 when American Tobacco launched its legendary "Reach for a Lucky instead of a Sweet" campaign. Thereafter, cigarette manufacturers pursued male and female customers with equal aggression. (American Tobacco soon began suggesting not only that women smoke, but that they also inhale, preferably the "purified" smoke of Lucky Strike.) However, by the time the manufacturers began overtly advertising to women, the female market was already a sizeable one. Endorsements by debutantes and female celebrities may have helped make public smoking more acceptable; but on the whole, advertising simply reinforced, more than initiated, the use of cigarettes by women.[48]

The real causes of the increase lay deep in the economic and social structure of postwar America. The war encouraged female smoking in several ways, beginning with changes in the formulation of cigarettes. The concept of "women's sphere" expanded to include a variety of roles, including some once reserved for men only. New social conventions bubbled up and displaced the old. More women were going to college, where they were relatively free of parental constraints. Whether women in the aggregate experienced appreciably altered lives is a matter of debate, but there is ample anecdotal evidence to suggest that many found an increased sense of autonomy during the war and that this translated to greater willingness to experiment with new behaviors, including smoking.[49]

The war helped lower not only the social but the physical threshold that had limited smoking by women. A significant share of the pre-war cigarette market was held by brands made with strong Turkish tobaccos, such as Fatima, Murad, and Helmar. Imports from Turkey were cut off during the war (beginning with the outbreak of hostilities in Europe in 1914) and were restricted thereafter by high import and revenue duties. This provided an opening for a new type of cigarette, made with blends of milder, mostly domestic tobaccos. Camel, introduced by R. J. Reynolds in 1913, claimed 35 percent of the national market by 1917; American Tobacco's Lucky Strike and Liggett and Myers's Chesterfield followed closely behind. By 1925, these three blended brands accounted for 82.3 percent of all cigarette sales in the United States.[50]

Milder cigarettes reduce the level of physical discomfort that discourages many novice smokers. This was one factor in the tremendous growth of the cigarette industry after the war; the newer blends were more appealing to both men and women. The industry itself attributed the increase in smoking by women to the large-scale manufacture of cigarettes more suited to their "delicate" constitutions.[51]

More women had money to experiment with cigarettes because of economic changes associated with the war. They found new employment opportunities because the war diverted men to military service, on the one hand, and increased the demand for domestic production, on the other. The war also reduced the flow of immigration to the United States, compounding the labor shortage. These developments did not bring large numbers of new women into the work force; the percentage of women employed outside the home stayed at roughly 25 percent from 1910 through 1920. Instead, they stimulated a shift within the existing female work force, setting in motion a kaleidoscope of job changes. On the whole, this rotation rewarded women with better wages than they had been earning.[52]

Women who had been working as domestics moved into jobs in sales, clerical work, light manufacturing, and specialized industries such as food processing and telephone communications. Maurine Weiner Greenwald points out that this pattern of change had already been established, in response to the standardization of factory work, business consolidation and expansion, and other changes in the American economy; the war simply amplified it. Some women moved into jobs traditionally held by men, including streetcar conducting, police work, and metalworking, but most remained in traditionally female jobs. Their wages, however, increased, by a total of 20 percent between 1914 and 1918.[53]

Job listings in the classified advertising sections of American newspapers reflected the expanded opportunities available to women. The *Cincinnati*

*Enquirer*, for example, carried five columns of advertisements for female job openings at the end of May 1917, compared to seven columns for men. Two years later, the paper published an equal number of openings for both men and women (twelve columns each). The number of jobs for women in the field of domestic work had declined slightly, by about 3 percent, while those in sales and office work increased by 100 percent and 40 percent, respectively. Openings for female factory workers increased by 92 percent. In terms of sheer numbers, factory jobs replaced domestic work as the largest single category of employment open to women.

In 1917, the *Enquirer* advertised very few jobs for women beyond the categories of domestic, factory, office, and sales. There were a handful of openings for dressmakers, restaurant cooks, waitresses, and commercial laundry workers. One company asked for "a writer of motion picture plays"; another sought a model (with measurements of 39–26–41) for a coat factory. Two years later, the "Help Wanted, Female" columns included openings for an assistant manager of an insurance company, a cashier, a draftsman, an artist to do hand coloring for a publishing company, a piano player ("good on pictures"), an assistant in a dental office, linotype operators, nurses, teachers, telephone switchboard operators, upholsterers, photofinishers, writers, and baseball players ("Girls. Real Ball Players. Bloomer Girl Ball Club. Must be willing to travel"). Not only the wages but the variety of work available to women had improved.[54]

Wartime labor shortages coupled with increased demands worked together to open up more jobs for women in the tobacco industry itself, particularly in retail sales. Women had long been involved in the production end of the industry, but they were virtually invisible in retailing before the war. Although the trade journals occasionally mentioned women who owned cigar stores, female proprietors rarely worked behind the counter; the public face of the industry was almost exclusively male. (Legend had it that "one naughty cigar store" employed female clerks around the turn of the century; stored most of its stock on shelves that could be reached only by tall ladders; and attracted customers with the prospect of a glimpse of an ankle when the clerks used the ladders to retrieve stock.) When rumors first surfaced that the United Cigar Stores, the country's largest cigarette and tobacco retailer, planned to hire women clerks, the trade press discounted them. "There are too many obstacles in the way of this plan," the leading journal, *Tobacco*, editorialized, citing labor laws which limited the hours that women could work, along with the reluctance of men to buy tobacco products from women.[55]

The Tobacco Manufacturers Association worried that the proximity of women to tobacco would call down the wrath of the reformers. "If the cigar store is maintained strictly as a man's store there will be less danger of its patronage being used as evidence that the sale of all tobacco should be discontinued," it argued. One area of concern involved "the element of sex-attraction." Miss S. I. Entwisle, hired by United Cigar Stores to supervise the new female workforce, said she planned to avoid such problems by offering jobs only to "serious-minded" women over age twenty-five. By the end of August 1918, the company had put more than 500 women to work in its 1,200 outlets, and proclaimed, "What started as an experiment is now a fixture." Indeed, some retail managers complained bitterly during the 1918 influenza epidemic that the "mask laws" (requiring people in most large cities to cover their faces in public) were depriving men of the smiles of the "Carmens" in their shops.[56]

Many of these women lost their jobs at the end of the war, as did other women who had moved into traditionally male positions. The Judge and Dolph Drug Company, which employed women in its three drug and tobacco stores in St. Louis, Missouri, replaced all of them with men after the demobilization of the American Expeditionary Forces. However, several of the women promptly found jobs operating competing cigar stands. Myrtle Wade, who replaced her cousin at a United Cigar Store in San Francisco, lost her job to him when he returned from military service; but she, too, found another.[57]

Although women had a lower profile in tobacco retailing after the war, they continued to have a presence. It is likely, if impossible to prove, that this made other women feel more comfortable as customers. Industry observers speculated that women would be more willing to enter the previously male bastion of the cigar store (and buy products both for the men in their lives and for themselves) if another woman were standing behind the counter. With this aim in mind, a large Philadelphia store established a separate department to cater to an exclusively female clientele. Several tobacco stores added lines of merchandise intended to tempt women, such as candy, stationery, and hosiery. Some tobacconists competed for female customers by furnishing their shops with thick rugs, Chinese prints, and overstuffed couches, so women could sample the wares in comfort.[58]

The war helped lower the social barriers that inhibited female smoking by stimulating a rebellion against bourgeois values, particularly among the young. Middle-class Victorians interpreted pleasure in primarily spiritual and moral rather than physical or sensual terms; they valued self-restraint more than self-indulgence. Their descendants sought immediacy, self-gratification, and sensuality. For women, smoking was one expression of departure from the past. Red mouths, bobbed hair, short skirts, strappy city shoes: these, along with cigarettes in long thin holders, helped define the modern woman in the 1920s.[59]

The war also raised issues of equality, which the industry's defenders quickly applied to tobacco use. "The charter of freedom was never meant to be used as an engine of oppression. Our women are going to powder their noses, paint their cheeks, chew gum, and smoke cigarettes if they want to," a trade journal editorialized. An editorial writer for the *Sacramento Star*, commenting on a divorce petition filed by a Houston, Texas, man who said his wife caused him mental anguish by smoking in public, wondered: "If it is legitimate for a man to make the air around him blue with the smoke of his cigar or cigaret, why should the same right be denied a woman? Equal rights for all; special privileges for none, is one of the very foundation stones of our government." A member of a women's club in New York City complained that anti-smoking measures were "Germanic."[60]

Female smoking expanded both socially (into the middle classes) and spatially (into more public places) after the war. Women who once smoked on the sly were increasingly welcomed into hotels, restaurants, theaters, railroads, and other public facilities. A *New York Times* canvass of the city's hotels and restaurants in 1919 found few where the managers prohibited smoking—a reversal of the pattern that prevailed just a few years earlier. Dozens of theaters in New York and elsewhere opened special smoking rooms for women; the amenities included complimentary cigarettes for patrons who had forgotten to bring their own. At the Woods Theatre in Chicago, women could smoke in luxury in a room appointed with $10,000 worth of marble, Persian rugs, and leather furniture. By the late twenties, female smokers had become so common that automatic cigarette vending machines were being installed in urban department stores for their convenience. (One store, in Boston, finally closed its posh smoking room because, the manager said, it was too popular: "It was a haven for all the girls who wanted to smoke without fear of interruption. They hogged the place and our own customers didn't have a chance.")[61]

Railroads and train stations also provided smoking facilities for women, sometimes to protect the sensibilities of men. A writer for the *Greensboro News* reported that the male occupants of a smoking car on a train en route to Raleigh, North Carolina, were alternately amazed and disgusted when a woman joined them. The Canadian Pacific and the Chicago, Milwaukee, and St. Paul Railroads were among those that responded to male concerns by adding women's smoking compartments. Others opened their existing smoking cars to women, although women did not always feel at ease in them. On one train leaving New York for Philadelphia during the holiday season of 1922, ten women had seats in the smoking car; but only one of them had dared to smoke by the time the train reached Philadelphia. Of the male passengers, "one and all of them appeared to have a regular Babbitt reaction to a woman smoking in a smoking car," the *New York Times* reported. (Babbitt, in the 1922 Sinclair Lewis novel of that title, regarded the smoking car as a haven for men and cigars; he took umbrage at even men who smoked cigarettes there.)[62]

After the manager of the Detroit municipal railway announced that women would be allowed to smoke on streetcars, saying there was no reason why women should not be permitted to do what men did, the *New York Times* asked, "Is there no limit to these encroachments?" The answer appeared to be no. The San Francisco Woman's Athletic Club not only opened its premises to smoking, it commissioned a local manufacturer to produce a special blend, stamped with the club's monogram, for members' use. The Young Women's Christian Association, which had vowed in 1919 to never, ever open its doors to smokers, acquiesced in 1922. Directors of the association decided that "women of the present day" were going to smoke whether permitted to or not; and that it would be better to allow them to do it openly rather than sneakily. The administrator of Paragon Park at Nantasket Beach, near Boston, installed several benches marked "Reserved For Ladies—Smoking Permitted" in response to "feminine demands." The advance of the female smoker even reached into the United States Military Academy at West Point, where a long-standing ban on the possession and use of cigarettes was repealed under pressure from cadets who said they were humiliated by not being able to supply their girlfriends with "fags" at academy dances.[63]

Women smokers also were accepted in lesser locales, including prison. The warden of Chicago's Cook County Jail extended smoking privileges to women in 1920, ending a decades-long policy under which only male prisoners were allowed to smoke. "We are living in an age of 'women's rights' and what's good for the men must be good for the women," he said. The Illinois State Penitentiary at Joliet also lifted a ban on smoking by women prisoners. In New York, the state commission on prisons ruled there was no reason to prevent smoking by the women under its jurisdiction when a recent survey at Vassar College showed that almost half of the students ("girls to the manor born") smoked.[64]

Another measure of changing attitudes was a joke that popped up late in the war and made the rounds for several years thereafter. In the most common version of the story, an elderly gentleman approached a boy smoking cigarettes and asked him what his mother would think if she saw him. The boy replied that she would probably be angry, since they were *her* cigarettes. Joking implies tolerance on some level: people do not find humor in the truly repugnant or unthinkable.[65]

Nonetheless, the triumph of the female smoker was far from complete. Even in New York City, some hotels and restaurants refused to tolerate smoking by women. The owner of the Yates Hotel and the Lussier Restaurant on West Forty-third Street said he did not want the type of woman who smoked in public as a customer: "All they have is a lot of wild, Bohemian ideas that never get them anywhere." The manager of the Woodstock Hotel, also on West Forty-third Street, said he had no personal objections to the habit, but his patrons came mostly from smaller towns and cities in upstate New York and New England and "[p]eople of that type would object to a woman's smoking in the same room with them, just as they would object to having a cabaret performance given at the hotel at which they were stopping. Very well, then. We omit the cabaret, and we omit the smoking—for women."[66]

Throughout the twenties, smoking by women was a highly charged issue, provoking responses that sometimes bordered on violence. For example, when a woman tried to smoke a surreptitious cigarette in a Baltimore hotel dining room in 1921, another woman, claiming to believe that the smoker was on fire, doused her with a glass of water. A year later, a policeman walking his beat on Eighth Avenue between Twenty-third and Twenty-fourth Streets in New York City told a nineteen-year-old woman who was smoking outside a soda shop that that sort of thing was not allowed in his jurisdiction. When she resisted, pointing out that there was no law against it, he rapped her knuckles with his nightstick, knocking the cigarette from her hand. His superiors upheld his action.[67]

In 1922, the New York City aldermen made a fourth attempt to prohibit smoking by women in public. An ordinance sponsored by Alderman Peter J. McGuinness of the Greenpoint section of Brooklyn would have imposed a fine of $5 to $25 and/or a jail term of up to ten days on the proprietor of any public facility that permitted women to smoke. "The morals of our young girls are menaced by this smoking," McGuinness said. "The young fellows lose all respect for women and the next thing you know the young fellows, vampired by these smoking women, desert their homes, their wives and children, rob their employers and even commit murder so that they can get money to lavish on these smoking women. It's all wrong and I say it's got to stop." Mary Garrett Hay of the National Woman's Party and Ruth Hale of the feminist Lucy Stone League were among those who said it was ridiculous and insulting to permit only men to smoke. The *New York Times* mocked the measure as a product of "the zeal of Dogberry." On the other hand, J. F. Sanderson, manager of the Ritz Hotel, said he thought it was a good idea, as did the managers of Delmonico's, the Hotel Ambassador, and the Commodore Hotel.[68]

New York police continued to arrest women for smoking despite the defeat of the ordinance. In the borough of Brooklyn, police charged an eighteen-year-old with disorderly conduct for smoking in public; she was found guilty in police court but won an appeal in county court. Police subsequently arrested her on a charge of corrupting the morals of a minor by smoking in the presence of a fifteen-year-old girl. A policeman who arrested a twenty-one-year-old schoolteacher for smoking on a street in Greenwich Village told her that while it was not a crime for a woman to smoke, "It wasn't nice." When she refused to stop, he escorted her, and her male companion, to jail. They were released by a magistrate the next day. Women who lit cigarettes in designated nonsmoking areas sometimes paid greater penalties than men who did the same thing. After fining a young woman $5 for smoking on a ferryboat when men were typically fined only $3, a New York magistrate told her, "The extra two is for having the nerve to do it."[69]

Female smokers encountered even greater opposition outside New York City. They faced penalties ranging from being fired (particularly if they were schoolteachers) to finding themselves in divorce court. In one notable case that eventually reached the New Jersey Supreme Court, the Secaucus school district fired teacher Helen M. Clark for impairing the morals of her pupils by smoking in public. The court overturned the school district, but the teacher never regained her job. Chauncey E. Cole of Lockland, Ohio, sued his wife, Viola, for divorce on the grounds that she had become a "cigarete [sic] fiend" and spent most of her time smoking rather than preparing his meals and otherwise attending to household duties. Smoking also figured in a divorce and child custody case involving a Flatbush, New York, couple, their five-year-old son, and his paternal grandmother. The wife successfully defended herself against a suit for divorce brought by the husband. She then petitioned for physical custody of the child, saying the grandmother—with whom he had been staying—was unfit to care for him because she smoked cigarettes. The court agreed, and ordered the boy returned to the non-smoking mother.[70]

When George Day of Wichita, Kansas, sought a divorce from his wife, Lavona, in 1923, he charged that she was an unfit wife because she smoked cigarettes in large quantities. District Judge Thomas E. Elcock dismissed the case, ruling that even the habitual use of cigarettes was not sufficient grounds for divorce. The ruling was probably less a vindication of female smoking than a demonstration of resistance to divorce; at the time, Kansas state law made it illegal for anyone to sell, possess, give away, or advertise cigarettes (or cigarette papers).[71]

The novelist Sherwood Anderson dramatized the perspective of rural America in a scene in *Winesburg, Ohio* (1919). Curtis Hartman, the town's minister, glanced out of the window in his room in the bell tower of his church and was rocked to his soul to see his next-door neighbor, lying on her bed, smoking a cigarette. She was a woman of some sophistication, one who had been to Europe and had lived in New York City for two years. Although willing to concede that "[p]erhaps after all her smoking means nothing," Rev. Hartman was still "horror stricken at the thought of a woman smoking." In Sinclair Lewis's *Babbitt*, the only women who smoked were those who had skated beyond the edges of propriety, among them the "dreadfully naughty" Tanis Judique, with whom Babbitt had an affair.[72]

The old taboos endured in smaller communities until well into the 1930s. The first reliable contemporary survey of gender patterns in tobacco use, conducted by *Fortune Magazine* in 1935, found that only about 8 percent of rural women smoked, compared to 40 percent of women living in urban areas. The survey showed that smoking varied with age as well as locality. Women under age forty were far more likely to smoke than those over forty. In their classic study *Middletown* (Muncie, Indiana), Robert S. Lynd and Helen Merrell Lynd found that middle America in 1935 still believed that smoking was "more appropriate" for men than for women, even though female smoking was noticeably more prevalent than it had been ten years earlier.[73]

These were the underlying attitudes that gave rise to a renewed battle against cigarettes, one that was focused on women and inspired in part by the success of the campaign for national prohibition. Although many supporters defected from the anti-cigarette movement during the war and never returned, new ones appeared, brought in by the "menace" of female smokers. The National Council of Women, the Business and Professional Women's Club, the Brooklyn Women's Club, and the Daughters of the American Revolution all joined the campaign for the first time. New support also came from the nation's granges. For example, the Michigan State

Grange condemned the use of women's pictures in cigarette advertisements and the employment of women teachers who smoked. The Oregon State Grange was appalled that "present-day feminism demands every privilege for woman that man claims for himself" and concluded that smoking by women was "a menace to the nation." The Non-Smokers' Protective League of America, a New York–based group founded in 1911, announced a special drive to convert women smokers. Even the Boy Scouts got involved, politely asking women to stop smoking.[74]

Reformers agreed that smoking was more harmful for women than for men, primarily for reasons that had something to do with the nervous system. United States Surgeon General Hugh S. Cumming, in an edict issued from Washington in 1920 telling the women of the country to stop smoking, explained it in this way: "The woman's nervous system is more highly organized than the man's. The reaction, therefore, is more intense. . . . If American women generally contract the habit, as reports now indicate they are doing, the entire American nation will suffer." (Cumming, a cigarette smoker himself, had no objection to men who smoked.)[75]

Other commentators said the problem was not that the female nervous system was highly organized but that it was underdeveloped or immature, like that of an adolescent boy, and thus easily damaged. The problem was compounded by periodic "nervous disturbances," due to pregnancy and menopause. Women who smoked during menopause were said to be particularly at risk, since they invariably became "nervously unstrung, sometimes to the point of insanity." The father of a young Boston woman who committed suicide in 1924 claimed his daughter had had a nervous breakdown brought on by cigarette smoking. Governor E. F. Morgan of West Virginia cited the father's statement in a speech urging women's clubs to "take up the fight" against the "alarming" increase in cigarette smoking among women.[76]

Some members of the medical profession, normally reserved on the topic of smoking, ventured to express concern about its neurological effects on women. An Indianapolis physician, writing in the November 1921 issue of the *Journal of the Indiana State Medical Association*, warned that "[t]he generally recognized emotional instability of the female sex indicates a type of nervous constitution in which chronic cigarette toxemia is more likely to act with disastrous results than in men." Among the consequences of this toxemia, he added, was "loss in beauty," due to "impaired physical, mental and moral tonus." Eighty percent of physicians surveyed by *Good Housekeeping* in 1929 said smoking was more harmful for women because "the nerves of women are less able to stand abuse than those of men." This idea percolated throughout the lay community. As late as 1938, a Seattle weekly magazine claimed that boys who began smoking were responding to normal instincts while girls were more often motivated by "a neurotic impulse." In other words, boys will be boys, but girls who smoke are neurotic.[77]

Beyond the direct effects on individual female smokers was the issue of "race degeneracy." This was a phrase that resonated even more deeply in the 1920s than it had when it was first introduced as an offshoot of Social Darwinism in the 1880s. It showed up in everything from grange publications to medical journals to the tobacco trade press. Reformers warned that the harmful effects of smoking would pass from mother to child, producing, over time, "an apparently new and a physically inferior race of men and women." The trade press gave surprising attention to such claims. For example, *Tobacco* quoted Dr. Granville N. Ryan, president of the Iowa Clinical Medical Society, as saying that smoking by women "is bound to have a bad effect on the next generation."[78]

Concern about this issue led Mrs. John B. Henderson, widow of a prominent United States senator from Missouri and a "luminary" of Washington society, to lend her considerable influence to the postwar anti-cigarette campaign. In a statement sent to newspapers in New York, London, and Paris, and signed by several other Washington social leaders, Mrs. Henderson said cigarette smoking—particularly by women—would "inevitably lead, sooner or later, to physical bankruptcy and race degeneracy." As a starting point for the avoidance of such a fate, she called upon women's colleges to expel students who smoked.[79]

Underscoring all these arguments was the lingering belief that women should set a good example for men. "Anything that is suggestive or immoral in women is detrimental to the welfare of the country," said Representative Paul B. Johnson, a Democrat from Mississippi, sponsor of a 1921 bill to prohibit "female persons" from smoking cigarettes in public in Washington, D.C. "The women can not save this country by trying to get down on a level with men; they must pull the men up to where they are, and they can not do it by smoking cigarettes and wearing only half enough clothes." A Baptist minister, in an anti-cigarette lecture broadcast over radio station wjay in Cleveland, Ohio, declared that smoking "brings a woman down to the level of man." Such equality "brings us a little nearer to the jungle. It is a part of the return to savagery."[80]

The Johnson bill was one of several postwar efforts to impose legal sanctions on female smokers. Although none succeeded, it is noteworthy that even people who supported the right of women to smoke in principle often expressed disapproval of the actual practice. For example, in testifying against a Massachusetts bill to prevent women from smoking in hotels and restaurants, a representative of the Association for the Preservation of Personal Liberty remarked that decent women did not smoke. During a congressional hearing on the Johnson bill banning female smoking in the District of Columbia, a director of the Anti–Blue Law League conceded it was "bad taste" for women to smoke in public. "I am willing to say there are many things done in public that should not be, even to a broad-minded woman," she added. "But where can you draw the line?" Representative Johnson passionately insisted the line should be drawn in front of cigarette-smoking women. One of Johnson's colleagues asked him how he felt about the pipe-smoking grandmother of earlier eras. "She is dead and gone," he replied. His bill suffered a similar fate, dying in committee.[81]

The opposition to female smoking was essentially nostalgic in nature. It represented one of two conflicting impulses that marked the postwar era: a rush to embrace the new, coupled with a retreat to the familiar (to "normalcy"). "Men who have an idea of the proprieties resent the idea of women smoking, especially in public," a Missouri state legislator remarked, while introducing an anti-smoking bill in Missouri in 1919. "I know our mothers didn't sit around in cafes smoking." The flapper, with her short hair, short skirts, and cigarette holder, may have been in a minority, but she captured the public imagination. By attempting to exert control over her, at least to the extent of snuffing out her cigarette, anti-smoking activists sought to restore one small piece of order to a world upended.[82]

Much of this battle took place on the campuses of women's colleges, where administrators struggled to uphold the old moral order against assaults from students who were forging new standards of behavior. Most women's colleges, from the elite institutions of the east to the normal schools of the midwest, prohibited smoking at the beginning of the decade. In many cases, smoking was grounds for expulsion. For example, the Michigan State Normal School at Ypsilanti expelled seventeen students and put thirteen others on probation for smoking in 1922. One of the students appealed, in a case that reached the state Supreme Court. The court not only refused to reinstate the student, it praised the dean of women, Mrs. Bessie Leach Priddy, for "upholding some of the old-fashioned ideals of young womanhood." (In addition to smoking, the list of forbidden practices at Michigan State included riding in automobiles without permission; accepting attentions from strange men; and "gaining access to rooming houses by way of windows.")[83]

The anti-smoking policies were far more popular with parents and administrators than with students. A survey of parents by the dean of students at Methodist-affiliated Boston University in 1925 showed nearly universal support for the school's ban on smoking by women; of 450 responses, only one expressed opposition. More than 60 percent of the parents, faculty, and prominent women in the community questioned by Antioch College around the same time said the school should continue to prohibit female smoking. The habit "lowers a girl's moral tone," one respondent wrote, in a typical comment. At both these colleges, male students were permitted to smoke.[84]

The very fact that smoking was officially prohibited at many colleges gave it an appeal that an increasing number of young women found hard to resist. A cigarette served as a badge of identification with a generation that was rather self-consciously rejecting the proprieties of the past. More than 45 percent of students at Vassar said they smoked. One-third of the coeds at Ohio State University admitted smoking at least occasionally. A fraternity leader at Rhode Island State College claimed, "Practically all the girls smoke." While this was a clear exaggeration, by the late twenties most college administrators had come to accept female smoking as a perfume that was out of the bottle. Bryn Mawr capitulated and rescinded its ban in 1925, followed by Vassar, Smith, Stanford, and many other schools. The new standards were celebrated in song: "She doesn't smoke / she doesn't pet / she hasn't been to college yet."[85]

These were the daughters of the upper and middle classes; by adopting a habit once confined to women on the periphery of society, they helped diffuse it throughout the broader culture. Still, residues of disapproval persisted. In 1927, two women brought a murder trial in Cincinnati, Ohio, to a halt by lighting cigarettes in court. According to a newspaper report, the sheriff insisted there would be no smoking by women in the courtroom, even though most of the men present, including the lawyers, were smoking. Amelia Earhart was one of a number of prominent women who provoked censure by being associated with cigarettes. After her pioneering solo flight across the Atlantic in 1928, Earhart "wickedly" (her word) appeared in an advertisement that claimed, "Lucky Strikes were the cigarettes carried on the 'Friendship' when she crossed the Atlantic." In fact, Earhart did not smoke, but the assertion that she did generated so much adverse publicity that she lost a job as a columnist at *McCall's*. "I suppose you drink too," one irate correspondent wrote to Earhart. She did not drink, nor did she ever endorse cigarettes again. Her quick retreat shows that female smoking remained a morally ambiguous issue for many people at the end of the decade.[86]

# 5

## *The*

## *"Triumph" of*

## *the Cigarette*

CLEARS CIGARETTES AS CANCER SOURCE
*New York Times* (1928)[1]

*I*n 1925, a tobacco trade journalist named Carl Avery Werner wrote an article for the *American Mercury* celebrating "The Triumph of the Cigarette." Werner reminded his readers that cigarettes had once been called "coffin nails," that many states had prohibited their sale, and that medico-ethical opinion at the highest levels had held them to be forerunners of disease and sin. This was all in the past, he concluded, largely because "the agitators had agitated not wisely, but too well." The more violently they had attacked the cigarette, the more popular it had become. The net effect of nearly half a century of crusading was that no fewer than 90 percent of American men over age twenty-one were smoking cigarettes "as regularly as they brush their teeth," as were at least 5 percent of all American women.[2]

Werner greatly overestimated the number of male cigarette smokers, probably underestimated the number of women who smoked, and was only about half right in dismissing the anti-cigarette movement as an antediluvian relic. Cigarette smokers have never enjoyed majority status in the United States. In 1925, only about a third of the adult population used tobacco of any kind, and less than 30 percent of all the tobacco they consumed was smoked in the form of cigarettes. Although women were smoking in greater numbers, and more and more men were switching from pipes and cigars, cigarettes had yet to eclipse other forms of tobacco. Forty years later, when per capita consumption of cigarettes reached its highest point, only about four out of ten adults smoked them: still a minority.[3]

If Werner was overly sanguine about the "triumph" of cigarettes, he aptly depicted the feeble state of the opposition as it appeared in the mid-twenties. Most of the people speaking out by that point were aging progressives, fighting a rearguard action against a steadily advancing foe. Just a few years earlier, however, Werner himself thought cigarettes might yet be swept aside by the same tide of reform that had outlawed alcohol and given the vote to women. By his own count, ninety-two measures to restrict or prohibit cigarettes were pending in twenty-eight states in 1921. Idaho and Utah both banned the sale and manufacture of cigarettes that year, becoming the fourteenth and fifteenth states to do so since Washington adopted the nation's first cigarette prohibition law in 1893.[4]

The resurgence of opposition to cigarettes proved to be temporary. Little of the proposed legislation was adopted; of the laws that were enacted, only those intended to protect minors survived the decade. Idaho legalized cigarettes less than two weeks after prohibiting them; and Utah followed suit two years later, at the very next session of the legislature. By mid-decade, cigarettes were fully legal for adults in every state but Kansas, which finally capitulated in 1927.[5]

Yet even as the first anti-cigarette movement was dying out, the groundwork was being laid for another, one fueled more by biostatistics and the young science of epidemiology than by moral issues. After largely ignoring the issue for decades, the medical profession began giving more attention to the impact of smoking on health in the late 1920s. The *New England Journal of Medicine* published the first of a new generation of studies showing a statistical link between smoking and cancer in 1928. The next year, an article in the *Journal of the American Medical Association* suggested that "sidestream smoke" (emitted by the burning tip of a cigarette) might be harmful to nonsmokers. "Simply holding a lighted cigaret in the hand, it appears, produces more toxic materials in the room air than result from active smoking," the researcher concluded. By 1940, more than forty studies identifying cigarettes as a health risk had been published. These reports, carrying the imprimatur of modern science, provided the basis for the modern campaign against cigarettes.[6]

The postwar crusade was heralded and to a large degree defined by *Nicotine Next*, the seventy-three page booklet published by economics professor Frederick W. Roman shortly after the armistice. Roman tried to shift the debate over smoking away from concerns about individual morality toward those involving public health and economics. He considered such unsentimental topics as allocation of capital, productivity in the workplace, and destruction of property due to fires caused by smokers. Roman's arguments would become common currency in another sixty years. At the time, however, it was the book's title—not its arguments—that gained attention. Both opponents and defenders of the use of cigarettes took it as evidence that moral reformers, having defeated King Alcohol, would now go after Lady Nicotine.[7]

Certain pronouncements by prohibition leaders reinforced this perception. "Prohibition is won," said Rev. William "Billy" Sunday, the best-known evangelist of his day, after the ratification of the Eighteenth Amendment in 1919; "now for tobacco." The fight against cigarettes "will be a longer and a harder fight than that against alcohol," a speaker told a WCTU conference on "scientific temperance education" that same year, "but it is a fight that needs to be made." Clarence True Wilson, a leader of the Anti-Saloon League as well as a Methodist Episcopal Church official, attacked cigarettes as "a stench in God's nostrils" and bitterly criticized relief organizations for giving them to soldiers. In one speech, to a gathering of about 20,000 Disciples of Christ in Cincinnati in late 1919, he said it was disgusting that "young men, trained at great expense by the government to fight its battles, had to be led out of the fighting ranks to have cigarettes stuffed into their mouths before they could stand up and hold a gun." He called upon reformers to take advantage of the momentum created by the prohibition campaign and "strike while the iron [is] hot" against cigarettes. The Presbyterian Church's Board of Temperance and Moral Welfare and the Northern Baptist Conference both pledged their support to such an effort.[8]

It was widely assumed that the professional organizers and lobbyists who had helped bring about national prohibition would be emboldened by victory, on the one hand, and in need of new employment, on the other. According to a writer for the *Atlantic Monthly*, prohibition had "dumped" a great deal of reform energy on "the sociological market." As proof that prohibitionists were looking for new fields to conquer, he pointed to *Nicotine Next*. The booklet reflected the "modern method of sociological propaganda utilized so effectively by the Anti-Saloon League." The writer also found it significant that Edwin C. Dinwiddie, national legislative superintendent of the league, had resigned to become general superintendent of the Southern Sociological Congress, which was said to be interested in taking up the anti-tobacco banner.[9]

Variations on this theme appeared in many other periodicals. The *Portland Oregonian* suggested that the death of "John Barleycorn" had put prohibitionists "in the unfortunate position of a soldier of fortune after the peace is signed." The *San Francisco Call and Post* claimed prohibitionists would go after tobacco "cunningly, to make a good living out of it." The *Cincinnati Enquirer* agreed that financial motives would send the "proponents of compulsory goodness" after other targets. The *New York Times* could see a Nineteenth Amendment, aimed at tobacco, shoving "a saintly nose" above the horizon.[10]

This theme provided fodder for many newspaper cartoonists. The *Los Angeles Times* depicted a "Professional Prohibitionist" holding a note from the Anti-Saloon League while casting a calculating eye on a nearby smoker. The note read, "Now that the Demon Rum is dead your services are no longer required." Another *Los Angeles Times* cartoon showed a smoker walking nervously past an establishment labeled "Dry Cleaning," where a suit marked "Rum" had been hung out to dry. In a similar vein, the *New York World* had a needle-nosed reformer in a stovepipe hat forcing a bottle of beer off a cliff at bayonet-point, while a cigarette, a pipe, and a cigar ("The Anxious Survivors") glumly awaited their turns. A subsequent article in the *World* pointed out that thirty-five states had already adopted anti-smoking laws, which it mistakenly claimed were "enough to ratify another amendment to the Federal Constitution" (actually, thirty-six states were needed to ratify an amendment to the Constitution at the time). Only the careful reader would have noticed, in the state-by-state accounting that followed, that the great majority of those laws applied just to minors. The newspaper's point, in large type, could be taken in at a glance: "The unprotesting generation that lost its right to drink may yet lose its right to smoke, and also, if it submits gracefully, its right to walk under a full moon or sit on the grass."[11]

No doubt these warnings were colored to some degree by self-interest, given the increasing prominence of cigarette advertising in American periodicals after the war. Manufacturers were spending nearly $20 million a year to promote their products, with some 90 percent of the money going to newspapers and magazines. Kansas had already outlawed the sale of publications containing cigarette advertising, and several other states had considered such legislation. Editors and publishers may have consciously exaggerated the possibility that cigarettes would be "next" in an effort to arouse public opinion and thereby forestall any further restrictions on a lucrative source of income.[12]

However, anti-cigarette activists expressed the same degree of confidence that their cause, at long last, was about to receive powerful reinforcements. "We have been holding back our agitation during the war for patriotic reasons," Roman told the *New York Tribune* in 1919, "but now that the war is over we intend to push it vigorously." With the return of peace and the elimination of the "liquor traffic," reformers would no longer be "lethargic" about cigarettes, said one of the speakers at a conference sponsored by the Anti-Cigarette League in 1920. Dr. Charles G. Pease, president of the Non-Smokers' Protective League, believed "a national revulsion against tobacco" was imminent.[13]

The Anti-Cigarette League demonstrated its optimism by expanding its operations, opening new chapters in California, Utah, Colorado, Nebraska, Indiana, Connecticut, Minnesota, and Ohio. A new field secretary, Manfred P. Welcher of Hartford, Connecticut, campaigned in twenty-seven states between 1921 and 1924, speaking to groups as varied as the Christian Endeavor Society of the Baptist Church and the New England Tobacco Growers Association. West coast operations were directed by James A. Walton, an energetic Presbyterian minister based in Los Angeles. In one typical month, Walton traveled 3,000 miles and lectured on the evils of cigarettes to more than 7,000 school children. To support his efforts, the league shipped five railroad carloads of pamphlets, fliers, and pledge cards to California. The goal was to raise the league's profile, demonstrate its viability, and convince prohibitionists and like-minded reformers that it was worthy of greater financial backing. Meanwhile, the redoubtable Lucy Page Gaston, freshly fired as superintendent of the league because of her impolitic intractability, was busy trying to organize a competing anti-cigarette group. She appealed for help from the prominent prohibitionists who had underwritten her activities in the past, promising to launch an invigorated "Clean Life" campaign "if friends of the movement rally to the support of this project as we believe they will."[14]

In fact, leaders of the prohibition movement ended up distancing themselves from the anti-cigarette campaign. They recognized that the furor over their alleged designs on smokers was eroding support for the enforcement of prohibition. However much they may have disliked cigarettes (or tobacco in general), they were willing to ignore them in the interest of protecting what they had already won. Both the Anti-Saloon League and the WCTU eventually issued statements disavowing any interest in restricting the use of any form of tobacco by adults. "The tobacco habit may be a private or personal bad habit, but it is not in the same class as intoxicating liquor," said Wayne B. Wheeler, general counsel and legislative superintendent of the Anti-Saloon League. Representative Andrew J. Volstead, author of the Prohibition Enforcement Act, insisted he had no interest in suppressing tobacco. Indeed, Volstead created a little stir by taking a slab of chewing tobacco out of his pocket and biting off a piece before rising to address his congressional colleagues during the debate on his bill in 1921. Even Mrs. Bogart, the Bible-thumping moral uplifter of Sinclair Lewis's *Main Street*, gave up the fight against cigarettes, saying, "Now we've got prohibition it seems to me that the next problem of the country ain't so much abolishing cigarettes as it is to make folks observe the Sabbath."[15]

The WCTU had been in the forefront of the anti-cigarette crusade since 1887, when it passed the first of many resolutions calling for cigarette prohibition. After considerable debate at the annual meeting of 1919, the organization rejected a proposal to seek a constitutional amendment to ban cigarette sales, manufacturing, and imports. The WCTU continued to disseminate anti-smoking literature, to protest the use of cigarettes by women, and to push for enforcement of laws forbidding the sale of tobacco to minors, but it made no further efforts to restrict smoking by adults. "Men have smoked for years," one spokeswoman told the *New York Times*. "We are not taking it upon ourselves to tell them at this late day that it is not good for them." The WCTU even dropped the inflammatory word "next" from subsequent editions of *Nicotine Next*; after 1921, the pamphlet was simply titled *Nicotine*.[16]

Clarence True Wilson, as editor of the *World Digest of Reform News*, devoted most of an entire issue in 1921 to repudiating claims that reformers intended to take cigarettes away from adults. He insisted the Methodist

Episcopal Board of Temperance, Prohibition, and Public Morals "recognizes the fundamental difference between the traffic in tobacco and that in alcoholic liquor." Speaking for the reform community in general, he said, "Nobody—at least nobody of any consequence—is asking for laws prohibiting the personal use of tobacco by adults." Delegates to the 1924 General Conference of the Methodist Episcopal Church rejected a proposed resolution condemning cigarettes. William E. "Pussyfoot" Johnson, a famous prohibitionist who earned his nickname by leading stealthy raids on bootleggers, refused to defend a cigarette prohibition law that was under attack in Kansas in 1927. Billy Sunday also retreated, claiming, "I never have been a crank about tobacco."[17]

Even if prohibitionists had been fully engaged in the campaign against cigarettes, it is unlikely they would have enjoyed much success. For one thing, their influence dissipated rapidly after America went legally dry in 1920. As K. Austin Kerr has shown, the Anti-Saloon League—the most powerful of the prohibitionist groups—was weakened by internal disputes and declining revenues. One faction envisioned the league as a police agency, overseeing enforcement; another wanted to leave law enforcement to the government and concentrate on an educational campaign to promote general public uplift. Behind a facade of strength was an organization crumbling under the weight of its own apparent success. The WCTU, with a geriatric membership and an ever-longer list of leaders who had been called to their celestial rewards, was even less effective as a force for reform in the twenties.[18]

These weaknesses were not immediately evident in the early postwar years. The very difficulties inherent in amending the United States Constitution indicated that prohibitionists had amassed considerable strength. When the Eighteenth Amendment was ratified in 1919, it was only the fifth time the Constitution had been modified since the end of the Civil War. The change was approved by all but two of the existing forty-eight states—far in excess of the thirty-six needed for ratification. There was nothing in the dimensions of this victory to suggest a movement in decline.[19]

Moreover, the number of individual prohibitionists who were speaking out against cigarettes overshadowed the wariness of some of their leaders. Among them was a minister in Knoxville, Tennessee, who wrote an impassioned letter to William Jennings Bryan, saying:

> Dear old valiant comrade, it would seem that no sooner do we fill up one slough of infamy than another is opened up by the arch fiend: We are about to place a tombstone over the carcass of Old Rye, but lo, a new Goliath of Vice has grown up like Jack's beanstalk, during the four years night of the war. . . . I allude to the pernicious vice of cigarette smoking. This hydra-headed vice is spreading by leaps and bounds over the whole world, due mainly to the crime of the International YMCA who spent literally *millions* of money sacredly *committed* to them for *constructive* service for *destructive* cigarettes![20]

The minister went on to say that he had started an anti-cigarette crusade and hoped Bryan would support it, at least to the extent of writing a brief letter for publication. Bryan declined, although he personally opposed the use of tobacco. Just two years earlier, he had reminded his grandson that men of good character did not smoke, drink, or gamble.[21]

Several other influential prohibitionists were less reticent than Bryan. Irving Fisher, the noted economist and longtime anti-tobacco crusader, organized the Committee to Study the Tobacco Problem in late 1918. He hoped it would do for tobacco what the Committee of Fifty on the Liquor Problem had done for alcohol twenty-five years earlier: provide scientific support for the anti-smoking movement. The committee financed the publication of two books exploring the effects of tobacco. Fisher also wrote his own anti-tobacco book. In *Tobacco, A Three-Fold Study*, he argued that economists should be interested in whether people spend their money on things that have value to society. He concluded that tobacco, especially cigarettes, "takes away our money but gives us in return little or nothing except illusion and distress."[22]

Like many other critics of cigarettes, Fisher had maintained a discreet silence on the topic during the war. In a letter to the *New York Sun* shortly after the first American troops arrived in France, he vaguely called upon Americans to "relinquish all indulgences and habits which impair the power to work." He did not mention cigarettes or tobacco as possibly impairing habits. Nor did he criticize the "smokes for soldiers" funds established by the *Sun* and many other American newspapers. It was only after the armistice that he publicly renewed his opposition to smoking.[23]

Likewise, Thomas Edison suspended his opposition during the war, accepting cigarettes as a military necessity. He even made a small contribution to the *New York Sun*'s smoke fund. In 1921, however, he again attacked cigarettes as poisonous and addictive, at the same time defending his beloved cigars. "Tobacco aside from cigarettes does no harm to society," he said. "It is not dangerous like narcotics and whiskey and few smoke it to excess." A few years later, he announced that a ban on cigarette smoking in his laboratories, instituted long before the war, would be continued; pipes, cigars, and chewing tobacco were acceptable, but anyone caught with a cigarette would be fired immediately.[24]

Harvey W. Wiley also rejoined the anti-cigarette chorus after the war. "I think the habit of using tobacco is the most reprehensible to which the human animal is addicted," he wrote, adding: "I do not believe there is a worst [sic] form in which tobacco can be used than in the form of a cigaret." After leaving the Food and Drug Administration, he joined the staff of *Good Housekeeping*; he later said he was proud of having worked to keep cigarette advertising out of the pages of that magazine. Wiley served as keynote speaker at the First National Anti-Tobacco Convention, held in Washington, D.C., in 1925. He subsequently joined the board of a new anti-cigarette group, the Anti-Cigarette Alliance of America.[25]

Many of the newly vocal critics buffered their remarks with tactful concessions to the value of cigarettes to soldiers in wartime. Clarence E. Woods, a minor federal functionary and a former mayor of Richmond, Kentucky, began an attack on cigarettes by saying he did not want to appear disloyal to "our boys" and that he supposed smoking may have helped promote soldierly valor among those who were accustomed to it. He then went on to assert that the manufacturers, the War Department, and the military service organizations had conspired to virtually force cigarettes on all soldiers, even those who had never smoked them before. As a result, many nonsmokers had acquired a habit that would follow them "to their premature graves." Dr. John B. Huber, professor of pulmonary diseases at Fordham University Medical School and a frequent contributor to *Association Men*, the national magazine of the YMCA, wondered, "Who would have spoken an untoward word, that has seen the cigaret being inserted by a comrade between the anguished lips of the sideswiped hero?" But now the war was over, the special needs of the war were over, and one did not need to be a "spoilsport" to question the effects of cigarette smoking. Another contributor to *Association Men* said the cigarette looked innocent enough, but was "a let-down" from high standards. An editorial in the magazine gently suggested that while "smoking seemed necessary" in the military camps and on the front lines, books, movies, singing, wrestling, and boxing were more appropriate diversions in peacetime. To that end, the YMCA resumed publishing anti-smoking posters, including one showing a soldier sighting down a rifle barrel, above text warning that "Smoking Affects Marksmanship."[26]

Writing for the *Sacramento Star* in 1921, Grove L. Johnson, father of Hiram Johnson (progressive governor and later senator from California), said it "probably was true" that cigarettes soothed the soldiers' nerves and otherwise helped them endure the hardships of war. Since the war, however, so many men were smoking that it had become almost impossible to walk down the street without encountering their irritating exhaust. He thought "Lady Nicotine has too strong a hold upon the present generation to be dethroned from her present proud position," but hoped that something could be done to save the younger generation.[27]

Although cigarettes had acquired the patina of patriotism, many Americans remained ambivalent about them. Sinclair Lewis captured these conflicting attitudes in *Babbitt*. George Babbitt, real estate magnate in the fictional prairie metropolis of Zenith (based on Minneapolis), occasionally smoked cigarettes himself. Indeed, he "knew himself to be of a breeding altogether more esthetic and sensitive" than his old-fashioned father-in-law precisely because he did so. He even kept a silver cigarette box in a prominent spot on a table in his living room. Initially, however, he confined his cigarette smoking to his car, preferring cigars for all other occasions; he regarded habitual cigarette smokers as effeminate. Babbitt did not begin to smoke cigarettes regularly until after he temporarily adopted the life of a libertine and began consorting with "the Bunch," Zenith's version of a Bohemian set. He had an affair with a woman who smoked (including in bed) and encouraged him to smoke with her. Cigarettes symbolized his rejection of conventional values. Once restored to the path of propriety, Babbitt returned to cigars, the preferred smoke of the "Regular Fellows" of Zenith. Naturally, the wives of the "Regular Fellows" did not smoke at all (although they did accept a bootleg cocktail now and then).[28]

Ambivalence was evident, too, in policies regarding cigarette smoking in the workplace. While some employers accommodated smokers to the point of setting aside times and places for them to indulge, many others still refused to hire them. A shoe factory in Marlboro, Massachusetts, instituted smoke breaks in an effort to increase efficiency, but the Guaranty Trust and Savings Bank of Los Angeles and the First National Bank of San Fernando said cigarette smokers should seek employment elsewhere. When Marshall L. Cook, editor and publisher of the *Hastings (Michigan) Banner*, needed a new press operator in 1919, he stipulated that cigarette smokers need not apply. "We would like to get a man of good clean habits," he wrote in a letter to a business associate in Chicago. "We do not care if he smokes but we do not want him to smoke cigarettes." Hastings was an inconspicuous little town of no more than 5,000 residents at that time, but cigarette smokers faced discrimination even in the supposed cultural centers of the United States. As late as 1924, they were unwelcome in most Wall Street brokerage houses, according to a report by Cameron Beck, personnel director of the New York Stock Exchange.[29]

Early in the postwar period, then, cigarettes still appeared vulnerable to both the vagaries of public opinion and the aims of reformers. This could be seen in the debate over a proposal to raise the federal excise tax on cigarettes in 1919. Anti-cigarette activists lobbied vigorously for higher taxes, expecting they would lead to retail price increases and thus discourage consumption. The industry's defenders hoped that the experiences of "tens of thousands of soldiers *who are voters*" [emphasis in original] would override "the vituperations of professional reformers and honest lunatics." It is not possible to determine whether lawmakers were influenced more by the arguments of the reformers or the need for new revenue, but they increased the tax, from $2 per 1,000 cigarettes to $3. Manufacturers of the three most popular brands—Camels, Lucky Strikes, and Chesterfields—immediately boosted their prices by a nickel, to twenty cents a package. Sales dipped slightly during the recession of 1920, for the first time in fifteen years; but by 1921 they had fully recovered.[30]

The campaign for higher taxes was part of a surge of cigarette-related legislation after the war. It also represented a new direction for the anti-cigarette movement. Leaders of the movement once had argued that cigarettes should not be taxed at all, on the grounds that they were not legitimate articles of commerce and should not be countenanced as such through taxation. For example, the WCTU protested the imposition of higher taxes on cigarettes and other tobacco products as part of the War Revenue Act of 1917, arguing that by accepting such revenue, the government was endorsing tobacco. In the twenties, reformers gave less emphasis to prohibiting cigarettes and more to taxing them, restricting their advertising, reducing the number of places where they could be smoked publicly, and encouraging voluntary abstinence through education.[31]

Most anti-cigarette activists in the 1920s also toned down their rhetoric. Warnings that cigarettes would shrivel brains and produce idiotic children gave way to more rational arguments, often emphasizing the rights of nonsmokers. James R. Day, chancellor of Syracuse University, stressed the hazards of fire, the health of smokers, and the comfort of nonsmokers when he defended a long-standing ban on smoking on campus in December 1920. Vida Milholland, a social reformer and radio commentator in New York City, recommended "a sharp line of demarcation" between smokers and nonsmokers in order to protect the latter from involuntary exposure to nicotine. "If people must indulge in this sensuous, mind-destroying habit, let them do it in private," she said.[32]

James A. Walton, superintendent of the Anti-Cigarette League of California, insisted he and his supporters were not—as the *Los Angeles Times* had put it—"crusade cranks" who wanted to "take the cigarette away from the young man by force." They were, instead, "a group of wholesome people" whose primary goals were to educate the public, limit cigarette advertising, and enforce existing laws restricting sales to minors. Arkansas Governor Thomas C. McRae, originally a strong supporter of cigarette prohibition, came to believe "the persuasion of kindly warning" was more effective in discouraging smoking than "the penalties of the law."[33]

Of more than 100 legislative proposals concerning cigarettes between 1919 and 1925, only nine would have banned their sale to adults. In Oregon, a retired truant and probation officer attempted to bypass the state legislature and ask the voters to prohibit cigarettes through an initiative, but he failed to collect enough signatures to qualify for the ballot. The only tobacco-related bill presented to the Oregon legislature during that period was one that would have made it illegal to advertise cigarettes through billboards, posters, signs, or any other "public display." The bill was defeated in committee by a vote of seventeen to eleven.[34]

Several states considered legislation to restrict public smoking to one degree or another. In South Carolina, a proposed ban on smoking in restaurants passed the Senate but was killed in the House. Two anti-smoking measures were introduced in Massachusetts. One would have made it illegal for anyone to smoke cigarettes or cigars anywhere in public; another would have applied only to women. A Minnesota bill would have banned smoking in most enclosed public places, including restaurants, theaters, streetcars, railway coaches, train stations, buses, taxis, barber shops, and all state, county, and city buildings. Maryland attempted first to ban smoking in theaters and then to allow fire commissioners to prohibit smoking in all public buildings. None of these proposals passed. Only a Michigan bill to ban smoking at boxing and wrestling matches won approval during this period, and this was more an effort to avoid the risk of fire—and possibly to exert control over dubious enterprises—than an expression of concern about cigarettes or tobacco.[35]

In 1921, Senator Reed Smoot of Utah asked Congress to prohibit smoking in most buildings owned by the federal government. Smoot was a leader in the Church of Jesus Christ of Latter–day Saints (Mormon), which condemned the use of both alcohol and tobacco. He initially defended his anti-smoking proposal on the grounds of safety. He pointed out that a recent fire in the basement of the Commerce Building (which had destroyed important census records) had been ignited by a discarded cigarette stub. When his colleagues scoffed at that argument, Smoot offered another: that smoking by government employees was a waste of time and an impediment to efficiency. Banning the practice would save the government millions of dollars. His proposal was rejected in favor of one giving department heads the authority to establish their own smoking policies. Not until 1997 would President Bill Clinton be able to do, by executive order, what Smoot had attempted to do in 1921.[36]

Of all the bills introduced to restrict the sale and use of cigarettes by adults in the postwar era, only two were enacted (in heavily Mormon Utah and Idaho), and both were quickly repealed. Some contemporaries suspected that the legislators who sponsored the bills did not really expect, or even want, to have them approved. According to this view, the proposals were either "cinch bills" (so called because such a bill supposedly was a "cinch" to elicit bribes from an affected party in return for votes against it); or they were intended to discredit prohibition. It seems more likely that the legislative record simply reflects the waning influence of anti-cigarette activists. They still had enough political power to put their agenda before legislators, but not enough to get it implemented—with two short-lived exceptions.[37]

The Idaho legislature prohibited the sale and manufacture of cigarettes in 1921 at the urging of a state senator from Oneida County, where the Mormon Church was very influential. The sponsor claimed to have received letters and petitions of support from more than 6,000 businessmen, educators, and club women. Regardless, on the very day that the bill was signed into law by the governor, the legislature began debating its repeal. Ten days later, cigarettes were once again legitimate articles of commerce in Idaho.[38]

The anti-cigarette law in Utah attracted little notice, either inside the state or out, when it was enacted that same year. According to historian John S. H. Smith, the law might well have remained on the books, safely ignored, but for the zeal of a Salt Lake County sheriff who was elected to office two years later. Under his orders, deputies arrested a dozen or so smokers in Salt Lake City in February 1923. This brought the state the kind of attention that the business community found embarrassing and annoying. Snickering news stories and indignant editorials appeared in newspapers as far afield as Boston and San Francisco. The *Salt Lake Tribune* (whose manager, A. N. McKay, was among those arrested) quoted out-of-town papers at length to demonstrate the degree to which the anti-cigarette bill had made Utah a laughingstock. The chamber of commerce, the Lions Club, the Utah Manufacturers Association, and other civic groups demanded that the law be repealed. Less than two weeks after the arrests, the legislature did exactly that.[39]

In language that recalled Wilson's description of cigarettes as "a stench in God's nostrils," a group of Salt Lake City businessmen demanded that cigarettes be legalized in Utah, lest the state become "a stench in the nostrils of the free peoples of America." The difference in phrasing is revealing. It shows that the debate over cigarettes had moved away from questions of morality and settled instead on the issue of personal liberty. This freedom was generally defined as the right of the individual to smoke, even if it meant infringing on the rights of other individuals not to smoke.[40]

Lucy Page Gaston, for years the most outspoken foe of the cigarette, was increasingly out of step with the times, although she continued to make her voice heard. She complained bitterly that the "smokes for soldiers" campaign had removed the stigma from cigarettes, especially among people with "self-indulgent tendencies." She reiterated her demand that the Food and Drug Administration regulate cigarettes as "a habit-forming drug." After the Anti-Cigarette League fired her in 1920, she announced her candidacy for the presidency of the United States, running on a platform of "[c]lean morals, clean food, and fearless law enforcement." Among her qualifications, she said, was the fact that she looked a little like Abraham Lincoln. If he could free the slaves, she could emancipate the nation from the cigarette. Residents of Lacon, Illinois (where she was reared), wished her well. "Go to it, Lucy," they telegraphed; "we're with you, and don't forget to invite us to the White House if you are elected." The *New York Times* thought it was unlikely that Gaston would ever enter the White House—at least, not as a resident—but it pointed out that "a few years ago it seemed no more likely that a 'dry' amendment would be added to our Constitution, and the fact that one has been added to it should lend caution to what will—and won't—come next."[41]

Gaston actually filed as a candidate in only one state—South Dakota—and she formally withdrew six months later, "in favor of any one who will endorse the moral reforms for which I stand." Evidently that was William Jennings Bryan. She was one of the delegates when the Prohibition Party nominated Bryan by acclamation during its national convention in Lincoln, Nebraska. Bryan declined the honor. Gaston must have felt some discouragement when Warren G. Harding was elected president, even though she once said of herself that the word was not in her vocabulary. Harding, a tobaccophile, was the first president to be photographed smoking a cigarette. She wrote to him, saying he was setting a bad example and asking him to stop. Reacting to news reports about her letter, a group of men in Atchison, Kansas, sent Harding a carton of cigarettes, violating the stringent anti-cigarette law in effect in Kansas at the time. Gaston promptly demanded that they be prosecuted. Harding's office later made public a letter to Gaston in which the president commended her dedication, but evaded any pledge to quit.[42]

She made several attempts to set up a rival to the Anti-Cigarette League, but her sources of funding—lean under the best of circumstances—had all but vanished. Even David Starr Jordan, who had supported her for nearly two decades, ignored her last request for a donation. "The hour seems to have struck to press the battle hard, and we need all of our forces in line," she told him. He did not reply. A few years later, when Gaston's successor at the Anti-Cigarette League asked Jordan for permission to use one of his early anti-cigarette aphorisms in a poster ("The boy who smokes cigarettes need not be anxious about his future: He has none"), Jordan stipulated that the quotation should be applied only to "youth below college age."[43]

Rebuffed in Chicago, Gaston found a refuge with the Anti-Cigarette League of Kansas, headquartered in Topeka. However, she was soon wrestling with that group's board of directors over whether its mission would be to "discourage" or "prohibit" the use of cigarettes. Her pronouncements became even more shrill. "I know many oppose the work I am doing," she said at one point, "but I am like Jesus Christ. I will forgive and forget the past if the people will try to do better in the future." This kind of talk was too much, even for Kansas. After little more than two months on the job, she was fired again. She returned to Chicago, where she cobbled together a new organization, called the National Anti-Cigarette League. Six months later, this group, too, fired her, saying, "Miss Gaston's methods were more drastic than the methods approved by the league Board of Managers."[44]

Gaston was not entirely bereft of disciples in the last years of her life. During the debate over her methods in Kansas, D. M. Fisk, dean of sociology at Washburn University in Topeka, was quoted as saying, "Let's do away with the pious namby-pamby way of doing things and get down to business and stamp the cigarette out. We need a million Miss Gastons." This was a minority view. The spirit of compromise permeated the reform community during the 1920s, and the overly zealous tended to be either ridiculed or ignored.[45]

With no regular salary, Gaston was forced to rely on handouts from relatives and charities. Her brother Edward said later that she often walked for lack of money to take a streetcar. She lived mostly on graham crackers, supplemented by a daily five-cent glass of milk from a lunchroom and an occasional holiday food basket from the Salvation Army.[46]

Even in these reduced circumstances, Gaston continued her crusade. She harangued women smokers; collared boys she saw smoking on the street corners; and handed out news releases and gentian root (her favorite cure for smoking) to reporters. "We are out to put the cigarette business out of business," she told a correspondent for the trade journal *Tobacco*. After this pronouncement, one of her last allies, the Methodist Episcopal

Board of Temperance, Prohibition, and Public Morals, moved to distance itself from her. The board issued a statement saying it had no interest in tobacco other than restricting its use by minors and educating the general public as to the dangers of smoking. Meanwhile, incensed by press reports that Queen Mary of Great Britain was fond of a cigarette after lunch, Gaston wrote a letter scolding Her Royal Highness for setting an "exceedingly unfortunate" example.[47]

She had promised to wage "a stubborn, unyielding and desperate fight" against the cigarette, and she kept it up until January 1924, when she was struck by a streetcar while on her way home from an anti-cigarette rally in Chicago. She died six months later—at the Hinsdale Sanitarium, a Seventh-Day Adventist institution—at the age of sixty-four. Ironically, the cause of death was throat cancer, a disease long associated with smoking. At her request, her body was cremated after her funeral and the ashes taken to her adopted hometown of Harvey, Illinois, where her ninety-two-year-old mother still lived.[48]

Her illness and death attracted the notice of newspapers around the country, in an echo of the prominence she had once achieved. The *San Francisco Call* described her as "a formidable lady and not popular," but nonetheless wondered, "[H]aven't you a little admiration to spare for Lucy Page Gaston?" Many editorial writers did, including some from the tobacco trade press. The *Tobacco Leaf* praised her "fine character and splendid ability." The *Chicago Examiner*, the *San Francisco Examiner*, the *Mobile (Alabama) Register*, and a dozen other papers all paid tribute to her courage and dedication. The *Idaho Statesman (Boise)* thought she had not been given the credit she deserved. The *Ann Arbor (Michigan) News* pointed out that "[f]rom the viewpoint of the smoker, Miss Gaston was wrong, but no one can state positively that, in a broader sense, she may not have been right." The word "uncompromising" crept into many of her eulogies. "Her zeal occasionally became too strong for other professional reformers," commented the *Daily Pantagraph* in Bloomington, Illinois, where she went to college. In the end, she had little left but her zeal. Reporting on her funeral, the *New York Times* noted that "[o]f the thousands of friends Miss Gaston had made during the long years of her work, only a handful were present at the simple rites." Among them were four children, who knelt by her coffin during the ceremony and solemnly pledged never to smoke cigarettes.[49]

By the mid-twenties, it was clear that the anti-cigarette movement had crested. Tennessee and Nebraska both repealed laws prohibiting the sale of cigarettes in 1919, followed by Arkansas and Iowa in 1921, and by North Dakota in 1925. An attempt to legalize cigarettes in Kansas failed in 1925 but succeeded two years later. Gaston's death in 1924, followed the next year by that of her nemesis, James B. Duke, symbolized the end of an era. Gaston's mother and brother both sent impassioned pleas to Herbert Hoover—then a spokesman for the American Child Health Association—to memorialize her by endorsing the Anti-Cigarette League. By that point, however, Hoover had developed a serious interest in the presidency, and he did not want to offend either the manufacturers or the consumers of cigarettes. He ignored the appeals. Identification with the anti-cigarette cause had become a political liability. A dwindling cadre of true believers carried on, but even they seemed to recognize themselves as part of the last flickers of a nearly dead fire.[50]

The Anti-Cigarette League survived into the 1930s, after a fashion, along with the Indiana-based No-Tobacco League, incorporated with a new board of directors in 1920; and the Anti-Cigarette Alliance, founded in Xenia, Ohio, in 1927. All three groups moderated their initial goals, emphasizing public education rather than individual coercion, and focusing on youth rather than adults. The Non-Smokers' Protective League dwindled to a membership that apparently did not extend much beyond its founder, Dr. Charles G. Pease of New York City. Pease continued to write occasional anti-cigarette letters to the editor of the *New York Times* until shortly before his death in 1941, but he attracted few supporters. He had never quite lived down an earlier scandal in which he claimed that one Annette Hazelton, "a pure young woman," had endorsed his ideas and would spread his gospel. It turned out that there was no such person; Pease himself had written the letters purportedly written by her.[51]

The surviving groups produced some anti-cigarette literature for distribution to adults, but they put most of their energy into programs aimed at school children. They went into classrooms as guest lecturers, armed with lurid slides depicting the diseased organs of smokers, along with various devices for capturing the "deadly poisons" in cigarette smoke and charts comparing smokers to nonsmokers (and finding them wanting) in terms of physical development, intelligence, and earnings potential. One popular classroom demonstration involved soaking a cigarette in water, straining the liquid through a white handkerchief (or blowing cigarette smoke through the handkerchief), and dramatically identifying the resultant yellow stain as nicotine. (The stain was actually caused by tar.) Some presentations were more complex, using laboratory-like equipment with vacuum tubes and other scientific trappings. Cautionary tales were told of how many drops of tobacco oil it would take to kill a cat, and how quickly, and of leeches dropping off dead from the skin of cigarette smokers. The lesson typically ended with the students chanting something along the lines of:

> I'll never smoke a cigaret,
> It injures health and brain;
> I'll not be caught in habit's net,
> With much to lose, and naught to gain.[52]

Years later, a public health physician could still vividly recall the ulcerated stomachs, hobnailed livers, grotesque hearts, and other "perfectly dreadful pictures" that "were shown to us horror-stricken kids" during his school days in Indiana. He also remembered the impressively stained handkerchief, the primary effect of which was to encourage students to try to replicate the demonstration. He wondered if there had ever been, in the history of education, lessons that were more futile and misleading. Later, some school boards began refusing to allow anti-cigarette speakers into their schools. The District of Columbia board explained that "lectures on the use of cigarettes might be construed as dealing with a controversial subject." Other boards apparently just found the lectures ineffective.[53]

By the end of the decade, fund-raising, never easy, became increasingly difficult. Wiley and Jordan, two of the more dedicated supporters of the cause, ignored pleas for additional contributions to the Anti-Cigarette League. At one point, the No-Tobacco League was paying solicitors a commission of 70 percent on any donations they managed to secure. Even then, few were interested in the work. Ever-hopeful organizers scheduled conventions and rallies, but they could not convince many people to come. After a particularly disappointing rally in Minneapolis in 1929, Charles M. Fillmore, superintendent of the No-Tobacco League, tried to reassure Anthony Zeleny, then president of the league's Minnesota chapter, with the following comment: "While it did not turn out finally in as big and effective a way as we both hoped, I know that you were not in the least to blame for that, and I flatter myself in believing that I was not to blame, either." Conditions for reform were simply "unfavorable" at the moment, he added.[54]

As Willa Cather once remarked, "The world broke in two in 1922 or thereabouts." The reformist energy that had characterized America during the Progressive Era was overshadowed in the twenties by consumerism and a sort of studied cynicism. Many Americans left the ranks of active reformers. However, those who remained seemed to become more determined even as they became more unfashionable. The more unpopular their cause, the greater their sense of mission.[55]

Evidence of this can be found in the papers of Zeleny, a prominent physics professor at the University of Minnesota, once described by the student newspaper as "grand archon of the mystic order of non-smokers." Zeleny abhorred not only cigarettes but all forms of tobacco; and he did not think much of dancing or drinking either. Shortly after he joined the faculty in 1897, he began embellishing his physics lectures with brief "sermonettes" on these topics; he continued doing so until he retired in 1938. He joined the No-Tobacco League in the twenties, served as national president in the thirties, and remained active in it until his death in 1947. As time passed, Zeleny became increasingly uncompromising on the issue of tobacco. When three young men sought his help in organizing a "Minnesota Anti-Snuff and Cigarette Society" in 1924, he politely but firmly declined, saying, "I am not entirely pleased with the name of your society because tobacco in any form is injurious." He found the society's focus too narrow. In another expression of his convictions, he reneged on a pledge to contribute to the construction of a new 50,000-seat stadium at the university in 1929 because the administration refused to set aside a no-smoking section.[56]

Reed Smoot was another stalwart. As a leader of the Mormon Church, he objected to smoking on religious grounds. He often condemned the habit in the sermons that he periodically delivered in his home state. He took this message to the Senate (and, he hoped, to the nation at large) on June 10, 1929, with a speech proposing that the federal government restrict cigarette advertising and regulate all tobacco products under the Pure Food and Drugs Act. Using the kind of oratory reminiscent of Bryan at his most flamboyant, Smoot denounced contemporary cigarette advertising as "an orgy of buncombe, quackery, and downright falsehood and fraud," devised by manufacturers "whose only god is profit, whose only bible is the balance sheet, whose only principle is greed." Smoot was particularly concerned about the use of testimonials ("disgusting" and "a great libel upon American business ethics") and about cigarette ads on the radio, a new medium with apparently greater impact than newspapers or magazines. The government had a duty to protect its citizens from such "insidious" campaigns, he said.[57]

In proposing that the Food and Drugs Act be amended to include tobacco, Smoot was echoing arguments made years earlier by Gaston and other officials of the Anti-Cigarette League. The act, adopted in 1906, gave the government the authority to regulate only those drugs listed in the *Pharmacopoeia of the United States of America*. Tobacco was once included in the *Pharmacopoeia* but had been removed in 1905. Smoot called this "only a fine technicality" that should be corrected. (Some modern critics of the tobacco industry have suggested that tobacco was removed in a deliberate attempt to avoid federal regulation. Smoot himself saw no indications of conspiracy. Of the exclusion, he said simply, quoting from the newly revised *Pharmacopoeia*, that tobacco "was formerly highly esteemed as a vulnerary, but is little used as a drug by intelligent physicians.") He was so pleased with the speech that he distributed 20,000 copies of it, printed at his own expense. His colleagues in the Senate, less impressed than he was, ignored his calls to action.[58]

One year later, in 1930, Oregon voters provided a coda for the first anti-smoking crusade by defeating an initiative to prohibit cigarette manufacturing, sale, purchase, possession, importation, and advertising. The Oregon legislature had rejected a similar measure in 1917. To collect the 16,000 signatures necessary to put the issue before the voters in 1930, the Anti-Cigarette League contracted with a professional petitioner in Portland. He, in turn, hired women to circulate petitions for the initiative in public markets and shopping districts. There were rumors that tobacco retailers and candy manufacturers were secretly financing the effort. Both those groups had reasons to hope for its success. The retailers did not like the low profit margin on cigarettes; and they resented the power of the oligopoly that had supplanted the old American Tobacco trust. Candy manufacturers had blamed cigarettes for a slump in their business even before the American Tobacco Company launched its "Reach for a Lucky Instead of a Sweet" advertising campaign in 1928. "There are some honest supporters of the (initiative) measure, but they are not much in evidence," the *Oregon Voter* concluded.[59]

On the other hand, the *Portland Oregonian*, the state's leading newspaper, thought the initiative's supporters were "wholly sincere and imbued with the crusading spirit" but misguided. "Many thousands of Oregon people consider cigarette smoking to be harmless and their view is not without support of medical authority," the paper commented. "Excessive smoking of cigarettes is harmful, to be sure, but so is excessive eating of meat or potatoes or pie." Voters, given a chance for the first time to express their sentiments on cigarettes, rejected the measure by a margin of nearly three to one (156,265 opposed, 54,231 in favor).[60]

More than 120 billion manufactured cigarettes were sold in the United States that year, along with the makings for about 13.5 billion roll-your-owns. Taxes paid on those cigarettes were second only to the income tax as a source of revenue for the federal government. In the years since World War I, cigarettes had become almost as essential to contemporary life as traffic cops and divorce courts; ambivalence had become, at some level, active acceptance. One affirmation of this came from California, where the state supreme court ruled that a construction worker who burned his hand while lighting a cigarette was entitled to workmen's compensation because he could not properly perform his job without smoking. Ashtrays replaced cuspidors in banks, post offices, police stations, and other public places. President Herbert Hoover, an avid cigar smoker, bowed to the changing times by retracting an anti-cigarette statement that had been attributed to him for years.[61]

It was a measure of the triumph of the cigarette that not only did the next president smoke, so did his wife. Franklin D. Roosevelt's cigarette, invariably held at a jaunty angle in a long holder, seemed as much a part of him as his spectacles and confident grin. (Roosevelt reportedly once joked that he used the holder because his doctor had told him to stay as far away from cigarettes as possible.) Years earlier, when he was assistant secretary of the navy, Roosevelt had irritated a senior congressman by smoking while waiting to testify before an appropriations subcommittee. The congressman brusquely told him to "throw that cigarette away; it's offensive to me." By the time Roosevelt was elected president, cigarette smokers rarely encountered such public censure.[62]

Prohibition, advertising, and the movies worked together to break down the remaining prejudices against cigarettes. The *Magazine of Wall Street*, in an optimistic article about the future of the tobacco industry in 1919, had confidently predicted that "when prohibition becomes general the consumption of tobacco will be greatly increased." In fact, the overall consumption of tobacco on a per capita basis hardly changed at all during the decade. Department of Agriculture figures show Americans used about seven pounds of tobacco a year in 1920 and just slightly more in 1930.

However, the amount consumed in the form of cigarettes doubled, from 20 to 40 percent. The elimination of legal drinking created a cultural void that cigarette smoking helped to fill. The manager of a New York hotel restaurant told a trade journal that men who formerly drank a cocktail and perhaps smoked one cigarette while waiting for their dinners were now smoking half a dozen, and more often than not, their female guests were lighting up too. Prohibition may have helped popularize cigarettes simply by encouraging unconventional behavior: people who ventured into speakeasies seemed more inclined to break other rules. At the least, it increased the number of places where cigarettes were sold, since many saloons were converted into sandwich shops or tearooms with counters for the sale of various sundries, including cigarettes.[63]

Meanwhile, the manufacturers of the "Big Three" (Lucky Strike, Camel, and Chesterfield) were spending millions to bombard Americans with images of people smoking their products—although the effect of this is not as easy to measure as it may seem. As the economist Richard B. Tennant pointed out in his landmark study of the cigarette industry in 1950, there is little quantifiable evidence that advertising actually recruits new smokers. Marked out on a graph, annual cigarette sales and traceable spending on advertising follow the same upward curve from 1900 to 1965, but so do many other factors, from the number of people living in cities to the number of women in the workforce. Per capita cigarette consumption has declined steadily since 1965 despite the fact that manufacturers have devoted proportionately greater amounts of money to advertising and promotion. Cigarettes were never as extravagantly advertised in Europe as they have been in the United States, yet nations such as Great Britain, France, Greece, and Finland embraced cigarette smoking long before Americans did, and they have been much slower to give it up. On the other hand, cigarettes had more cultural hurdles to overcome in the United States than elsewhere. The large-scale advertising campaigns of the 1920s may have helped lower those hurdles. Their volume and reach—on billboards, in periodicals, in store windows, on the radio—made cigarettes seem less a habit of a deviant minority and more a part of everyday life.[64]

As cigarettes became more popular, the number of cinematic smokers—and their social status—also increased. Cigarettes were rare in American films until the early twenties, and usually signified villainy or vampishness. The Tobacco Merchants Association, ever sensitive to imagery, protested in 1922 that only "the villain and every low type of character in the cast" smoked cigarettes, which suggested that the habit was "confined to that class, hence is debasing. This is wrong, absolutely; it is unjust."[65]

Even so, cigarette smoke clung to the wicked women of the early movies like ectoplasm, beginning with Theda Bara as *Carmen* (1915), and again as *The Vixen* (1917). In *On the Banks of the Wabash* (1923), J. Stuart Blackton, a pioneering director, filmed a young man (newly arrived in the sinful city) entering an apartment. The camera panned the back of a sofa; smoke curled upward from the other side. Then the audience saw the head of a glamorous vamp, rising to meet (and presumably seduce) her visitor. Greta Garbo became a star on the basis of a scene in *Flesh and the Devil* (1926), when she took a cigarette from the mouth of John Gilbert and then arched her beautiful neck backward in a startlingly sexual gesture.[66]

Among male characters, a cigarette was often visual evidence of degeneracy. It was the evil Lejaune, not the noble Beau Geste, who smoked in the silent film version of *Beau Geste* (1927). Rudolph Valentino smoldered his way through one film after another with a cigarette dangling from his lips. Depending on the perspective of the viewer, he was either dangerously seductive or effete.[67]

In later films, heroes and heroines were far more likely to smoke cigarettes than villains and villainesses. When Paramount Pictures remade *Beau Geste* with Gary Cooper in the title role in 1939, Beau Geste not only smoked, he smoked nobly (at one point, offering one of his last two cigarettes to his brother, as they awaited the dawn and certain death from the Saracens). The tyrannical and sadistic Sergeant Markov (the Americanized version of Lejaune) did not smoke at all. A study of films of the late twenties and early thirties showed that 65 percent of movie heroes smoked, compared to only 22.5 percent of the scoundrels. Among women, 30 percent of the "good" ones smoked, but only 2.5 percent of the "bad." Heroines smoked more than the bad guys, male or female. This trend was foreshadowed in *A Woman of the World* (1926), in which Pola Negri played a worldly countess who visits relatives in a small midwestern town. The countess, smoking a cigarette in a long black holder, arrives just as an anti-vice district attorney finishes delivering a lecture on the evils of smoking. She eventually humanizes and then marries him. He gives up intolerance and provincialism; she continues smoking.[68]

Will H. Hays, head of what became known as the Production Code Administration of the Motion Picture Producers and Distributors of America, rejected several requests to censor the use of cigarettes in films. Reformers had hoped he would order smoking limited to "discreditable" or "derelict" characters. The mayor of Lynn, Massachusetts, took matters into his own hands in 1929 by banning movies that showed women of any kind smoking, but it hardly mattered by then. Filmmakers were putting more smokers into their movies because more people were actually smoking. In turn, images of smokers on the screen reverberated through the broader culture, creating a sort of harmonic curve, with the reality and the reflection magnifying each other. Countless young women learned how to smoke by watching movie stars. Young men tried to emulate the heroes who could talk with a cigarette in their mouths, light matches one-handed in the wind, and light two cigarettes at once (passing one to a compliant woman). Another trick, admired by both sexes, was the so-called French inhale, in which smoke was held in the mouth, then released and breathed in through the nostrils in one sinuous stream.[69]

The depression of the 1930s provided another boost to cigarette smoking. The capitalistic cigar lost ground to the democratic cigarette, although the reasons probably had less to do with symbolism than with economics. When people have to struggle to pay their bills, they either switch to a less expensive form of tobacco or give it up altogether. Sales of both factory-made cigarettes and cigars declined after the collapse of the stock market in 1929. However, by 1934, the cigarette industry had fully recovered, while cigar sales continued to slump. Meanwhile, consumption of homemade ("roll-your-own") cigarettes doubled and nearly doubled again, from an estimated 12 billion in 1929 to more than 40 billion in 1933.[70]

As for the organized opposition to cigarette smoking, few would have argued with the assessment of one historian in 1932: "Although the fight between the smokers and non-smokers still drags on, a glance at statistics proves convincingly that the latter are but a feeble and ever-dwindling minority." While apt enough at the time, in the long run this turned out to be a profound miscalculation. The evidence that would rekindle the battle was already accumulating, although much of it was still hidden in the pages of medical journals.[71]

In October 1920, a University of Minnesota pathologist named Moses Barron performed an autopsy on a forty-six-year-old male patient and determined that he had died of lung cancer. Like most other physicians at the time, Barron had never personally seen a case of lung cancer. Although the disease had been described in European medical journals in the early 1800s, it was so rare that it was not codified in the International Classification of Diseases until 1923. A few weeks after encountering his first case, Barron found another. Checking the university's records, he discovered that a third case had been identified by a fellow pathologist a few months earlier. Barron subsequently reported to the Minnesota State Medical Society that the university's pathologists had found eight cases of lung cancer in the twelve months between July 1, 1920, and June 30, 1921, compared to only five in the preceding twenty years. These were the "index cases," in the argot of the newly emerging field of epidemiology: pebbles tossed into a pond, with ever-widening consequences.[72]

By the late twenties, a few scientists were beginning to hypothesize that the increasing prevalence of lung cancer and other degenerative diseases was related to the continuing rise in cigarette consumption. A German researcher cautiously observed in November 1928 that "[t]he increase in cancer of the lungs observed in this and many other countries is in all probability to a certain extent directly traceable to the more common practice of cigarette smoking." Dr. William McNally of Rush Medical College was less tentative, asserting that cigarettes were "an important factor" in lung cancer. Several studies identified tobacco as a carcinogen, although the main focus was on the role of smoking in cancers of the mouth or throat. Others looked at smoking and heart disease. Scientists also were beginning to speculate about why cigarettes might be more dangerous than other forms of tobacco. Some suspected it had something to do with inhalation: since cigarette smokers were more likely to inhale, they might be more likely to absorb any deleterious substances present in tobacco smoke. A few of these reports circulated in the popular press, including one predicting that the incidence of cancers of the mouth would rise as a result of increases in the number of women smokers.[73]

The volume of cigarette-related research increased in the next decade. Among some of the more notable reports was one by Drs. Alton Ochsner and Michael DeBakey, prominent surgeons in New Orleans, who concluded "more persons are dying of cancer of the lung than ever before, probably because more persons are smoking and inhaling tobacco smoke than ever before." Dr. Raymond Pearl, a distinguished professor of biometry at Johns Hopkins University, associated cigarettes not only with lung cancer but with "impairment of life duration" in general. Meanwhile, the Bureau of the Census reported that deaths from lung cancer increased by 36 percent between 1934 and 1938.[74]

Despite the mounting evidence, the prevailing opinion within the medical community was that smoking (of cigarettes as well as pipes and cigars) was a harmless indulgence. Many doctors defended it as a mild sedative, useful against the pressures of living in the modern world. A few still regarded smoking as a prophylactic against certain infectious diseases. (According to this latter theory, the process of combustion transformed nicotine into a sort of germicide.) William J. Mayo, famed surgeon and cofounder of the Mayo Clinic in Rochester, Minnesota, disapproved of female smokers but believed that "the large majority of men who smoke appear to get a great deal of comfort from it, and, generally speaking, without demonstrable harm." A Michigan doctor who thought he saw a link between maternal cigarette smoking and high infant mortality in 1927 was roundly denounced by his peers. In a 1928 article titled "On the Use of Tobacco in Prolonging Life," one physician concluded, "A goddess, at whose shrine the whole world worships, must have some good in her." This appeared in *Hygeia*, the American Medical Association's magazine for general audiences. The next year, the *Journal of the American Medical Association* said only cultists and intemperate reformers believed cigarettes were harmful to expectant mothers or their offspring. Dr. James A. Tobey, author of a popular book on cancer, decided "[t]here is no scientific evidence to show that My Lady Nicotine has any deleterious effect," when used "in reasonable moderation" by the average person.[75]

Some doctors cautioned their patients not to smoke "excessively"; and some were concerned that constant chewing on a pipe or cigar stem could irritate tender tissues in the tongue, mouth, and throat and thereby cause cancer. But probably most would have agreed with the following remarks by a New York physician, in a paper presented at the 1926 annual meeting of the American Laryngological, Rhinological, and Otolaryngological Society:

The idea that . . . it is unhealthy to smoke is in strong contradiction to physiological knowledge and our experience in medical practice. Such an idea, made popular in many parts of the Union, is nothing but a popular delusion. . . . [M]edical opinion will agree that tobacco is as harmless as ice cream *if* taken moderately.[76]

Doctors were particularly reluctant to accept evidence of an apparent connection between lung cancer and cigarette consumption. One school of thought held that lung cancer only *seemed* to be increasing, because of better diagnostic tools. According to another, the increase was real but caused by something besides smoking, such as airborne pollution or even delayed reactions from the flu epidemic of 1918–19. A group of researchers in Great Britain announced that cigarette smoking could not possibly cause lung cancer because all attempts to produce the cancer by blowing smoke on laboratory animals had failed (the *New York Times* headlined this as "CLEARS CIGARETTES AS CANCER SOURCE"). Dr. Evarts Graham, a surgeon and professor at Washington University in St. Louis, once remarked that the parallel between lung cancer and the sale of nylon stockings was just as strong as that between lung cancer and the sale of cigarettes. In the 1940s, Graham and one of his students directed a major epidemiological study documenting the statistical correlation between lung cancer and cigarettes. Even then, it was another two decades before organized medicine fully enlisted in the battle against smoking.[77]

The tobacco industry itself seemed more sensitive to concerns about smoking and health than many doctors. Few issues of the leading trade journals in the twenties did not include at least one article related to the topic, usually carefully edited to remove any hints that smoking might be unhealthy. For example, when *Tobacco* reprinted an article written for the YMCA's *Physical Training* magazine by Dr. P. K. Holmes, director of the Department of Public Health and Hygiene at the University of Kentucky, it excised passages suggesting that cigarettes were addictive and harmful to the heart, lungs, metabolism, and immune system. In his original article, Holmes weighed the available evidence and found more to be said against cigarettes than for them. As presented in *Tobacco*, he virtually endorsed smoking as beneficial to health. Any defense of smoking in a medical journal, no matter how mild, was likely to appear in truncated form in one of the trade journals, to reinforce the claim that "[s]cience has come to the rescue of the reputation of tobacco. Chemists, physicians, toxicologists, physiologists and experts of every nation and clime, have given tobacco a clean bill of health and pronounced it a great God-given boon to mankind." Another common theme in the tobacco journals was that the American government, by supplying troops with cigarettes during World War I, had proven they were safe.[78]

The fact that the industry was making efforts to counter the image of smoking as dangerous suggests that such an image was somehow being conveyed to the public, despite the medical profession's indifference. One trade journal explained that it published articles on the issue of health "in order that those members of the trade who may be interrogated on the subject may be in a position to appease any scruples that may have arisen

among their customers." At that point, the "scruples" were being generated largely by the reform community, not organized medicine, but the
industry still feared the potential effect on consumers.[79]

The journals advised their readers to pass on to their customers stories
about implausibly aged people who smoked incessantly: a Nebraska tobaccophile who was "cut off by the grim reaper at the early age of 126 years";
a 118-year-old Milwaukee woman who "smoked a pipe whenever she
could fill it and was fond of cigars and cigarettes"; a Jewish centarian who
told a reporter, "All this stuff about what you should eat and drink and
smoke is all foolishness. It is making old people out of young ones." The
trade press also provided sample scripts to be used by retailers when customers asked questions about the effect of smoking on health ("I was talk-
ing to a doctor the other day, and I asked him the identical question you
have asked me. The doctor said . . .")[80]

In addition, the industry tried to dispel doubts by using medical themes
in its advertising. Prior to the late 1920s, any health-related messages in
cigarette ads tended to be subtle. Fatima was "truly comfortable to your
throat and tongue"; there was not a "cough in a carload" of Old Golds;
Lucky Strikes caused "[n]o throat irritation—no cough." The American
Tobacco Company supported its claims about Lucky Strikes with a pamphlet citing tests by three independent laboratories that allegedly proved
that "toasting" removed "acrid substances" from tobacco, making it "non-
irritating to the mucous membranes." Since it was widely believed that
cancer was somehow linked to "irritation," this was a way of saying that
Lucky Strikes, having been "toasted," could not possibly cause cancer.[81]

The claims became more overt in the thirties and forties. R. J. Reynolds
maintained that "[m]ore Doctors smoke Camels than any other cigarette,"
while American Tobacco reported that 20,679 physicians believed Lucky
Strikes were less irritating than other brands; L & Ms were "[j]ust what
the doctor ordered," and Philip Morris cigarettes were "recognized by eminent medical authorities." The *Journal of the American Medical Association*
criticized such claims as "hooey" in 1928, but from the early 1930s until
the mid-1950s, it accepted advertising that implied smoking was healthful,
as did most other medical journals.[82]

The white-coated, stethoscope-equipped doctor remained a fixture in
cigarette advertising until just a few years before the 1964 publication of
the seminal *Smoking and Health: Report of the Advisory Committee to the
Surgeon General of the Public Health Service* (commonly known as the first
Surgeon General's Report on Smoking and Health). The report was 387
pages long, listed 916 scientific references, and concluded that cigarette
smoking was "a health hazard of sufficient import in the United States to
warrant appropriate remedial action."[83]

The first generation of anti-cigarette crusaders had come to a similar con-
clusion decades earlier. With the exception of lung cancer, they had already
ploughed the major fields later reworked by medical science, from emphysema to heart disease. While they did not specifically address the issue of

lung cancer, they had long speculated that smoking was harmful to lungs. As a 1929 newsletter published by the Anti-Cigarette League pointed out, "If the inhalation of coal smoke causes such serious chronic irritation and so blackens the lungs, how much more serious must be the effect of the almost constant inhalation of tobacco smoke direct into the lungs." More than two decades before epidemiologists began collecting biostatistics on smoking and mortality, the reform community was circulating data from the New England Life Insurance Company suggesting that smokers had shorter life spans than nonsmokers. A mortality study of graduates of the Dartmouth College class of 1868, conducted in the 1920s under the aegis of Irving Fisher's Life Extension Institute, showed that nonsmokers could expect to live an average of seven years longer than smokers. When the National Health Bureau reported increased rates of death due to heart disease and cancer in 1929, one longtime foe of the cigarette noted that he had predicted that very development twenty years earlier.[84]

The fact that early scientific reports about the effects of cigarettes echoed the claims of reformers made it difficult for doctors to accept them. Since the mid-nineteenth century, organized medicine had sought to separate itself from the "irregulars" who promoted alternative therapies, many of which involved the avoidance of alcohol and tobacco. Health reformers such as Joel Shew (developer of the "water cure"), Sylvester Graham (whose name has been immortalized by the graham cracker), and John Harvey Kellogg had been in the forefront of the anti-smoking movement. Shew, for example, believed tobacco use contributed to eighty-seven individual diseases, including cancer, heart disease, blindness, apoplexy, insanity, acne, and tooth decay. To the medical establishment, such claims were fictions, woven by "cranks" from the trappings of religion and morality, unrelated to the truth as revealed by science. The tradition of denial created psychological barriers for many doctors. They had become so convinced, in their own minds, that the reformers had no legitimate case against smoking that they could not easily turn around and admit they had been wrong.[85]

As the scientific evidence began to develop in the late twenties, even those physicians who were inclined to accept it took steps to distance themselves from the reformers. "Many pamphlets and books have been written about the terrible effects of cigarette smoking, but few of them contain anything like scientific proof of their claims," Holmes complained in his article in *Physical Training*. The crusaders were "silly"; much of what they had to say was "ridiculous." Nonetheless, it was true that "the so-called diseases of degeneration" had become more common since cigarette smoking had become more popular. The *Journal of the American Medical Association* might have been moved to defend smoking by expectant mothers in 1929 just because the Methodist Episcopal Board of Temperance, Prohibition, and Public Morals had recently attacked the practice.[86]

An exchange of letters between Raymond Pearl of Johns Hopkins University and Anthony Zeleny illustrates the tension between medical science and early opponents of smoking. Zeleny apparently felt that Pearl was overly cautious in his conclusions about the effects of smoking on longevity in 1938. "I have been wondering whether I would have given your conclusions so little weight had I been able to discuss them with you last summer as I had planned," he wrote to Pearl. In his reply, Pearl sniped, "Your whole discussion of my work carries the implication that either I am a fool or a knave. . . . Now the fact is that I am certainly not a knave and I do not think that I am quite that big a fool."[87]

No doubt many doctors resisted the suggestion that cigarettes were harmful because they themselves smoked. Zeleny suspected this was the reason Dr. Louis I. Dublin, vice president and chief statistician of the Metropolitan Life Insurance Company in the 1930s and a former vice president of the American Medical Association, thought it improbable that smoking could affect longevity. Martin Arrowsmith, hero of Sinclair Lewis's novel about a science-driven doctor, started smoking cigarettes in medical school to counter the reek of formaldehyde, and never gave them up. Charles Buckley Hubbell, president of the Board of Education of Greater New York in the early 1900s and the founder of an anti-cigarette group, said he rarely met medical students who did not smoke. Once acquired, he added, the habit was not easily relinquished. Consequently, "a very large number of physicians in every community are addicted to the cigaret and the inhaling habit, and naturally are handicapped in the influence that they should exert in advising and suppressing this alarming evil." A tobacco trade journal, outlining strategies to defend the industry in 1919, asserted that "[m]ost doctors are addicted to tobacco." One study, completed in 1950, showed that 53 percent of physicians smoked—compared to less than 40 percent of all adults. Cigarette manufacturers demonstrated their awareness of the market by offering physicians free samples of their products and by advertising in medical journals.[88]

The inherent difficulty of proving causal connections in the study of disease was another factor in the medical community's reluctance to accept the early scientific data about cigarettes. The researchers could point out statistical correlations between smoking and, say, lung cancer, but they could not say what actually caused smokers to develop lung cancer. Some wondered if the new insecticides used to treat tobacco caused the cancer, rather than the tobacco itself. Not until 1953 did scientists succeed in isolating tars from tobacco and using them to induce cancer in laboratory animals. Even then, their methods were criticized because the tars were painted on the animals' skins, rather than being absorbed through smoke. Sometimes the evidence itself was contradictory. For example, experiments at the University of Minnesota's medical school and at Antioch College in Yellow Springs, Ohio, in the mid-twenties seemed to exonerate cigarettes as a cause of heart disease. Earlier, researchers at the Cornell University Medical School concluded that smoking was just as likely to lower blood pressure as to raise it.[89]

The reformers who powered the first campaign against cigarettes had ventured into the arena of health without adequate evidence to support their claims. By the time the evidence they needed was available, they had lost their influence. This suggests something about the mixed legacy of the Progressive Era. Progressivism was driven by evangelical fervor, on the one hand, and by faith in science, on the other. Of these conflicting impulses, it was science that prevailed.

This fact served to promote organized medicine while undercutting both organized religion and the eclectic, laymen-dominated health reform movement—the two most important sources of early opposition to cigarettes. Higher standards for admission to medical schools; more demanding, science-based curricula; tighter requirements for licensing; the proliferation of professional groups such as the American Medical Association: these progressive reforms gave physicians a certain mystique in American society. As James T. Patterson has noted, the real gains made by doctors in their ability to control disease were less important than public perceptions about their powers. The public had confidence in the ability of experts to decide what should be done; and medical experts said it was not necessary to restrict the use of cigarettes by adults.[90]

In one sense, the first anti-cigarette movement was both a product and a victim of progressivism. It was fostered by one manifestation of the reform spirit, and then subverted by another. However, by elevating the status of the medical profession, reformers of the Progressive Era provided the framework for the resuscitation of the campaign against cigarettes in the late twentieth century. When organized medicine finally entered the battle over smoking, it did so with the moral authority once held only by the church. The publication of the 1964 surgeon general's report ushered in a new round of opposition, one far more successful than its predecessor. Still, more than thirty years later, it is too early to write a requiem for the cigarette.

# *Conclusion*

The cigarette today is the most vilified product available legally in the United States, blamed for causing the premature deaths of more than 400,000 Americans a year, banned from most public buildings, besieged in the courts, and subject to increasing restrictions on advertising, promotion, and sales. Nonetheless, one out of four adults continues to smoke, a figure that has remained virtually unchanged since 1989.[1]

This suggests that victory over "the little white slaver" will not be as complete or as permanent as two generations of reformers have hoped. Although cigarettes probably never will enjoy the same degree of cultural acceptance they once had, neither are they likely to vanish from the American scene. Significant numbers of Americans will smoke however stringent the marketing limitations and however insistent the public condemnation. Indeed, the more vigorous the attacks on cigarettes, the more attractive they become as symbols of rebellion and independence, particularly to young people. It is not surprising that the prevalence of smoking among high school students increased by nearly one-third between 1991 and 1997 despite intensive anti-smoking efforts in the schools and elsewhere.[2]

Many critics attribute the persistence of smoking to the devious marketing practices of a wicked industry. They imply that if the manufacturers were only properly restrained, demand for their products would evaporate. That explanation has the virtue of simplicity, but it fails to recognize the complex role of cigarettes in the modern world. Although the industry has been aggressive, clever, even corrupt in promoting cigarettes, its behavior alone does not explain why the percentage of smokers in the adult population has hardly budged in nearly a decade, or why the percentage of youthful smokers has begun to creep up. Nor can these facts be explained solely by the addictive properties of the nicotine in cigarettes; after all, two out of every three people who start smoking give it up. For those who continue, cigarettes serve a number of important psychosocial functions—as self-medication for either depression or excitability, as emblems of solidarity with peers, as expressions of identity. Cigarettes are simply too useful in too many ways to make a "smoke-free America" more than wishful thinking on the part of the anti-smoking lobby.[3]

Organized opposition to cigarettes began in the late 1880s, reached an apogee around 1917, and faded by the end of the 1920s. A second wave began in the late 1960s, built momentum over the next two decades, and now runs the risk of engendering a backlash. There are striking similarities as well as marked differences between the two campaigns. Both developed as offshoots of broader reform movements, generated by widespread social unrest; both took on the qualities of crusades in the classic sense, including a commitment to total victory over a demonized enemy; and both put faith in the power of government to regulate the behavior of individuals. The early crusaders had the advantage of challenging a product that was just beginning to establish a foothold in American culture. Their successors had to confront a product that had gained wide acceptance. However, medical science has handed today's reformers potent weapons, including the argument that secondhand smoke is dangerous to the health of nonsmokers. Even many smokers now consider the act of lighting a cigarette in public—once considered a social act—to be antisocial.[4]

The first anti-cigarette campaign was a manifestation of the reformist spirit of the Progressive Era, which, in turn, was a response to the social tensions arising from the transformation of a rural, agrarian nation into an urban, industrial one. The campaign was closely tied to the drive for national prohibition. As Norman Clark has pointed out, most progressives—whether they were involved in efforts to regulate industry, promote female suffrage, improve playgrounds, or democratize government; whether living in urban centers or rural villages, whether Protestant or Catholic—also advocated prohibition. The religious leaders, social workers, health reformers, educators, and businessmen who sought to banish cigarettes during this period did so in the belief that their use contributed to other social problems, from "race suicide" to drug use to juvenile delinquency to, above all, use of alcohol. They also argued that cigarettes were addicting and unhealthy; that secondhand smoke could harm the health of nonsmokers; and that exposure to parental smoke was dangerous to children, including unborn children. None of these health-related arguments carried as much weight at the time as those connected to moral issues.[5]

The anti-cigarette movement enjoyed a measure of success in the years before the United States entered World War I largely because it was part of a chain of reform. The war dissolved the matrix that held this chain together. Reformist energy shifted to new priorities: winning the war, and winning it with an army that was chaste and sober. The ambitious agenda of earlier years gave way to a tightly focused effort to prohibit the manufacture and sale of beverage alcohol, at least as an emergency war measure. Progressives justified wartime prohibition on the grounds that alcohol wasted grain and fruits needed to feed the allied armies and also curtailed the efficiency of soldiers and munitions workers. Such claims made it difficult to counter arguments advanced by the industry that cigarettes helped conserve food by suppressing the appetite, and improved efficiency by simultaneously sedating and stimulating men denied other comforts. By linking the general cause of reform to patriotism, progressives helped undermine the specific case against cigarettes.

The anti-cigarette movement lost important allies and gained new enemies during the war. Many groups—including the YMCA and the Salvation Army—not only suspended their opposition to cigarettes, they actually began to promote them as useful to the war effort. Although Congress banned the sale of alcohol to men in uniform and tried to outlaw alcohol and prostitution in zones around military camps, it included cigarettes in the rations issued to soldiers overseas and it subsidized their sale at post exchange stores both at home and abroad. Hundreds of civic, business, social, and religious organizations joined in the effort to make sure "Johnny" had plenty to smoke. These actions, carried out in the name of military efficiency, helped endow a once-despised product with a new aura of legitimacy.

The changes in the political barometer were reflected in a keynote speech by Representative James R. Mann during the 1920 convention of the Tobacco Merchants Association. Mann, a Republican from Lucy Page Gaston's Congressional district in Illinois, stood before the delegates, held a cigarette aloft, and declared that it had won the war. Not to be outdone, Representative Henry M. Goldfogle, a Democrat from New York, then took the podium to denounce "anti-tobacco propaganda" and pledged to support lower taxes on all tobacco products."[6]

After the war, the only groups with the potential power to mount an effective campaign against cigarettes were preoccupied with ratifying and then enforcing the Eighteenth Amendment. The Anti-Saloon League, the WCTU, and other prohibitionist organizations made a calculated retreat from the issue of smoking in order to gain support for national prohibition. Although many Anti-Saloon League officials believed that any kind of tobacco use detracted from "the development of man at his best," they were unwilling to press the point. The WCTU had been in the forefront of the anti-cigarette crusade since 1887, when it passed the first of many resolutions calling for cigarette prohibition. After considerable debate at the annual meeting of 1919, the organization rejected a proposal that it seek a constitutional amendment banning the sale and manufacture of cigarettes. Moderates, including Anna A. Gordon, national president, argued that such a stand would erode public sympathy for pro-hibition.[7]

Despite the defection of the prohibitionists, anti-cigarette crusaders ral-lied briefly after the war, pushing proposed legislation onto the agenda in dozens of state legislatures. By that time, however, their opponents in-cluded the American Legion and the Veterans of Foreign Wars, both of which lobbied for the defeat of proposed anti-cigarette laws and the repeal of existing ones. Manufacturers exploited the association between ciga-rettes and soldiers by using military themes in their advertising. Posters for Camels featured a doughboy's helmet and the slogan "Ask the Man Who Wore One"; Lucky Strike quoted a commander of the American Ex-peditionary Forces as saying, "An Army man must keep fit—reach for a Lucky instead of a sweet"; Chesterfield showed two veterans reminiscing over the smokes they had shared in the trenches (Chesterfields, of course). By selecting such themes, advertisers underscored the fact that cigarettes had become symbols of democracy, making them more impervious to the assaults of reformers. Five years after the armistice, only two states still had laws restricting the sale of cigarettes to adults: North Dakota and Kansas, which at the time had a combined population less than that of Brooklyn and Queens.[8]

Perhaps just as compelling as patriotism in the decline of political op-position to cigarette smoking was the need to replace revenue lost to pro-hibition. For example, Chicago, home of the Anti-Cigarette League, col-lected about $8 million from licenses issued to about 5,400 saloons in 1918; that source of income vanished as of July 1, 1919, when a local-option prohibition law went into effect. To compensate, the city coun-cil repealed an ordinance banning the sale of cigarettes within 600 feet of schools. The action was taken on the recommendation of the deputy tax collector, who pointed out that by making it easier for retailers to get licenses, at annual fees of $100 a year, the city would make up some of the funds lost to prohibition.[9]

Any residual hostility toward cigarettes among legislators quickly lost ground to pragmatism. The North Dakota legislature replaced a thirty-year-old ban on the sale of cigarettes in 1925 with a new law that re-quired sellers to buy annual licenses and pay state taxes. In recommend-ing that the law be approved, Governor Arthur G. Sorlie predicted that it would add more than $500,000 a year to the state's treasury. After sign-ing a 1921 bill making it legal to buy cigarettes in Iowa for the first time since 1896, Governor N. E. Kendall said, "[I]f the present volume of cig-arette consumption be maintained, revenues will accrue to the state ag-gregating annually several hundred thousands of dollars." Kendall's re-mark suggests not only the lure of new sources of revenue for governments whose finances had been "disordered" by prohibition, but something about the degree to which the ban on cigarettes had been en-forced in Iowa. Obviously, people had managed to buy cigarettes despite the law.[10]

Kansas, too, imposed state taxes when it legalized cigarette sales in 1927. Responding to an opponent who argued, "Kansas don't need this dirty cigaret money," the state treasurer said: "The question is not whether or not cigarets are going to be sold in Kansas but whether they are going to be sold legally or illegally. The question is not whether the smoker is going to be gouged, but whether he is going to pay five or ten cents to a bootlegger or two cents to a reputable dealer." The legislature opted for the latter, imposing a two-cent per package tax on cigarettes.[11]

Taxes on tobacco were second only to the income tax in the amount of revenue generated for the federal government after the enactment of national prohibition in 1920. By 1925, the greatest share of this revenue came from cigarettes. It is notable that Ohio, which began taxing cigarettes in 1893, rejected at least six efforts to outlaw their sale. Vermont was one of the few states to resist the temptation to tax cigarettes, at least until the 1930s. That state's legislators consistently voted down proposals for such taxes on the grounds that southern tobacco growers used Vermont maple syrup to cure their products, and a tax on tobacco would lead to a retaliatory tax on syrup.[12]

Cigarettes also were attractive as a source of revenue because more and more people were smoking them. In 1865, the first year that the federal government collected taxes on cigarettes, only about 20 million were sold—less than one per capita. Sixty-five years later, American manufacturers produced more than 120 billion cigarettes for the domestic market, enough to supply every man, woman, and child with nearly 1,000 smokes a year.[13]

This extraordinary growth was the result of a convergence of factors. Certainly one influence was the cohesion and aggressiveness of the industry. Cigarette manufacturing and distribution was dominated by a single company from 1890 until 1911, and thereafter by an oligopoly of three companies. In comparison, there were 1,248 breweries and 440 distilleries in the United States when the drive for national prohibition began in 1890. The alcohol industry was fragmented, highly competitive, and slow to recognize the threat posed by the prohibitionists. Cigarette manufacturers took the threat seriously from the outset, fighting back with a carefully planned, well-financed offensive, using everything from old-fashioned bribery to the new science of public relations.[14]

During his tenure at the American Tobacco Company, James B. Duke himself monitored the activities of reformers and personally directed countermeasures. His successor, Percival Hill, was equally vigilant. When Thomas Edison condemned cigarettes as poisonous and addictive in 1914, Hill sent him a letter complaining about his "unwarranted attacks," and insisting, "Aside from the overwhelming weight of scientific testimony, common sense alone will convince any reasonable man that the cigarette is not injurious." He then had the letter printed up as a pamphlet for distribution by tobacco retailers. Hill gave no less attention to Lucy Page Gaston, inviting her to tour one of his factories at one point. When she persisted in attacking cigarettes anyway, he wrote an extensive rebuttal for the press. Hill also played a central role in convincing the rest of the tobacco industry to close ranks around the cigarette, through trade groups such as the Tobacco Merchants Association (founded in 1915) and the Allied Tobacco League (1919). For years, manufacturers of other forms of tobacco had regarded the cigarette as an unwelcome competitor. There are reasons to suspect that cigar and plug tobacco interests spread rumors about the contents of cigarettes and helped finance other anti-cigarette activities in the 1890s and early 1900s. By the late teens, however, the industry was presenting a united face to the public.[15]

Cigarette manufacturers won the support of their competitors by maintaining that cigarettes were merely the point of entry for an all-out war against the entire tobacco industry. They appealed to growers, leaf dealers, unions, wholesalers, retailers, salesmen, and manufacturers of other tobacco products to avoid the "delusion" that the "antis" would stop with cigarettes. The cigarette had been "singled out for direct attack" only because "it is regarded by the reform element as the weakest link in the tobacco chain." Under the influence of such assertions, the tobacco industry avoided the discord that set beer, wine, whiskey, and gin interests against each other.[16]

A number of other factors contributed to the decline of the first anti-cigarette movement, beginning with the seemingly prosaic nature of cigarettes themselves. The consequences of excessive smoking were less immediate and more difficult to detect than those resulting from overindulgence in alcohol. There were no stories to be told of sad-eyed children waiting by the tobacconist's door, begging a smoke-besotted father to come home; no reports of cigarettes converting an amiable Dr. Jekyll into a low-browed, villainous Mr. Hyde. In her address to the annual meeting of the WCTU in 1889, Frances Willard could tell her followers about "[t]he drunkard in Chicago who pounded his sick wife to death with the body of their new-born child" and be believed; but not even the most credulous would accept a story about comparable evils caused by smoking. "Men don't smoke cigarets and go home to beat their wives," a Kansas legislator commented in arguing for the repeal of that state's cigarette prohibition law in 1927. "Nor do they squander their wages for cigarets on Saturday night." The very ordinariness of cigarettes helped undercut the initial opposition to them.[17]

The movement also was weakened by poor leadership and internecine squabbling over goals, tactics, and turf. Gaston, for all her determination, had none of the charisma of Willard of the WCTU; or the political acumen of Ernest H. Cherrington and Wayne B. Wheeler of the Anti-Saloon League. Neither she nor any of the lesser figures in the battle against cigarettes could command the depth of commitment from their followers or the financial support needed to prevail against a well-organized, economically powerful, and politically skilled industry. "Brother This and Sister That do not dig down deep into their pocketbooks as they did when the foe was the Demon Rum," one observer noted.[18]

Compounding these factors were social changes that favored increased smoking, including urbanization, broader opportunities for women, and generational dissonance. Cigarettes were convenient (when Americans were embracing convenience); could be smoked quickly (when time was becoming a valuable commodity) and easily (without the rapt attention required by pipes or cigars); and were less offensive to nonsmokers in enclosed spaces (when more people were working in offices rather than outdoors, and riding to work in subways, streetcars, or automobiles instead of walking). "Short, snappy, easily attempted, easily completed or just as easily discarded before completion—the cigarette is the symbol of a machine age in which the ultimate cogs and wheels and levers are human nerves," the *New York Times* editorialized in 1925.[19]

Cigarettes also fulfilled several important social functions. For one thing, they provided a frame of reference for personal relationships at a time when the traditional avenues of discourse were being rearranged. Both smokers and nonsmokers participated in the new ballet of manners. "Got a light?" and "Mind if I smoke?" were pathways to companionship, to connections in a disconnected world. For women, who comprised the fastest growing segment of the market after the war, cigarettes were tokens of equity with men. Additionally, as symbols, cigarettes had the advantage of being amorphic: they made men more manly, women more womanly.

Perhaps above all, cigarettes were useful as generational markers. A retrospective study based on interviews conducted in the late 1970s by the United States National Center for Health Statistics showed that people who were between the ages of twenty-five and thirty-four in 1925 were far more likely to smoke cigarettes than people who were older. This was the generation that had come of age during World War I. For many of them, the war was a transforming experience that set them apart from previous generations. They challenged the authority of the past by adopting new styles and new behaviors, including cigarette smoking. The very fact that cigarettes had been identified with unconventional behavior made them attractive to a generation that was throwing off the fetters of the past. Not until another reform-minded generation came of age, during the Vietnam War era, would cigarette smoking again face serious opposition.[20]

The myriad challenges to the social and political order of the 1960s provided the context for the second anti-cigarette movement. Blacks challenged whites; women challenged men; environmentalists challenged polluters; students challenged their parents, teachers, and administrators; and, most relevant to the campaign against cigarettes, consumers challenged big business. John F. Banzhaf III was still a student at the Columbia University Law School in 1964 when he began earning a reputation as a legal-action gadfly in the mold of consumer-rights advocate Ralph Nader. As a twenty-five-year-old associate in a New York law firm in 1967, Banzhaf filed a complaint with the Federal Communications Commission that eventually led to a ban on cigarette advertising on radio and television. He went on to organize Action on Smoking and Health (ASH), the modern counterpart to Gaston's Anti-Cigarette League. In late 1969, Nader himself made the rights of nonsmokers a national issue by petitioning the Federal Aviation Administration to ban smoking on airline flights.[21]

The modern campaign differs from its predecessor in two key areas: the degree to which medical science has enlisted in the crusade and the attention given to the issue of passive smoking. Although the first issue of the *Journal of the American Medical Association (JAMA)* in 1883 included an anecdotal account of the harmful effects of tobacco, organized medicine took little interest in cigarettes as a health issue until the late 1920s. Since then, researchers have developed increasingly convincing medical arguments against both active and passive smoking. Historian Allan Brandt points out that these arguments are based not only on a simple accretion of evidence but also on new ways of looking at it. Older "lab bench" standards of research required that theories be proven in the laboratory. The upstart science of epidemiology built the case against smoking by using biostatistics, inferential thinking, and new models of causality. The result is that if there are any physicians who would be willing to defend cigarettes today—as *JAMA* did as late as 1948—they are keeping a low profile.[22]

The well-credentialed researchers who began studying cigarettes in the late twenties uncovered little new ground; for the most part, their reports merely confirmed the speculations that had been floating around in the reform literature for decades. But in a society that was both health-conscious and inclined to respect expertise, the judgments of organized medicine carried far more weight than those of the "cranks." This was perhaps the most durable legacy of the progressive spirit that launched the opposition to cigarettes in the first place. The progressives deeply admired professionalism. Under their influence, the ever-expanding middle class became increasingly deferential to experts in all aspects of life, including medicine, business, education, social work, even motherhood and child rearing. When medical professionals finally challenged cigarettes, they spoke from a position of enormous cultural authority.

The Non-Smokers' Protective League and its allies in the first anti-smoking movement raised the issue of "second-hand smoke"—a phrase in use by 1923—but they failed to convince the public that the exhalations of those who smoke could be anything more than a passing irritation to those who do not. With his 1986 *Report on the Health Consequences of Involuntary Smoking*, Surgeon General C. Everett Koop helped change public perceptions about what was by then being called "environmental tobacco smoke." Although the report itself was more tentative than Koop implied in his preface and in subsequent speeches, it was promoted as proof that nonsmokers could contract cancer or other diseases from exposure to other people's smoke. A controversial 1993 report by the Environmental Protec-

tion Agency classified tobacco smoke as a Class A carcinogen and estimated that 3,000 nonsmokers die from it every year. The new evidence,
however contested, shifted the focus of the debate from what smokers do
to themselves to what they do to others.[23]

Today, cigarettes are even more stringently regulated than alcoholic
beverages—just as Marshall Cook, the cigarette-detesting publisher of the
*Hastings (Michigan) Banner*, predicted some eighty years ago. At the same
time, there are signs that anti-smoking efforts have reached their limits.
At least fifteen states have enacted so-called "smokers' rights" laws, prohibiting employers from discriminating against workers who smoke outside
the workplace. "The days when the employer could dictate what you could
do outside the place of employment (are) over," a New Hampshire state
senator said in urging his colleagues to vote for such a bill in 1991. Re-
ferring to the state's famous license plate, he added, "[I]t says 'Live Free
or Die,' so let's live free and make (our) own decisions at home and not
have the employer dictate to us." The measure passed.[24]

On nearly any college campus, groups of self-consciously defiant smokers can be seen in front of buildings or under trees ("the tree people," some
students call them). Also becoming more visible are so-called social smokers, who light up only occasionally and favor specialty brands, including
one marketed to the health-conscious as an "all natural" cigarette. The
1995 movie *Smoke* celebrated tobacco as a test of liberality and suggested
that longevity is not the measure of a good life. Meanwhile, a few advertisements for high-fashion women's clothing have featured models holding
cigarettes.[25]

One of the lessons to be learned from the first campaign against cigarettes is that any successful social reform movement carries within it the
seeds of a backlash. Incessant warnings can fade into the ozone of the
commonplace, unheard by those they are intended to reach. "Men are so
habituated to the outcry against smoking that there are few who do not
ignore it," *Harper's Weekly* observed—in 1906. The cultural excesses of the
so-called Roaring Twenties came partly in response to the web of restrictions laid down during the Progressive Era. People began to chafe about
the limits on freedom in the supposed land of the free. The United States
had just fought a war to protect democracy; this gave the issue of liberty
at home greater resonance. "You Americans talk liberty like it was God
Almighty," complained a Catalan immigrant who subsequently returned
to Spain, "but you can't get a drink of wine without breaking the law.
And look at the places where you can't go to the theater or a ball game
on Sunday, or drive an auto—some where you can't even buy a package
of cigs!" The new mood of the country penetrated even to Evanston, Illinois, home of the WCTU, where city attorney William Lister asked that
members of that organization be barred from trials of tobacco dealers
charged with selling cigarettes to minors. Lister said he thought the dealers
were being acquitted because jurors resented the presence of WCTU workers in the courtroom.[26]

Five hundred years of the history of tobacco in western culture also show it is risky to venture into prophecy where smoking is concerned. A minister in Dayton, Ohio, was certain in 1882 that "the time is not far distant when the use of tobacco will be generally looked upon with disfavor and admit of no apology whatever." Forty years later, another writer was equally confident that "[t]he cigarette smoker of the future is the leper of the future." Forty years after that, a popular children's game called "Go to the Head of the Class" included cigarette jingles in its list of what elementary students were expected to know. If today it seems as if the earlier prophecies are coming to pass, it is useful to keep in mind another, voiced by an Italian physician who was one of the first to study the effects of smoking on tobacco workers: "This vice will always be condemned and always clung to." The date was 1713.[27]

# $Coda$

My mother was a smart woman. As a high school student in Dumas, Texas, she set a record on a statewide math test and held it until the test was discontinued some thirty years later. She graduated at age fifteen (one year after she first experimented with cigarettes). By twenty, she was working as a laboratory technician. In her forties, she entered the then-new field of computer programming. Some of the programs she helped design for the student services department at the University of Washington in the late 1970s are still in use today.

She was, she once said of herself, a strong woman with many weaknesses. One of them was cigarettes. She smoked at least one pack every day for nearly fifty years, from her early twenties until her death in 1994 at age seventy-two (except during her eight pregnancies, when cigarettes always tasted unpleasant to her), and yes, she died of lung cancer. After years of nagging her to quit, I was the one who lit her last cigarette for her and urged her to smoke it. By that point, she could no longer inhale deeply enough to light one for herself. I knew she was really dying when she lost interest in cigarettes—her steady, faithful companions for all those years.

Smoking shaved five or six years from her life, by her reckoning, but she did not seem to begrudge it. I never heard her say she wished she had taken her father's advice and stayed clear of what he had called "coffin nails," any more than she wished she had eaten more tofu and less red meat, exercised more, kept her weight down, substituted white wine for bourbon, or made other sacrifices in the pursuit of a longer life.

This is what she did say, about ten years before she was diagnosed with lung cancer: "I'm glad that most of my children don't smoke. I hope that none of my grandchildren start to smoke. I'm pleased when people who do smoke stop. And I think that the government should encourage people not to smoke, and it sure as hell should not be subsidizing tobacco farmers, helping them grow tobacco the government says is going to kill you. But I choose to smoke. I can't imagine being without cigarettes. It would be very frightening for me. It would be hazardous to my mental health."

# $\mathcal{A}ppendix$

*State Cigarette Prohibition Laws*
*(in Order of Adoption)*

*Washington:* Sale and manufacture of cigarettes banned 1893; repealed 1895; reenacted 1907; sale, manufacture, and possession banned 1909; repealed 1911.

*North Dakota:* Sale banned 1895; repealed 1925.

*Iowa:* Sale and manufacture banned 1896; repealed 1921.

*Tennessee:* Sale and giving away of cigarettes banned 1897; repealed 1919.

*Oklahoma:* Sale and giving away of cigarettes banned 1901; repealed 1915.

*Indiana:* Sale, manufacture, and possession banned 1905; repealed 1909.

*Wisconsin:* Sale, manufacture, and giving away of cigarettes banned 1905; repealed 1915.

*Arkansas:* Sale and manufacture banned 1907; repealed 1921.

*Illinois:* Sale and manufacture banned 1907; law declared unconstitutional by Illinois Supreme Court six months after enactment, but not formally repealed until 1967.

*Nebraska:* Sale, manufacture, and giving away of cigarettes banned 1909; repealed 1919.

*Kansas:* Sale banned 1909; law amended to ban advertising and possession as well as sale in 1917; repealed 1927.

*Minnesota:* Sale and manufacture banned 1909; repealed 1913.

*South Dakota:* Sale, manufacture, and giving away of cigarettes banned 1909; repealed 1917.

*Idaho:* Sale of cigarettes banned and then legalized by the same session of the legislature, 1921.

*Utah:* Sale and advertising banned, 1921; repealed 1923.


## Cigarette Prohibition Laws Considered

*Colorado:* 1911
*Alabama:* 1892, 1897, 1899, 1900, 1903, 1907
*Arizona Territory:* 1895, 1901
*California:* 1895, 1917
*Delaware:* 1901, 1917
*Georgia:* 1919
*Kentucky:* 1896, 1898
*Maine:* 1897, 1909
*Massachusetts:* 1892, 1902, 1907, 1912, 1915
*Michigan:* 1892, 1901
*Missouri:* 1897, 1913
*Montana:* 1901
*Nevada:* 1907
*New Hampshire:* 1897, 1901, 1903, 1907, 1913
*New York:* 1899, 1905
*North Carolina:* 1897, 1901, 1903, 1905, 1911, 1913, 1917
*Ohio:* 1906, 1910, 1911, 1913, 1923, 1925
*Oregon:* 1917, 1925, 1930
*Pennsylvania:* 1917
*South Carolina:* 1897, 1901, 1902 (bill to ban smoking in public eating places considered 1920)
*Texas:* 1923 (bill to make cigarette smoking grounds for dismissal of public school teachers and administrators considered 1929)
*West Virginia:* 1917


For sources, see Cassandra Tate, "The American Anti-Cigarette Movement, 1880–1930" (Ph.D. diss., University of Washington, Seattle, 1995), appendix.

# *Notes*


List of Abbreviations

*Manuscripts*

Archives, Washington, D.C.; xeroxed copy available in JBD
Papers

JHK    John Harvey Kellogg Papers, Bentley Historical Library, University of Michigan, Ann Arbor

JR    Julius Rosenwald Papers, University of Chicago Library, Chicago, Illinois

MHC    Michigan Historical Collections, Bentley Historical Library, University of Michigan, Ann Arbor

UNC    University of North Carolina, Chapel Hill

WCTU    Woman's Christian Temperance Union Annual Meeting Minutes, Temperance and Prohibition Papers, microfilm edition, University of Michigan, Ann Arbor

WKD    William K. Dingledine Papers, Alderman Library, University of Virginia, Charlottesville, Virginia

WP    West Point Papers, U.S. Military Academy Archives, West Point, New York

YMCA    Young Men's Christian Association (YMCA of the USA) Archives, University of Minnesota, St. Paul

*Periodicals*

AM    *Association Men* (YMCA)
CE    *Cincinnati (Ohio) Enquirer*
HB    *Hastings (Michigan) Banner*
JAMA    *Journal of the American Medical Association*
NYS    *New York Sun*
NYT    *New York Times*
TW    *Tobacco World*
US    *Union Signal* (WCTU)

Introduction

1. U.S. Department of Health and Human Services, Public Health Service, *Health United States, 1995* (Hyattsville, Md., 1996), 173.

2. *Binghamton (New York) Press*, Oct. 15, 1904 (see also *NYT*, Oct. 18, 1904); *Seattle Post-Intelligencer*, July 3, 1909 (divorce); June 1, 1909 (prenuptial agreement). For cigarette legislation, see appendix.

3. *Spokane (Washington) Spokesman Review*, Oct. 8, 1890. For the Secaucus case, see *NYT*, Nov. 21, 1923; Mar. 17, June 6, 1926; Jan. 26, 1927.

4. 52nd Cong., 1st sess., 1892, Senate Report 1001; see also *NYT*, July 21, 1892 (both the news report, p. 8, and the accompanying editorial, p. 4); *U.S. Reports* 179 (1900), 367; James J. Jeffreys, *The Curse of the Nation: A Knock-out Blow for Tobacco in Six Rounds* (Marshall, Mich., 1912), 1, 58–62; *Saturday Review*, May 4, 1889, 528; Mark Sullivan, "Roosevelt of the 1880s," *Our Times: The United States, 1900–1925*, vol. 2 (New York, 1927), 228–29.

5. U.S. Department of Health and Human Services, Public Health Service, *National Household Survey on Drug Abuse, Population Estimates 1995* (Rockville, Md., 1996), 89; *Health United States, 1995*, 174.

6. Henry Ford, *The Case Against the Little White Slaver* (Detroit, 1914).

7. Richard B. Tennant, *The American Cigarette Industry: A Study in Economic Analysis and Public Policy* (New York, 1971; orig. New Haven, 1950), 143; JBD testimony, 3410; Allan M. Brandt, " 'Warning: The Surgeon General Has Determined . . . ': Cigarettes and the Culture of Risk," paper presented at "Altered States: Alcohol and Other Drugs in America," symposium sponsored by the Strong Museum, Rochester, N.Y., Nov. 13–14, 1992.

8. Larry C. White, *Merchants of Death: The American Tobacco Industry* (New York, 1988). The phrase "the tobaccoism holocaust" comes from an editorial in *JAMA* 255 (1986), 1923.

9. C. W. Baines, *The Cigarette* (Newport News, Va., 1913), 14.

10. *NYT*, Oct. 16, 1993; Patrick O'Neill, "Casualties in America's Nicotine War," Newhouse News Service, published in *Seattle Times*, Oct. 2, 1994; *Time*, Aug. 21, 1991; "Marketplace," National Public Radio, Sept. 16, 1997; Garrison Keillor, "Where There's Smoke There's Ire," *American Health*, Dec. 1989, 50.

11. Richard Corliss, "What's All the Fuming About?" *Time*, Apr. 18, 1994, 65.

## 1. Birth of the Coffin Nail

1. William A. Alcott, *Tobacco: Its Effects on the Human System, Physical, Intellectual, and Moral* (New York, 1883), preface.

2. Mrs. E. C. Marshall interview with Frank Rounds, Charlotte, N.C., 1963, 42, Duke Endowment Papers, DU; JBD testimony, 3480–81.

3. Jack J. Gottsegen, *Tobacco: A Study of Its Consumption in the United States* (New York, 1940), tables on 34, 36, 39, 43; *NYT*, Jan. 29, 1884.

4. JBD testimony, 3282; William K. Boyd, *The Story of Durham* (Durham, 1925), 76.

5. Sarah A. Dickson, *Panacea or Precious Bane: Tobacco in Sixteenth Century Literature* (New York, 1954), 106; Richard B. Tennant, *The American Cigarette Industry: A Study in Economic Analysis and Public Policy* (New York, 1971; orig. New Haven, 1950), 129–30; *The London World*, in *NYT*, Feb. 8, 1883.

6. Russell T. Trall, *Tobacco: Its History, Nature and Effects, with Facts and Figures for Tobacco-Users* (New York, 1854), 4; Schooler to Mary Eliza (Fleming) Schooler, Edge Hill, Virginia, Aug. 6, 1868, in Nannie Mae Tilley, *The Bright Tobacco Industry, 1860–1929* (Chapel Hill, 1948), 507–8.

7. U.S. Laws, Statutes, 38th Cong., 1st sess. (1864), chap. 173; Tennant, *American Cigarette Industry*, 16; A. McDonald, L. Schwabacher (doing business as McDonald & Schwabacher) v. William H. Watson (case file number 0993/1007, 1884), Frontier Justice Case Files, Washington Territorial Court Records, Washington State Archives, Olympia.

8. 52nd Cong., 1st sess., 1892, Senate Report 1001.

9. George Watts Hill, transcript of oral history interview with James Leutze, 1986, 42, UNC.

10. Washington Duke memoir, in *Raleigh News and Observer*, Apr. 5, 1896; JBD testimony, 3277; Robert F. Durden, *The Dukes of Durham, 1865–1929* (Durham, N.C., 1975), 18–19.

11. Ben Dixon MacNeill, "Duke," *American Mercury*, August 1929, 430–38, esp. 431.

12. J. B. Duke to B. N. Duke and Mrs. B. N. Duke, Aug. 18, 1880, JBD Papers.

13. JBD testimony, 3282–83; Tilley, *Bright Tobacco Industry*, 510.

14. Tilley, *Bright Tobacco Industry*, 18–22; William Bennett, "The Nicotine Fix," *Harvard Magazine*, July–August, 1980, 13.

15. JBD testimony, 3284.

16. Duke to D. B. Strouse, Mar. 16, 1888, JBD Papers.

17. Quote from *Alamance Gleaner*, Aug. 28, 1886, in Paul Escott, *Many Excellent People: Power and Privilege in North Carolina, 1850–1900* (Chapel Hill, 1985), 197.

18. B. N. Duke to D. B. Strouse, Mar. 30, 1886; Strouse to W. Duke Sons and Co., Aug. 23, 1886, both in JBD Papers; Tennant, *American Cigarette Industry*, 22–23.

19. JBD testimony, 3286; D. B. Strouse to W. Duke Sons and Co., Feb. 8, 1888; J. B. Duke to Strouse, Mar. 16, 1888; and reply, Mar. 23, 1888, all in JBD Papers.

20. Tilley, *Bright Tobacco Industry*, 565–67.

21. JBD testimony, 3286–88.; *NYT*, Jan. 22, 1890; Duke to D. B. Strouse, Nov. 26, 1885, JBD Papers. In 1887, Duke failed to convince major competitors to join him; Strouse to Duke, July 8, 1887; and reply, July 19, 1887, JBD. See also U.S. Bureau of Corporations, *Report of the Commissioner of Corporations on the Tobacco Industry*, part 2 (Washington, D.C., 1915), 96.

22. For an analysis of the trust's operations and profits, see Tennant, *American Cigarette Industry*, 49–57.

23. Mark Sullivan, *Our Times: The United States, 1900–1925* (New York, 1932), 4: 374; Frances M. Trollope, *Domestic Manners of the Americans* (New York, 1901; orig. 1832), 20, 164; Charles Dickens, *American Notes*, part 2 (London, 1842), 52.

24. Herbert Manchester, *The Diamond Match Company: A Century of Service, of Progress, and of Growth, 1835–1935* (New York, 1935), 14, 35–36, 46–47, 67; Robert Sobel, *They Satisfy: The Cigarette in American Life* (New York, 1978), 66–71.

25. "The World's Great Monarchs and Their Favorite Smokes," *London Express*, in *Seattle Post-Intelligencer*, June 27, 1909; *NYT*, May 11, 1914 (Edison); *Seattle Post-Intelligencer*, Jan. 23, 1903 (cigar-smoking legislator); *NYT*, Dec. 3, 1893 (pipe-smoking anti-cigarette activist).

26. Harris Lewine, *Goodbye to All That* (New York, 1970), 21; *The Truth About Cigarettes*, Cuyler Series 1 (Chicago, n.d.), 2, copy in HFF Papers. Sullivan quoted in Jerome E. Brooks, *The Mighty Leaf: Tobacco Through the Centuries* (Boston, 1952), 259.

27. Stephen Crane, *Maggie: A Girl of the Streets* (New York, 1988; orig. 1893), 22, 55; Charles and Mary Beard, *The Rise of American Civilization* (New York, 1943), 2: 392; Edward Hyatt, *The Cigarette Boy* (Sacramento, ca. 1913), 7.

28. *NYT*, Jan. 11, 1879; Carl Theophilus Odhner, *Tobacco Talk by an Old Smoker, Giving the Science of Tobacco: Its Botany, Chemistry, Uses* (Philadelphia, 1894), 49–50, 55–57; E. A. King, *The Cigarette and Youth* (Newport, N.Y., 1896), 5–6, copy in AC; *NYT*, Aug. 14, 1887. Headlines from *NYT*, Aug. 10, 1887; *Detroit Tribune*, Oct. 2, 1896. For the identification of nicotine, see Jordan

Goodman, *Tobacco in History: The Cultures of Dependence* (London, 1994), 116–17.

29. Lewine, *Goodbye to All That*, 80 ff; *NYT*, Apr. 7, June 17, 1907; May 31, 1914. In 1919, Ralph Sayre and Elias Yanovsky of Washington, D.C., patented a method of removing nicotine from tobacco; U.S. Patent Office, no. 1,294,310, reported in *Tobacco*, Mar. 27, 1919, 32. The term "coffin nails" was in common use by the 1890s; see King, *Cigarette and Youth*, 3. Its origin is not clear. According to Eric Partridge, *Dictionary of Slang and Unconventional English* (New York, 8th ed., 1984), it dates from about 1885. This would coincide with the mechanization of the cigarette industry.

30. *NYT*, May 15, 1910.

31. Josiah Strong, *Our Country: Its Possible Future and Its Present Crisis* (New York, 1885), 161, 170, 178.

32. Mastheads of the ACL show Strong on the advisory board in 1911 and 1912.

33. Mrs. John A. Logan, "The Evils of Cigarette Smoking" (copyrighted by William Randolph Hearst; reprinted by ACL, Chicago, [ca. 1902]), copy in HFF Papers; quotes are at 3, 4. John A. Logan served several terms in Congress and was James G. Blaine's vice presidential running mate in 1884. He died in 1886. Mary Logan was on the ACL advisory council in 1911 and 1912.

34. John Ellis, *The Deterioration of the Puritan Stock and Its Causes* (New York, 1884), was one of the first to mention "race suicide."

35. For example, see I. L. Kephart, *The Tobacco Question* (Dayton, Ohio, 1882), esp. 28–29, 159–61; Abiel Abbot Livermore, *Anti-Tobacco* (Boston, 1883), 32, both in AC; and Margaret Woods Lawrence, *The Tobacco Problem* (Boston, 6th ed., 1897), 208.

36. John Harvey Kellogg, *Tobaccoism, Or How Tobacco Kills* (Battle Creek, Mich., 1922), 123. Kellogg frequently reprinted as pamphlets anti-tobacco articles originally published in his magazine *Good Health*; see, for example, "The Physical Effects of Alcohol and Tobacco" (1882), "The Smoker's Heart" (n.d.), "The Smoker's Liver" (n.d.), "The Immorality of Smoking" (1922), and "Is Smoking Harmful?" (1927), all in JHK Papers.

37. Ellen G. White, unpublished manuscript, 1881, quoted in Ronald L. Numbers, *Prophetess of Health: A Study of Ellen G. White* (New York, 1976), 167. Kellogg described tobacco as a "race poison" in a speech at a conference on "Hygiene and Heredity," Calvary Baptist Church, Washington, D.C., May 5–7, 1884; program in JHK Papers, box 13. See also James C. Whorton, *Crusaders for Fitness* (Princeton, 1982), esp. 203–5.

38. Edward Bellamy, *Looking Backward* (New York, 1986; orig. 1888), 191.

39. Gottsegen, *Tobacco*, 147–48; Laurel Thatcher Ulrich, *Good Wives: Image and Reality in the Lives of Women in Northern New England, 1650–1750* (New York, 1980), 95, 100–101, 227 (note also the photograph of clay pipes used by colonial women, following p. 108); John S. Haller Jr., *American Medicine in Transition, 1840–1910* (Urbana, Ill., 1981), 159; "Narrative of the Captivity of Mrs. Mary Rowlandson, 1682," in Charles H. Lincoln, *Narratives of the Indian Wars* (New York, 1913), 134; Benjamin Ferris to Deborah Ferris, June 29, 1834, Ferris Collection, Friends Historical Library, Swarthmore College, Swarthmore, Pa.

40. Ivor Noel Hume, *Martin's Hundred* (New York, 1982), 295; Durand of Dauphine, *A Huguenot Exile in Virginia; or, Voyages of a Frenchman Exiled for His Religion, with a Description of Virginia and Maryland* (New York, 1934; orig. 1687), 111, 118; Virginia Ingraham Burr, ed., *The Secret Eye: The Journal of Ella Gertrude Clanton Thomas, 1848–1889* (Chapel Hill, 1990), 95; W. S. Kimball, "Ye 'Good Old Days': Historical Reminiscences of Early Day Casper," *Casper (Wyoming) Tribune Herald*, Dec. 2, 1945.

41. Nancy F. Cott discusses the "canon of domesticity" in *The Bonds of Womanhood: Woman's Sphere in New England, 1780–1835* (New Haven, 1977). See also Mary P. Ryan, *Cradle of the Middle Class: The Family in Oneida County, New York, 1790–1865* (Cambridge, 1981).

42. Frances Willard, *Glimpses of Fifty Years: The Autobiography of an American Woman* (Chicago, 1889), 642, 427; Ruth Bordin, *Frances Willard: A Biography* (Chapel Hill, 1986), 251.

43. Trall, *Tobacco*, 4; Charles A. Greene, *The Tobacco Slave and How to Be Liberated from Its Fetters* (Boston, 1889), 117, copy in AC.

44. C. K. True, *A Word to Lads on Tobacco* (Cincinnati, 1877), 25–26, copy in Museum of American History Archives, Washington, D.C.; *NYT*, Sept. 1, 1879; Montez photograph in Wolfgang Schivelbusch, *Tastes of Paradise: A Social History of Spices, Stimulants, and Intoxicants* (New York, 1992), 124; Lewine, *Goodbye to All That*, 58.

45. Sobel, *They Satisfy*, 21; Gay MacLaren, "Morally We Roll Along," *Atlantic Monthly*, Apr. 1938, 450.

46. Josephus Daniels, *Editor in Politics* (Chapel Hill, 1941), 239.

47. WCTU Annual Meeting Minutes (1893), 313; Joseph Hatton, *Cigarette Papers for After-Dinner Smoking* (Philadelphia, 1892), 258. "My Cigarette" was published in Hatton, 264–65; John Bain, *Tobacco in Song and Story* (New York, 1896), 55–56, and elsewhere.

48. Tobacco Collection, W. Duke, Sons, and Co., picture cabinet 4, drawer 3, DU (see also the Allen and Ginter picture collection, same location); Daniels, *Editor in Politics*, 393.

49. Washington Duke to J. B. Duke, Oct. 17, 1894, BND Papers.

50. *NYT*, Apr. 23, 1905.

51. Oscar Wilde, *The Picture of Dorian Gray* (New York, 1931; orig. 1891), 27, 90–91.

52. Greene, *Tobacco Slave*, 117; James J. Jeffreys, *The Curse of the Nation* (Marshall, Mich., 1912), 25; L. Bremer, *Tobacco, Insanity, and Nervousness* (St. Louis, Mo., 1892), 6, copy in AC; U.S. Department of Health and Human Services, *Preventing Tobacco Use Among Young People: A Report of the Surgeon General* (Atlanta, Ga.: U.S. Department of Health and Human Services, Public Health Service, Centers for Disease Control and Prevention, Office on Smoking and Health, 1994), 34–38.

53. David F. Musto, "A Brief History of American Drug Control," 12–14, and Dennis Joseph Pfennig, "Early Twentieth Century Responses to the Drug Problem," 25–26, both in *Magazine of History*, 6: 2 (1991); Upton Sinclair, *The Jungle* (New York, 1981; orig. 1906), 330.

54. *NYT*, Aug. 14, 1887; *Chicago Tribune*, Nov. 16, 1888; *Saturday Review*, May 4, 1889, 528; Thurman B. Rice, *The Hoosier Health Officer: A Biography of Dr. John N. Hurty* (Indianapolis, 1946), 326.

55. Richard G. Schlaadt, *Tobacco and Health* (Guilford, Conn., 1992), 9; Lawrence, *Tobacco Problem*, 163.

56. Harvey W. Wiley et al., *The Cigarette: What It Contains and What It Does Not Contain* (Boston, 1892), 11–12, 7.

57. For laws regarding "adulterated" cigarettes, see Washington, *Session Laws* (1895), 125; Minnesota, *Laws of Minnesota* (1907), 544; South Dakota, *Laws Passed at the Tenth Session of the Legislature of South Dakota* (1907), 95; and Michigan, *Public Acts of Michigan* (1909), 441. West Virginia, *Acts of the West Virginia Legislature* (1891), 14, and Kansas, *Laws* (1889), chap. 256, sec. 1, banned the sale of cigarettes and "other narcotics" to minors. The Supreme Court justice is quoted in *U.S. Reports* 179 (1900), 367. For the WCTU, see Lawrence, *Tobacco Problem*, 10; and WCTU Annual Meeting Minutes (1887), cciv. The Department of Narcotics was renamed the Anti-Narcotics Department in 1897.

58. Harvey W. Wiley, "The Little White Slaver," *Good Housekeeping*, Jan. 1916, 95; Charles B. Towns, "Injury of Tobacco and Its Relation to Other Drug Habits," *Century*, Mar. 1912, 770; Ford, *Little White Slaver*, 14.

59. John C. Burnham, *Bad Habits: Drinking, Smoking, Taking Drugs, Gambling, Sexual Misbehavior, and Swearing in American History* (New York, 1993), esp. 5–11; WCTU Annual Meeting Minutes (Presidential Address, 1886), 72; (1891), 86. For cigarettes and insanity, see *Laborer's Emancipator*, Dec. 22, 1892; *Spokane (Washington) Spokesman-Review*, Oct. 18, 1888; *NYT*, Jan. 29, 1893.

60. Jordan to C. L. Flatter, July 25, 1927, DSJ Papers.

61. Lawrence, *Tobacco Problem*, 152; Benjamin Rush, *An Inquiry into the Effects of Ardent Spirits upon the Human Body and Mind*, reprinted in *Medical Inquiries and Observations* (Philadelphia, 2nd ed., 1805), 1: 366; Rush, *Observations upon the Influence of the Habitual Use of Tobacco, upon Health, Morals, and Property* (Philadelphia, 1798), quoted in Lawrence, 84–85; William A. Alcott, *The Use of Tobacco; Its Physical, Intellectual, and Moral Effects on the Human System* (Boston, 2nd ed., 1847), 5, 26; Alcott, *Tobacco: Its Effects on the Human System*, preface.

62. *Raleigh News and Observer*, Jan. 30, 1901 (appeal to youth); *Sacramento Bee*, Nov. 3, 1910 (gift packages); E. Rodgers, J. N. Williamson Jr., and Paul Dillard to B. N. Duke, May 10, 1891, BND Papers; *Seattle Mail and Herald*, May 25, 1901.

63. *NYT*, Jan. 11, 1879; Oct. 27, 1905; Aug. 8, 1909; Nov. 23, 1887; Sept. 27, 1890; Jan. 11, 1891.

64. Lincoln Steffens, *The Autobiography of Lincoln Steffens* (New York, 1931), 244–45.

65. South Carolina, *Acts and Joint Resolutions of the General Assembly* (1889), 321.

66. Mary Earhart, *Frances Willard: From Prayers to Politics* (Chicago, 1944), 158; Willard, *Glimpses*, 392.

67. WCTU Annual Meeting Minutes (1891), 136; Willard annotation quoted in Earhart, *Frances Willard*, 297.

68. WCTU Annual Meeting Minutes (1897), 105; (1900), 249. Before Willard's death in 1898, the WCTU approved six resolutions calling for the pro-

hibition of cigarettes; Annual Meeting Minutes (1887), cc–cci; (1889), 164; (1890), 60; (1893), 314; (1895), 241; and (1897), 51.

69. Tax figures from Tennant, *American Cigarette Industry*, 55; WCTU Annual Meeting Minutes (1897), 343–433; (1899), 232.

70. Lawrence, *Tobacco Problem*, 389–92. In 1889, a "prominent cigarette manufacturer"—probably either James B. Duke or his brother Benjamin— promised a WCTU delegation that he would stop using "obscene pictures" in cigarettes produced for the domestic market; WCTU Annual Meeting Minutes (1889), ccli. For other anti-cigarette activities under the WCTU banner, see reports of the Anti-Narcotics Department, in the Annual Meeting Minutes for the 1890s.

71. Gottsegen, *Tobacco*, 11.

72. U.S. Bureau of Corporations, *Report of the Commissioner of Corporations on the Tobacco Industry*, part 3 (Washington, D.C.: 1915), 150. Tennant, *American Cigarette Industry*, cites the tax increase as one of several "adverse influences" at work on the industry during this period, along with "public hostility" and a ban on cigarette coupon advertising (55).

73. JBD testimony, 3306, 3397–98.

74. WCTU Annual Meeting Minutes (1900), 45, 108, 248.

75. Duke to D. M. Stansbury, Sept. 15, 1896; Duke to J. D. Stacy, Dec. 5, 1899, and June 8, 1904; see also J. R. Hutchings to Duke, July 9[?], 1894; all in JBD Papers.

76. Junius Parker, memorial address, Dec. 10, 1935, Williamson Whitehead Fuller Papers, DU.

77. Duke to W. C. Purdy, Aug. 7, 1900, JBD Papers. *A copy of The Truth About Cigarettes: Papers Read and Discussed by the Medico-Legal Society of New York* (New York, 1898; reprinted from *Medico-Legal Journal*, Dec. 1897, Mar. 1898) is in the rare book room, DU.

78. Duke executive quoted in Tennant, *American Cigarette Industry*, 139; *NYT*, Mar. 17, 1893.

79. *New York World*, Dec. 12, 1894; Duke to Levi P. Morton, Dec. 31, 1894; Duke to George W. Turner, Dec. 19, 1894, both in JBD Papers. The *New York Recorder* published from Feb. 18, 1891, until Oct. 11, 1896. Apparently, both James B. and Benjamin N. Duke invested in it; see J. R. Patterson to B. N. Duke, Aug. 14, 1891, BND Papers. The investment was not a profitable one, and James B. Duke refused to make any additional contributions in 1895; Duke to Balkley, Dunton, and Co., Jan. 10, 1895, JBD Papers.

80. *New York World*, Dec. 20, 1894 (see also *NYT*, Dec. 30, 1894); *Proceedings of the City Council of the City of Chicago, 1896–1897* (Chicago, 1897), 1714–15. For flavoring agents added to cigarettes, see B. N. Duke to William G. Emery, Dec. 16, 1893, BND Papers; and the formulas for "Satin" and "Pin Head" cigarettes, filed as miscellany, Aug. 12, 1912, May 13, 1916, Arthur Vance Cole Papers, DU.

81. *New York World*, Dec. 30, 1894; Duke to Levi P. Morton, Dec. 31, 1894, JBD Papers. For Duke's support of Republican causes, see Duke to F. P. Olcott, Sept. 22, 1900, and Duke to E. C. Stokes, May 19, 1904, JBD Papers.

82. *NYT*, Feb. 7, 1898.

83. "When Smoke Made Sparks in the Legislature," *Indianapolis Star Magazine*, Mar. 2, 1980, 28–29. A legislative committee made cursory efforts to file charges against the alleged briber; *NYT*, Mar. 23, 1909.

84. Durden, *Dukes of Durham*, 4–5, 110–11; Emma Pegram to George Pegram, Apr. 14, 1901, Nov. 18, 1900, Craven-Pegram Family Papers, DU. Josephus Daniels expressed a similar point of view; *Editor in Politics*, 118–19, 490. In his biography of the Duke family, Durden argues that self-interest was a minor motive in the Dukes' philanthropy. He concludes that the family's generosity came largely from its commitment to Methodism (with its emphasis on tithing) and to civic pride; *Dukes of Durham*, 82–83.

85. *Minutes of the Ninth Session of the Western North Carolina Annual Conference of the Methodist Episcopal Church South, Winston, N.C., Nov. 16–22, 1898* (Raleigh, 1898), 33, Divinity School Library, DU.

86. *Raleigh News and Observer*, May 25, 1901; Joseph L. Morrison, *Josephus Daniels Says: An Editor's Political Odyssey from Bryan to Wilson and FDR, 1894–1913* (Durham, 1962), 125–28; Josephus Daniels, *Tar Heel Editor*, (Chapel Hill, 1939), 471; Durden, *Dukes of Durham*, 158; Robert, *Story of Tobacco*, 162.

87. *Raleigh News and Observer*, Feb. 21, 1897; North Carolina, *Journal of the House* (1897), H.B. 52; (1903), H.B. 1313; (1911), H.B. 41; (1913), H.B. 564; (1917), H.B. 1500; *Senate Journal* (1901), S.B. 91; (1905), S.B. 711.

88. U.S. Bureau of Corporations, *Report of the Commissioner of Corporations*, part 3, 2; JBD testimony, 3297. One of the earliest and most successful of the diversification ventures was the Erwin Cotton Mills in Durham; see W. A. Erwin to B. N. Duke, Jan. 9, 1893, BND Papers. For a general reprise of Duke's business enterprises from a former associate, see John T. Woodside, unpublished autobiography, ca. 1933, Southern Historical Collection, UNC, esp. pp. 58–61. Durden, *Dukes of Durham*, examines the family's commercial interests at length; see esp. pp. 74–80, 128–33, 137–39, 148–51.

89. WCTU Annual Meeting Minutes (1898), 246.

## 2. The Clean Life Crusade

1. James J. Jeffreys, *The Curse of the Nation* (Marshall, Mich., 1912), 7.

2. ACL incorporation papers, filed Dec. 19, 1899; in Dissolved Domestic Corporation Charters, ISA; *NYT*, July 12, 1901.

3. Robert M. Sobel, *They Satisfy: The Cigarette in American Life* (New York, 1978), 55.

4. Herbert Asbury, *Carry Nation* (New York, 1929), 278–79.

5. *Chicago Tribune*, Aug. 25, 1919.

6. *NYT*, Feb. 22, 1922; Sinclair Lewis, *Arrowsmith* (New York, 1961; orig. 1925), 239–41.

7. Frances Warfield, "Lost Cause: A Portrait of Lucy Page Gaston," *Outlook and Independent*, Feb. 12, 1930, 244–47, 275–76 (quote at 244).

8. State of Illinois, Department of Public Health, Division of Vital Statistics, death certificate, Aug. 20, 1924; Peter Beck memoir, in Alex Kerr, ed., *History of the City of Harvey, 1890–1962* (Harvey, Ill., 1962), 35. See also *Daily Pantagraph* (Bloomington, Ill.), Aug. 21, 1924; and John William Leonard, ed., *Woman's Who's Who of America, 1914–1915: A Biographical Dictionary of Contemporary Women of the United States and Canada* (New York, 1914), 317–18.

9. Warfield, "Lost Cause," 244. Edward Page Gaston's activities were reported regularly in *US*; see esp. Feb. 4, 1887; Oct. 29, 1896; Aug. 3, 1899. See also Ernest H. Cherrington, ed., *Standard Encyclopedia of the Alcohol Problem* (Westerville, Ohio, 1930), 1073–74.

10. Illinois State University archives list Gaston as having attended for one term during the 1881–82 academic year; Jo Ann Rayfield, university archivist, letter to the author, Apr. 15, 1994; *Daily Pantagraph*, Aug. 21, 1924.

11. *Daily Pantagraph*, Aug. 21, 1924; Leonard, *Woman's Who's Who*, 317; Sobel, *They Satisfy*, 53.

12. Lucy Page Gaston, "Children's Temperance Work in Illinois" (n.d.), 5, copy in Frances E. Willard Memorial Library, Evanston, Ill.

13. *US*, Sept. 22, 1892; Oct. 29, 1891; May 5, 1892.

14. WCTU Annual Meeting Minutes (1893), 454. On Harvey, see James Gilbert, *Perfect Cities: Chicago's Utopias of 1893* (Chicago, 1991), 195–98.

15. Chicago Title and Trust Company as Trustee of Harvey Land Association, "Contract of Sale" (Chicago, 1893), Harvey Land Company Manuscripts, Thornton Township Historical Society, Harvey, Ill.; Gilbert, *Perfect Cities*, 197; Horace Holmes and Peter Beck memoirs, in Kerr, *History*, 32, 34.

16. Lucy Page Gaston, "Harvey's Danger," *US*, Aug. 22, 1895; see also Dec. 5, 1895; Oct. 7, 1897. For the Gaston family in Harvey, see Kerr, *History*, 29, 152. The first *Harvey City Directory* (1907) lists Alexander Hugh Gaston as a nurseryman. For Gaston's career in journalism, see Leonard, *Woman's Who's Who*, 318; and a report on the history of Harvey's newspapers, in *Harvey Star*, Jan. 4, 1990.

17. *US*, Jan. 30, 1896; Dec. 12, 1895; Mar. 4, 1897. Ruth Bordin, *Frances Willard: A Biography* (Chapel Hill, 1986), is the best source on Willard and her influence as a reformer in the 1890s. During most of this period, Willard lived in Evanston, headquarters of the WCTU, not far from Harvey.

18. *US* reported frequently on Gaston's activities during the 1890s; see esp. Dec. 3, 1896; Jan. 21, July 15, Aug. 5, 12, and Nov. 25, 1897. For her activities as national superintendent of the Christian Citizenship League, see WCTU Annual Meeting Minutes (1897), 14.

19. Margaret W. Lawrence, *The Tobacco Problem*, (Boston, 6th ed., 1897), 36; *US*, Dec. 5, 1895; Perry R. Duis, "Cigarettes and Sin: Lucy Page Gaston Led a Children's Crusade Against the Evils of the Weed," *Chicago*, September 1983, 142; U.S. Department of Commerce, Bureau of the Census, *Historical Statistics of the United States: Colonial Times to 1970* (Washington, D.C., 1975), Table H751–765, Institutions of Higher Education, Degrees Conferred by Sex, 1870–1970, 386.

20. Frank V. Irish to Herbert F. Fisk, Apr. 26, 1902, HFF Papers; *US*, Jan. 30, 1896.

21. Gaston to Jordan, July 21, 1908, Feb. 17, 1911, DSJ Papers. Jordan's epigrams are quoted in Edward Hyatt, *The Cigarette Boy* (Sacramento, 1913), 10; and elsewhere.

22. *US*, May 28, 1896; Edwin D. Wheelock, president of the National Christian Citizenship League, to John R. Tanner, governor of Illinois, Sept. 27, 1897, John R. Tanner Papers, ISA. No correspondence between Gaston and Clark or Crafts has survived, but both men are listed as officers of the Anti-Cigarette League on letterheads for the years 1912 to 1917.

23. *US*, May 7, Oct. 29, 1896; Illinois secretary of state, *Official Vote of the State of Illinois, General Election, 1896*, Vote for Trustees of the University of Illinois (Springfield, 1897), 16–18. One obituary described Gaston as "an ardent advocate of woman suffrage"; *Chicago Daily Tribune*, Aug. 21, 1924.

24. *The Boy*, Apr. 1, 1900, 6; *US*, July 9, 1908; Warfield, "Lost Cause," 245. See also Lawrence, *Tobacco Problem*, 36.

25. Illinois, 38th General Assembly (1893), S.B. 310, H.B. 185; 39th General Assembly (1895), S.B. 245, 307; 40th General Assembly (1897), S.B. 134, 245; 41st General Assembly (1899), H.B. 238.

26. For example, see James A. Walton, superintendent of the California Anti-Cigarette League, to David Starr Jordan, Nov. 11, 1925, DSJ Papers.

27. Josephus Daniels, *Tar Heel Editor* (Chapel Hill, 1939), 471–73; Jerome E. Brooks, *The Mighty Leaf: Tobacco Through the Centuries* (Boston, 1952), 253–54; Bernard M. Baruch, *Baruch: My Own Story* (New York, 1957), 110; *NYT*, Mar. 17, 1893. Retailers continued to complain about the low profit margin on cigarettes for many years; see *Tobacco*, Mar. 14, 1918, 29.

28. Washington, *Session Laws* (1893), 82; *NYT*, Mar. 17, 1893.

29. *Seattle Press-Times*, May 8, 1893.

30. *NYT*, June 15, 1893; Washington, *Session Laws* (1895), 125–27.

31. Lawrence, *Tobacco Problem*, 36; Illinois, 40th General Assembly (1897), Petitions in Favor of House Bill 221, ISA (quote from a petition submitted by teachers in Cairo, Ill., Mar. 26, 1897).

32. Illinois, 40th General Assembly (1897), H.B. 221, S.B. 245, 134; *Journal of the Senate* (1897), 671; Edwin D. Wheelock to John R. Tanner, Sept. 27, 1897, John R. Tanner Papers, ISA.

33. *Proceedings of the City Council of the City of Chicago* (1896–1897), 1714–15. Recipes for ten brands of cigarettes produced by the American Tobacco Company in the 1890s are included in the E. J. Parrish Memorandum Book, 1899–1900, E. J. Parrish Papers, Special Collections Library, DU. All contained glycerine; half also contained sugar.

34. "Why the Cigarette is Deadly" and "Maxim, Burbank, Edison, and Hamilton Attack the Cigarette," *Clean Life Series*, No. 1 and 2 (Chicago, n.d.), copies in CTCA Papers, entry 396, box 2; quotes from *The Boy*, Apr. 15, 1903, front cover, and *US*, Jan. 18, 1900.

35. *US*, Jan. 18, 1900.

36. *Raleigh (North Carolina) News and Observer*, Jan. 30, 1901; *US*, Feb. 2, 1899.

37. Anti-Cigarette League newsletter, May 1908, DSJ Papers.

38. Members of the original board of directors are listed in the ACL incorporation papers, ISA.

39. *US*, Dec. 28, 1899, Jan. 18, 1900; biographical sketch of Rep. Charles A. Evans, *Wisconsin Blue Book* (Madison, 1905), 1096.

40. Lucy Page Gaston, "The Deadly Cigarette," *National Series Leaflets* (Chicago, n.d.), 2, copy in DSJ Papers; D. H. Kress, "Why the Cigarette Is Deadly," *Clean Life Series*, No. 1 (Chicago, n.d.), 3, copy in CTCA Papers, entry 396, box 2; "Drugs and Drink," in *The Boy*, first quarter, 1914, 27; Edison to Henry Ford, April 26, 1914, in Ford, *The Case Against the Little White Slaver* (Detroit, 1914), 5.

41. *NYT*, Feb. 27, 1910. See also *Education*, Nov. 1907, 154–60; *Cigarette Papers* (Chicago, ca. 1915), copy in the Tobacco Collection, box 2, DU; and William A. McKeever, *The Cigarette Smoking Boy* (Lawrence, Kan., 1909) and *Training the Boy* (New York, 1913).

42. Harvey W. Wiley, "The Little White Slaver," *Good Housekeeping*, Jan.

1916, 91, 95; David Starr Jordan, "Three Counts Against Tobacco," *Temperance Educational Quarterly*, July 1912, 1. In Greek mythology, the waters of the river Lethe induced oblivion.

43. *US*, Jan. 28, 1909; Charles Larsen, *The Good Fight: The Life and Times of Ben B. Lindsey* (Chicago, 1972), 97; Ben B. Lindsey and Harvey J. O'Higgins, *The Beast* (Seattle, 1970; orig. 1910), 105–6. Lindsey advocated "companionate marriage" in a series of articles titled "The Revolt of Modern Youth," *Redbook Magazine*, Dec. 1926 through May 1927.

44. Irving Fisher and Eugene Lyman Fisk, *How to Live: Rules for Healthful Living Based on Modern Science* (New York, 1915); *US*, July 4–18, 1918; Fisher, *How to Live: Rules for Healthful Living* (New York, 21st ed., 1946), preface. For Fisher's reputation as an economist, see John Kenneth Galbraith, *The Great Crash* (New York, 1961; orig. 1954), 73, 148–49.

45. John Harvey Kellogg, *Tobaccoism, or How Tobacco Kills* (Battle Creek, Mich., 1922); William DeKleine memoir, chap. 4, William DeKleine Papers, MHC. Kellogg's anti-tobacco pamphlets, lectures, and a description of his 1922 film are in the JHK Papers. A collection of 77 lantern slides prepared by Kellogg's staff at Battle Creek in 1911, used in anti-tobacco lectures by James W. Fields, a Kansas dentist, is held by the Kansas State Historical Society.

46. [Samuel Bishop Goff], *Petition to Congress to Pass a Bill to Prohibit the Growing of Tobacco and the Importation of It* (Camden, N.J., 1913), 3; Lucy Page Gaston, letter to the editor, *NYS*, Sept. 2, 1919.

47. Jeffreys, *Curse of the Nation*, 65–66; *Seattle Post-Intelligencer*, June 2, 11, 1909. For a report on a typical Catholic Church "smoker," see *Seattle Post-Intelligencer*, Feb. 17, 1903.

48. *Christian Mission Magazine*, Oct. 1, 1870, 148, copy in Salvation Army Archives and Research Center, Alexandria, Va.; William Booth, *Orders and Regulations for the Soldiers of the Salvation Army*, 1890, cited in *The Case Against Smoking: The Salvation Army Point of View* (New York, 1974), 3. See also Herbert A. Wisbey Jr., *Soldiers Without Swords: A History of the Salvation Army in the United States* (New York, 1956), 20, 77, 150. The Salvation Army chapter in Spokane, Washington, was among those that sponsored local anti-cigarette leagues; *Spokane Spokesman-Review*, Feb. 7, 1909.

49. E. A. King, *The Cigarette and Youth* (Newport, Ky., 1896), 1, copy in AC; John Q. A. Henry, *The Deadly Cigarette* (London, 1906), 120; George J. Fisher, "Is Smoking Injurious?" *AM*, Dec. 1912, 122; L. R. Welzmiller, "Effects of Cigaret Smoking on Young Men," *AM*, May 1913, 393; *Official Bulletin*, Jan. 1914, 28 (on crime); "Letter from Connie Mack, Manager Philadelphia American Baseball Club," *Ohio Association News*, Aug–Sept. 1913, 8; speech by Henry W. Newkirk to the YMCA of Ann Arbor, Michigan, Mar. 31, 1902, Henry W. Newkirk Papers, MHC; Lucy Page Gaston, "The Anti-Cigarette Cause," *American Youth*, Dec. 1914, 307, 309. The YMCA also promoted Henry Ford's anti-cigarette book, *The Case Against the Little White Slaver*; see *Ohio Association News*, June–July 1915, 11.

50. Daniel H. Kress, "The Cigarette As Related to Moral Reform," *Interstate Medical Journal* 23 (1916), 485–89; *Literary Digest*, Dec. 6, 1913, 1118. See also Kress, *The Cigarette as a Physician Sees It* (Mountain View, Calif., 1931), esp. chap. 8, "Tobacco's Effect on Character"; John N. Hurty to

*Indianapolis Star*, Feb. 21, 1916; Hurty, "Some Health Points" (n.d.); "Conservation of the Human Race," speech to the National Conservation Congress, Indianapolis, Oct. 2, 1912, both in John N. Hurty Papers, Indiana State Board of Health, State Archives, Indianapolis; Thurman B. Rice, *The Hoosier Health Officer: A Biography of Dr. John N. Hurty* (Indianapolis, 1946), 286, 328, 351. For Kress's early work in the sanitary reform movement, see *NYT*, Oct. 30, 1898.

51. Anon., *Work for Chimny-sweepers: Or A Warning for Tobacconists* (London, 1936; orig. 1601), quote is on the page headed, "eight principall reasons and arguments" (opposing tobacco); A Counterblaste to Tobacco (Westminster, 1895; orig. 1604), 112; Benjamin Rush cited in Lawrence, 84–85; George Morton, graduating essay, University of Pennsylvania Medical School, 1822, copy in Morton Family Papers, University of Virginia Library, Charlottesville; J. R. Wigle, thesis submitted to the Medical School Faculty, University of Michigan, 1862; William H. Ralston, thesis submitted 1865; Eltham Watson, thesis submitted 1868, all in Medical School Theses, MHC. For a survey of sixteenth-century literature regarding tobacco, see Sarah A. Dickson, *Panacea or Precious Bane: Tobacco in Sixteenth Century Literature* (New York, 1954), esp. 66, 219–20, 196–99.

52. *Laws of the State of Illinois* (1907), 265; Missouri, 47th General Assembly (1913), H.B. 548. Two of the original seventeen directors of the Anti-Cigarette League were homeopaths: Frank W. Baker, a professor of materia medica at the Chicago Homeopathic College; and Julia Holmes Smith, a graduate of the college; Anti-Cigarette League incorporation papers, filed Dec. 19, 1899, in Dissolved Domestic Corporation Charters, ISA.

53. Bernarr A. Macfadden was among the people on the medical fringe who condemned smoking on grounds of health. See Macfadden, *The Virile Powers of Superb Manhood: How Developed, How Lost, How Regained* (New York, 1900), 62; and *The Truth About Tobacco* (New York, 1924), copy in pamphlet collection, DU.

54. Leonard K. Hirshberg, "Truth About Tobacco," *Harper's Weekly*, Jan. 4, 1913, 12–13; unsigned editorial, *JAMA* 138 (1948), 652–53.

55. Charles A. Greene, *The Tobacco Slave and How to be Liberated from its Fetters* (Boston, 1889), 112, copy in AC.

56. Ibid., 72, 110–13; Kellogg, *The Physical Effects of Alcohol and Tobacco* (Battle Creek, Mich., 1882), copy in JHK Papers, box 8; I. L. Kephart et al., *The Tobacco Question* (Dayton, Ohio, 1882), 22; Ethel Gofen, "Report on Smoking 1988," *Current Health*, Nov. 1988, 4–5; *JAMA* 269 (1993), 1069 ff. Lung cancer was not included in the International Classification of Diseases until 1923.

57. Julius Rosenwald to Lucy Page Gaston, May 6, 1912; Gaston to Rosenwald, June 11 and 13, 1912; Rosenwald to Gaston, June 14, 1912, all in JR Papers; *Chicago News*, in *Tobacco*, Jan. 9, 1919, 4; *US*, June 1, 1899.

58. Elbert Hubbard, "The Cigarette," *Cosmopolitan*, August 1913, 2; *NYT*, Nov. 29, 1907; Aug. 27, 1908; Mar. 14, 1909; Dec. 8, 1910 (railroads); *Ohio Association News*, June–July 1914, 9–10 (Colorado Fuel and Iron); *The Boy*, Dec. 15, 1900, 6 (Duluth).

59. John Wanamaker to Henry Ford, in Ford, *Little White Slaver*, 30–31; William Leach, *Land of Desire: Merchants, Power, and the Rise of a New American Culture* (New York, 1994), 46.

60. William R. Heath to Henry Ford, in Ford, *Little White Slaver*, 28; "Cigarette Smoking Prohibited," *Railroad Men*, July 1907, 380.

61. Ford, *Little White Slaver*, 32.

62. *Yakima Herald*, Feb. 12, 1908.

63. *NYT*, Aug. 8, 1909; see also editorial, Aug. 14, 1909.

64. Fisk's comments about the Keeley Institute are written on his copy of "The Evils of Cigarette Smoking," n.d.; *Michigan Advocate*, Oct. 10, 1896; Gaston to Fisk, Mar. 31, 1902, Oct. 30, 1903, all in HFF Papers. In the Old Testament, Moloch was a deity who demanded human sacrifice.

65. Undated note, HFF papers; Fisk quoted in *Quincy* (Michigan) *Herald*, Mar. 13, 1902. This is one of eleven clippings from newspapers around the country in Fisk's papers, all commenting favorably on his action. See also H. O. Smith to the Faculty of Northwestern University, Dec. 6, 1907; Helen Gray to Fisk, March 1, 1907; and "Anti-Cigarette Prog[r]am for the Use of Sunday Schools Appropriate for Anti-Cigarette Sunday, June 27, 1909" (n.d.), 3, all in HFF Papers.

66. *U.S. Reports* 179 (1900), 343; Florida, *Laws* (1907), 229–30; Nevada, *Statutes* (1911), 383. For laws banning cigarette smoking on school property, see West Virginia, *Acts* (1913), 123, and Kentucky, *Statutes* 1 (1915), 732.

67. W. S. Kimball, "Ye 'Good Old Days': Historical Reminiscences of Early Day Casper," *Casper (Wyoming) Tribune Herald*, Dec. 2, 1945; *Tobacco*, Sept. 6, 1917, 28.

68. *NYT*, July 25, Aug. 3, 1911; WCTU Annual Meeting Minutes (1914), 212.

69. David Starr Jordan, "Three Counts Against Tobacco," *Temperance Educational Quarterly*, July 1912, 1; Wiley quoted in "Bad Talk but a Good Purpose," *Life*, Aug. 3, 1911, 178; *The Boy*, first quarter, 1914, 19.

70. *NYT*, June 13, 19, 1913.

71. Tillman to Townsend, May 16,1913, Henry W. Newkirk Papers, MHC.

72. Jeffreys, *Curse of the Nation*, 12; *Reno (Nevada) Evening Gazette*, Aug. 23, 1912.

73. *Chicago Tribune*, Aug. 3, 1913; "Killing the Cigaret Habit," *Literary Digest*, Dec. 6, 1913, 1118; "Boys and the 'Cigaret Cure,' " *Literary Digest*, Feb. 21, 1914, 395–98; *NYT*, March 14, 1914.

74. *NYT*, Jan. 22, 29, Feb. 5, 1914; *Spokane Spokesman-Review*, Feb. 26, 1914; Charles Alma Byers, "A City Fights the Cigarette Habit," *American City*, Apr. 1916, 369–70; *Spokane Spokesman-Review*, Aug. 2, 1902.

75. Gaston to Julius Rosenwald, June 11, 1912, JR Papers; *Laws of the State of Illinois* (1907), 265; *NYT*, Dec. 19, 1907; *Illinois Reports* 231 (1907), 251. In its ruling, the Illinois Supreme Court quibbled only with the language, not the intent of the state's anti-cigarette law, saying, "It is clear, we think, under a proper title, the legislature has the right, under the exercise of its police power, to pass an act prohibiting the sale of cigarettes."

76. *Chicago Daily News*, Dec. 25, 1911; Document 219063, "Cigarettes or cigarette papers, prohibiting the sale or giving away of," brief prepared by Sampson and Putting, attorneys, submitted by Lucy Page Gaston; Daniel H. Kress, general secretary, Anti-Cigarette League, "Why the Cigarette is Deadly" (Chicago, n.d.); Charles Winfield (tobacco lobbyist) to Alderman Laughlin, June

29, 1914; John W. Beckwith (corporation counsel) to Francis D. Connery (Chicago city clerk), Mar. 11, 1915; all in Chicago City Council Proceedings Files, 1915–1916, Illinois Regional Archives Depository, Northeastern Illinois University, Chicago.

77. *Tobacco*, Jan. 25, 1917, 26; *Chicago News*, in *Tobacco*, Jan. 9, 1919, 4. Gaston also petitioned for laws to ban smoking on streetcars in Chicago; *The Boy*, first quarter 1914, 29.

78. Gaston to Rosenwald, June 11, 13, 1912, JR Papers; *US*, Nov. 23, 1911.

79. *The Boy*, first quarter, 1914, 3; Gaston to David Starr Jordan, Jan. 12, 1915, DSJ Papers; *US*, Apr. 24, 1902; *Institution Quarterly*, Sept. 30, 1913, 98.

80. *NYT*, Sept. 12, 1907. A report about Mrs. Vanderbilt's tea and cigarette room appeared in *The Boy*, Apr. 15, 1903, 15. Gaston made another effort to save New York City from the cigarette in 1910; *NYT*, July 20, 1910. A collection of opera and theater programs is in BND Papers, box 113.

81. Compiled from Annual Reports of the Commissioner of Internal Revenue and the U.S. Department of Agriculture, cited in Jack J. Gottsegen, *Tobacco: A Study of Its Consumption in the United States* (New York, 1940), 27, 42.

82. *NYT*, Aug. 8, 1909.

83. Washington, *Session Laws* (1909), chap. 249. For the arrests, see *Seattle Post-Intelligencer*, June 6, 12–15, 19–21, 23–28, 30, 1909; and *The Patriarch*, Aug. 7, 1909.

84. *Seattle Post-Intelligencer*, June 17, 18, 25, 1909; William D. Haywood, *Bill Haywood's Book: The Autobiography of William D. Haywood* (New York, 1929), 228; Washington, *Session Laws* (1911), chap. 133; *Journal of the Senate* (1911), 521–22; Collins quoted in *Seattle Press-Times*, Feb. 28, 1911.

85. G. H. A. Jenner, "Unenforced Legislation in Wisconsin," thesis submitted to the University of Wisconsin (1912), quoted in *Wisconsin Briefs* (Madison: Legislative Reference Bureau, 1985), 3–4; Wisconsin, *Laws* (1915), 130–32; Oklahoma, *Session Laws* (1915), 317–18.

86. Ford, *Little White Slaver*, 13; Wiley, "The Little White Slaver," 91.

87. *Chicago News*, in *Tobacco*, Jan. 9, 1919, 4; Gaston to David Starr Jordan, Dec. 24, 1919, DSJ Papers; pamphlet advertised in *The Boy*, first quarter 1914, 2; *Sioux Falls (South Dakota) Press*, Mar. 9, 1920.

88. Irish to Fisk, Apr. 26, 1902; Gaston to Fisk, Mar. 31, 1902, HFF Papers; *The Boy*, Apr. 15, 1903, 21.

89. Gaston to Baker, July 18, 1917; "War Bulletin No. 1"; Enlistment Blank for "A Clean Life Million Club"; *A Puff of Smoke, Why the Cigarette Is Deadly*, and *Maxim, Burbank, Edison, and Hamilton Attack the Cigarette* (n.d.), all in CTCA Papers, entry 396, box 2.

90. *New York Evening Sun*, July 13, 1917; *Chicago News*, in *Tobacco* Jan. 9, 1919, 4.

91. Warfield, "Lost Cause," 247; Duis, "Cigarettes and Sin," 143.

92. Gaston to Jordan, Jan. 11, 1912, DSJ Papers; Gaston to Rosenwald, June 13, 1912, JR Papers; Gaston to Thomas A. Hall, Jan. 29, 1906 (letter courtesy Terry Fife, History Works, Inc., Oak Park, Illinois); *Tobacco*, May 20, 1920, 28.

### 3. The Little White Slaver Goes to War

1. Lawrence Leslie, *The Seer and the Cigarette* (Greenfield, Ind., 1928), 115.

2. U.S. Department of Agriculture statistics cited in Richard B. Tennant, *The American Cigarette Industry: A Study in Economic Analysis and Public Policy* (New York, 1971; orig. 1950), 143.

3. *Omaha Sermons of Billy Sunday, September–October, 1915* (Omaha, 1915), 5.

4. Benedict Crowell, *America's Munitions, 1917–1918* (Washington, D.C., 1919), 449; *Tobacco*, Dec. 12, 1918, 5; Carl Avery Werner, "The Triumph of the Cigarette," *American Mercury*, Dec. 1925, 420.

5. *HB*, Jan. 3, 1918; 65th Cong., 1st sess., Selective Service Act (Washington, D.C., 1917), secs. 12, 13.

6. Henry Ford, *The Case Against the Little White Slaver* (Detroit, 1914).

7. *NYT*, Aug. 9, 11, 1927.

8. William Congreve, *The Old Bachelor*, act 3, quoted in H. L. Mencken, ed., *New Dictionary of Quotations on Historical Principles from Ancient and Modern Sources* (New York: 1942), 1123; Lasalle quoted in Richard Klein, *Cigarettes Are Sublime* (Durham, N.C., 1993), 139; Jerome E. Brooks, *The Mighty Leaf: Tobacco Through the Centuries* (Boston, 1952), 221, 233–34; Confederate States of America, Committee on Quartermaster and Commissary Departments, *A Report on the Subject of Tobacco Rations for the Army* (Richmond, 1865), copy in Rare Book Collection, Library of Congress, Washington, D.C.

9. Carl A. Werner, *Tobaccoland* (New York, 1922), 105; Nannie M. Tilley, *The Bright Tobacco Industry, 1860–1929* (Chapel Hill, 1948), 3–36; Robert F. Durden, *The Dukes of Durham, 1865–1929* (Durham, N.C., 1975), 12–18.

10. U.S. Military Academy, Special Order No. 178, Sept. 4, 1903; General Orders and Circulars, Adjutant General's Office, 1903, No. 42, involving Cadet Gibson T. Berry Jr. and Cadet Louis E. Kloeber, 1–5, both in WP Papers; *NYT*, Sept. 8, 1903.

11. Constitution and By-Laws of the Anti-Cigarette League of Rhodes Military Institute, 1905, 1, Rhodes Military Institute Records, Southern Historical Collection, Wilson Library, UNC; *Regulations for the U.S. Military Academy*, 1911, sec. 472, WP Papers.

12. *NYT*, Nov. 24, 1907.

13. Ibid., June 18, Aug. 8, 1909; *Seattle Post-Intelligencer*, June 18, 1909.

14. Surgeon's report to the superintendent, U.S. Military Academy, July 9, 1915; Morton F. Smith, commandant of cadets, to the superintendent, July 16, 1915, both in WP Papers.

15. U.S. War Department, "Home Reading Course for Citizen Soldiers," Lessons 4, 8, in *CE*, Aug. 16, 20, 1917; Raymond B. Fosdick to Walter Camp, June 11, 1917, regarding *How To Be Fit: Sound Advice Given by Walter Camp*, CTCA Papers, entry 195, box 1.

16. F. R. Lang, judge advocate, U.S. Army, to Dr. A. W. Herzog, editor of *Medico-Legal Journal*, in *The Truth About Cigarettes* (New York, 1918), 83; *Tobacco*, Oct. 11, 1917, 14.

17. Percy M. Ashburn, *The Elements of Military Hygiene: Especially Arranged for Officers and Men of the Line* (Boston, 1915), 28–29; Joseph H. Ford, *Elements of Field Hygiene and Sanitation* (Philadelphia, 1917), 10; Gerald B. Webb, "The

Effect on the Lungs of the Inhalation of Smoke from Cigarettes," *Military Surgeon* 42 (1918), 500.

18. W. A. Bloedorn, *Medical Record*, Jan. 21, 1920, reprinted in *Tobacco*, July 29, 1920, 12; Edward A. Spitzka, quoted in *Current Opinion* 67 (October 1919), 243.

19. Frank R. Keefer, *Military Hygiene and Sanitation* (Philadelphia, 1914), 281; *Minneapolis Morning Tribune*, Aug. 11, 1917; *Scientific American Supplement* 84 (1917), 291; G. J. S. Archer, "Cigarette Smoking and Nerves," *Journal of the Royal Army Medical Corps* 30 (1918), 233; *Los Angeles Times*, Nov. 15, 1917.

20. *NYS*, July 7, 1917; *NYT*, July 13, 1918; James Irving Crabbe, *Tobacconalia: Containing Medical, Moral and Social Reasons for the Moderate Use of Tobacco* (Portland, Ore., 1920), 16; Lawrence Stallings, *The Doughboys* (New York, 1963), 3.

21. *NYS*, July 28, Aug. 3, 19, 1917.

22. John Harvey Kellogg, "The Decay of American Manhood," *AM*, Oct. 1917, 115; Dr. John H. Quayle, "Easy to Make Fit 90 Per Cent of All Rejected in Draft," in *NYS*, Aug. 19, 1917, sec. 5, 9; *Sacramento Bee*, May 3, 1918.

23. *NYS*, July 8, 1917; Pershing's aides quoted in *NYS*, July 5, 7, 1917; for Wilson, see *NYS*, Sept. 2, 1917, May 19, 1918.

24. H. L. Mencken, " 'Reformers' Oppose Sanitary Measures Against Disease," *New York Evening Mail*, Sept. 18, 1917. Raymond B. Fosdick responded to this column by describing Mencken as "a superficial writer with no ideas"; Fosdick to Frederick H. Whitin, Sept. 26, 1917, CTCA Papers, entry 395, box 3.

25. Baker, May 26, 1917, filed with Fosdick to Chesley R. Perry, May 31, 1917, entry 396, box 2; J. H. McCurdy, M.D., "Recreation Recommendations from the American YMCA to the American Army General Staff in France," Nov. 22, 1917, 3, entry 397, box 4; Minutes of Meetings of the War Department Commission on Training Camps (May 5, 1917), 7, entry 403, box 57, all in CTCA Papers.

26. *AM*, Oct. 1917, 107; CTCA news release, Oct. 22, 1917; undated statement issued by Fosdick; Daniels to Newton D. Baker, June 20, 1917, all in CTCA Papers, entry 395, box 1. See also Raymond B. Fosdick, *Chronicle of a Generation: An Autobiography* (New York, 1958), esp. 144.

27. *Report of the First Corps of Moral Engineers, U.S.A., with Reference to the Commission on Training Camp Activities, U.S.A., and the Work of the New England Watch and Ward Society in the War Emergency*, typescript included with J. Frank Chase to Fosdick, Oct. 13, 1917; League of Christian Reformed Churches for the Spiritual Care of Our Soldiers to Woodrow Wilson, Sept. 29, 1917; E. W. Hart, pastor of Columbia Avenue Methodist Episcopal Church, Philadelphia, to Newton D. Baker, Oct. 13, 1917, all in CTCA Papers, entry 396, box 2. The quotes are from Petition from the Women's Section of the Navy League to Fosdick, May 23, 1917, entry 395, box 7; and Stanley B. Roberts to Baker, Sept. 19, 1917, entry 396, box 2. See CTCA Papers, entry 395, boxes 1–10, and entry 396, box 2, for "field reports" from groups appointed by Fosdick to monitor vice around the training camps.

28. A. J. Heyl, quoted in *TW*, July 1, 1918, 20; Jane Deeter Rippin, Confidential Outline of Organization and Methods, Law Enforcement Division, War

and Navy Department Commissions on Training Camp Activities, July 1, 1918, 11, CTCA Papers, entry 396, box 1.

29. 64th Cong., 2d sess., S.B. 1695, sec. 39, H.R. 20783 (Washington, D.C., 1917).

30. *CE*, Apr. 3, 1917; *NYT*, Apr. 8, 1917. Chamberlain reportedly intended the anti-tobacco clause to apply only to men in training, but opponents insisted it would have wider applications; *Tobacco*, Apr. 5, 1917, 11.

31. *NYT*, Apr. 7, 1917, from *Tobacco*, Apr. 5, 1917, 12.

32. *Chicago News*, Apr. 24, 1917; *Sacramento Bee*, Apr. 21, 1917; *CE*, May 28, 1917; *Cleveland Leader*, Mar. 27, 1917; *NYT*, Mar. 29, 1917; *Los Angeles Times*, Jan. 7, 1918.

33. *CE*, May 3, 1917.

34. George E. Chamberlain to Charles Dushkind, Apr. 7, 1917, in *Tobacco*, Apr. 12, 1917, 5; 65th Cong., 1st sess., Selective Service Act, quote in section 13.

35. WCTU Annual Meeting Minutes (1917), 171; *Tobacco*, Mar. 7, 1918, 4; General Orders No. 176, American Expeditionary Forces, May 11, 1918, CTCA Papers, entry 196; Crowell, *America's Munitions*, 449.

36. Report of Preston Herbert, chief of the Tobacco Section, Subsistence Division, War Department, in *TW*, Apr. 1, 1919, 6.

37. Crowell, *America's Munitions*, 449, 452; *TW*, Apr. 1, 1919, 22; July 1, 1919, 10. For the takeover of the Bull Durham production, see *Tobacco*, Apr. 4, 1918, 5; *NYT*, May 19, 1918.

38. *NYT*, July 15, 1918; *Tobacco*, July 18, 1918, 11; Bernard M. Baruch, *American Industry in the War* (Washington, D.C., 1921), 29; Baruch, *Baruch: My Own Story* (New York, 1957), 310. Cigarette production increased from 18 billion in 1917 to 45 billion by the end of the war; Tennant, *American Cigarette Industry*, 16.

39. WCTU Annual Meeting Minutes (1917), 171; *No-Tobacco Journal*, Oct. 1918, 4; *TW*, Mar. 15, 1918, 11, 22; Apr. 1, 1918, 13; *Tobacco*, Apr. 26, 1917, 6; Mar. 21, 1918, 33; Apr. 4, 1918, 9. Rhondda's remarks were reported in the *Los Angeles Evening Express* (under the headline "TOBACCO NEEDED AS FOOD SAVER"), Dec. 26, 1917; *NYT* ("CALLS TOBACCO NECESSITY"), Dec. 28, 1917, and elsewhere.

40. *Red Triangle Overseas*, Nov. 23, 1918, 7; *Official Facts Concerning the Red Triangle Overseas*, n.d., in YMCA Archives; *Tobacco*, Jan. 23, 1919, 18.

41. Daniel A. Poling, *Huts in Hell* (Boston, 1918), 54–55; also in *AM*, Nov. 1918, 259.

42. L. R. Welzmiller, "Effects of Cigaret Smoking on Young Men," *AM*, May 1913, 393; "Injuriousness of Tobacco," *Official Bulletin*, Oct. 1913, 26–27; "The Dormitory Problem in the Young Men's Christian Association," report presented at the annual meeting of the Association of General Secretaries, Asilomar, Calif., May 19–23, 1915, YMCA Archives.

43. Harold R. Peat, excerpt from *Private Peat*, in *AM*, Jan. 1919, 366, 376; *Red Triangle Overseas*, Nov. 23, 1918, 7.

44. *Red Triangle Overseas*, Oct. 16, 1918, 1–2; *AM*, Aug. 1918, 931.

45. *AM*, Oct. 1918, 126.

46. *NYT*, May 23, 27, 1918; *Tobacco*, May 16, 1918, 35; June 20, 1918, 6.

47. Statement of K. P. Keppel, third assistant secretary of war, report on prices charged for cigarettes in YMCA canteens overseas; *Official Facts Con-*

*cerning the Red Triangle Overseas*, 5; "American YMCA Price List for October, November, and December" (reproduction of the canteen price list), all in YMCA Archives. The dispute over prices is also examined in *Tobacco*, July 18, 1918, 11; *AM*, July 1918, 872; Sept. 1918, 27, 37; *NYS*, Dec. 16, 1918; and Katherine Mayo, *"That Damn Y"* (Boston, 1920), 380–82.

48. C. P. Paffley, first lieutenant, Quartermaster Corps, to YMCA, third division, American Expeditionary Force, Oct. 23, 1918, "Report on Gift Tobacco Sold at YMCA Canteens Overseas"; *Official Facts Concerning the Red Triangle Overseas*, 5–6, both in YMCA Archives; *AM*, Oct. 1918, 126; Jan. 1919, 376; *NYS*, Dec. 16, 1918.

49. Cable from unidentified YMCA representative to YMCA headquarters in New York, Oct. 19, 1918, Jane Addams Collection, Stanley R. Linn Family Papers, University of Illinois at Chicago Circle; *Red Triangle Overseas*, Aug. 3, 1918, 1; Mayo, *"That Damn Y,"* 134; *AM*, Aug. 1918, p. 950. For the YMCA's efforts to provide cigarettes to men going "over the top," see *Red Triangle Overseas*, Nov. 23, 1918, 7.

50. Minutes of Meetings of the War Department Commission on Training Camps (June 18, 1918), 73, CTCA Papers, entry 403, box 57.

51. *The War Cry*, May 23, 1908, cover; June 20, 1908, 9; Diary of Capt. Margaret Sheldon, Dec. 1918, 189, Salvation Army Archives and Research Center, Alexandria, Va. For reports on the quantity of tobacco distributed by the Salvation Army during the war, see *Tobacco*, Sept. 26, 1918, 64; Dec. 12, 1918, 5.

52. Lt. Col. P. H. Bagby to Brig. Gen. Avery D. Andrews, Nov. 5, 1918; Andrews to Bagby, Nov. 23, 1918; William S. Barker, director of Salvation Army activities in France, to Administrative Section, General Headquarters, May 20, 1918; all in American Expeditionary Forces General Headquarters, Adjutant General's Files, National Archives, Washington, D.C., box 160. For YMCA personnel and canteen operations, see the report by John R. Mott, chief executive of the national War Work Council of the YMCA, in *AM*, Jan. 1919, 376.

53. Letters published in *HB*, Oct. 21, Dec. 12, 1918.

54. *Tobacco*, July 10, 1919, 34; May 17, 1917, 13; May 8, 1919, 12.

55. American Red Cross, with the American Expeditionary Forces in France, cable number 2018, to American Red Cross national headquarters, Washington D.C., responding to cable number 6521, Feb. 1918, in *Tobacco*, Feb. 14, 1918, 3; Daniel Breck, vice president, Selden-Breck Construction Co., to William Howard Taft, chairman of the central committee, American Red Cross, Aug. 11, 1917; J. G. Blaine Jr., associate director, Red Cross bureau of development, to Commission on Training Camp Activities, Sept. 6, 1917; both in CTCA Papers, entry 396, box 1.

56. *Tobacco*, July 10, 1919, 34.

57. Ibid., Aug. 28, 1919, 4; July 10, 1919, 34.

58. *AM*, Aug. 1918, 391; *Tobacco*, Aug. 15, 1918, 9; Aug. 28, 1919, 4; Frank R. Bates to his mother, Mrs. Guy Golden, from a hospital in France, in *HB*, Oct. 14, 1918.

59. Patrick F. Gilbo, *The American Red Cross: The First Century* (New York, 1981), 53–55.

60. *NYT*, Aug. 1, 1917; *Butte (Montana) Miner*, Aug. 27, 1917; *HB*, Oct. 24, 1917; Jan. 1, May 9, July 4, 1918. For other examples, see *CE*, June 23,

1917; *NYS*, July 17, 27, 1917. One typical poster featured a distressed soldier looking into an empty cigarette box; another exhorted viewers to "Smoke the Kaiser Out" by contributing to a tobacco fund; posters for the Our Boys in France Tobacco Fund, US 5030, 5044, Poster Collection, Hoover Institution on War, Revolution, and Peace, Stanford University, Stanford, Calif.

61. *NYT*, Dec. 22, 1917 (Consolidated Stock Exchange); Mar. 17, 1918 (Cigarette Service Committee); Mar. 1, 1918 (Palm Beach party); *NYS*, July 3, 1918. For reports on prisons, see *Tobacco*, Jan. 17, 1918, 21; *Los Angeles Times*, Jan. 7, 1918; *NYT*, July 14, 1917; July 3, 1918.

62. *Tobacco*, Oct. 25, 1917, 5, 9 (Forestry Association); Aug. 29, 1918, 10 (Ambulance Company); May 23, 1918, 9; Jan. 2, 1919, 28 ("Our Boys in France"); *NYT*, Jan. 27, 1918 (Pennsylvania Railroad); *NYS*, Dec. 31, 1918 (final report on smoke fund); *Butte Miner*, Aug. 27, 1917. The *New York Times* was one of the few major newspapers that did not establish a tobacco fund; it did, however, publicize the fund at the competing *Sun*; see, for example, *NYT*, July 23, 1917.

63. *CE*, Aug. 10, 1917; *NYT*, Jan. 6, 1918; *NYS*, July 10, 1918. For the Espionage Act, see *NYS*, July 15, 1917; *NYT*, Dec. 12, 1917.

64. *Tobacco*, June 20, 1918, 31; Jan. 9, 1919, 24; *Los Angeles Times*, Jan. 7, 1918; *Tobacco*, Sept. 13, 1917, 26; May 23, 1918, 13; June 13, 1918, 29; Jan. 15, 1920, 29 (Pickford photo). For a sampling of stories about benefits featuring these and other well-known entertainers, see *NYS*, Sept. 8, 9, 1917; May 29, June 3, 14, 1918. "My Lady Nicotine" continued to be shown during the demobilization period, when it was used to raise money to buy cigarettes for returning or convalescent soldiers; *Tobacco*, Jan. 9, 1919, 24. Apparently, no copies of the film have survived.

65. *NYS*, Aug. 19, 1917; *NYT*, July 9, 1917; Apr. 26, 1918; Transport Tobacco Fund, US 5028, Poster Collection, Hoover Institution on War, Revolution, and Peace, Stanford University, Stanford, Calif. An account of the cigarette bombardment appeared in *NYS*, Aug. 31, 1917.

66. *Tobacco*, Dec. 27, 1917, 8; *NYT*, Oct. 3, 1917; *TW*, Apr. 1, 1918, 15.

67. Author unknown, published in *NYS*, July 16, 1917. For similar odes, see "Smokes," author unknown, *NYS*, June 11, 1918; L. C. Davis, "The Cigarette Comes Back," *St. Louis Post Dispatch*, Aug. 19, 1918; and Jack Turner, "Fags," *Scientific American* 118 (1918), 102.

68. Gaston to Baker, July 18, 1917, CTCA Papers, entry 396, box 2; Grace Hamilton Hicks to Daniels, Sept. 15, 1917, CTCA Papers, entry 396, box 1.

69. *HB*, Oct. 25, 1917; Sept. 5, 1918; *AM*, Dec. 1918, 279.

70. *Sacramento Bee*, Sept. 14, 1918; *No-Tobacco Journal*, Oct. 1918, 9, copy addressed to Mott in YMCA Archives.

71. H. L. Dodge, *Kaiser Nicotine and Its Effects on My Friends* (Long Beach, Calif.,1918), 43; WCTU Annual Meeting Minutes (1917), 171; *US*, Mar. 14, May 9, July 4–18, 1918; *NYS*, July 7, 1918; *NYT*, Mar. 15, 1918. For the Bibles from Hammond, see *CE*, May 29, 1917. Several other church groups opposed the distribution of cigarettes to soldiers, including the Chicago Methodist Ministers' Association, Women's Foreign Missionary Society, and Federation of Minneapolis Ministers; *Tobacco*, June 14, 1917, 25; Nov. 1, 1917, 16; Nov. 22, 1917, 33.

72. Frederick W. Roman, *Nicotine Next* (Evanston, Ill., 1918), 52–57.

73. U.S. Department of Commerce figures in *TW*, Sept. 1, 1918, 24. See also

Tennant, *American Cigarette Industry*, 41, 393. During the twelve months ending with June of 1919, Americans shipped 1.3 billion cigarettes to France and nearly 1 billion to England; no cigarettes were exported to those markets during the twelve months ending with June of 1914; *TW*, Aug. 15, 1919, 13. Two-thirds of total American cigarette exports went to China; most of the rest went to other Asian countries; and less than 3 percent went to Europe; *NYT*, July 7, 1917. For domestic sales, see U.S. Department of Internal Revenue figures, reported in the *Seattle Times*, Jan. 25, 1917. For the ratio between orders and production, see *Tobacco*, Nov. 1, 1917, 3.

74. *Tobacco*, Dec. 19, 1918, 31; July 4, 1918, 19; *TW*, Feb. 15, 1918, 11.

75. *TW*, Apr. 15, 1918, 9; Sept. 1, 1918, 5; Sept. 15, 1918, 15; *Tobacco*, Apr. 5, 1917, 25, 27; Aug. 30, 1917, 22; Oct. 24, 1918, 30, 31; Nov. 14, 1918, 19. Many such reports appeared in the trade press.

76. *Tobacco*, Nov. 14, 1918, 7; Sept. 13, 1917, 18. Detailed accounts of the American Tobacco Company's arrangements with the *Washington (D.C.) Times and the Albany (New York) Knickerbocker-Press* appear in Aug. 30, 1917, 27; Sept. 6, 1917, 14. Each of the five major cigarette manufacturers sold discounted "smoke kits" to the "Our Boys in France Tobacco Fund," sponsored by about 440 newspapers and 100 magazines; Nov. 29, 1917, 10–11.

77. Quote in *NYS*, Sept. 1, 1918, Sunday magazine, 5. For allegations of kickbacks, see *Tobacco*, Apr. 11, 1918, 33.

78. *Tobacco*, Aug. 2, 1917, 30; Aug. 9, 1917, 3; May 24, 1917, 23.

79. Ibid., Oct. 17, 1918, 28; Oct. 24, 1918, 13, 20, 32–33. Percival S. Hill was the chairman of the Tobacco Trade Committee of the United War Work Campaign, which raised money for seven groups designated as relief agencies by the War Department, including the YMCA and Salvation Army; ibid., Nov. 7, 1918, 3–4; Nov. 21, 1918, 8, 14, 25. George W. Hill went to France as an officer for the Red Cross in June 1917 and later served in Washington with the Motor Transport Corps. He did not return to American Tobacco until January 1919; ibid., Dec. 12, 1918, 4; Robert Sobel, *They Satisfy: The Cigarette in American Life* (New York, 1978), 80. For donations to relief agencies by other cigarette executives, see *CE* Aug. 7, 1917; *NYS*, May 16, 1918.

80. Modris Eksteins, *Rites of Spring: The Great War and the Birth of the Modern Age* (New York, 1989), 175; W. S. Kimball, "Ye 'Good Old Days': Historical Reminiscences of Early Day Casper," *Casper (Wyoming) Tribune Herald*, Dec. 2, 1945; industry executive quoted in *Los Angeles Times*, Jan. 19, 1918; *Tobacco*, Apr. 10, 1919, 30. When smoking could not be permitted, because a light would be a fire hazard or give away the position of troops, the officers distributed chewing tobacco.

81. *Washington (D.C.) Times*, Aug. 27, 1917; Gorgas quoted in Col. D. C. Howard, Medical Corps, to L. H. Higley, president, *No-Tobacco* League of America, Aug. 30, 1918, responding to Higley's letter to George Creel, chairman of the Committee on Public Information, Aug. 28, 1918, in *No-Tobacco Journal*, Oct. 1918, 3.

82. *AM*, Nov. 1918, 201; Sept. 1918, 11; *NYS*, June 19, 1918 (under the headline "GAS VICTIM CALLS TOBACCO FIRST AID / YMCA Worker, Back From Front, Tells of Solace of Cigarette").

83. George V. Z. Long, *War Diary*, Nov. 11, 1918, 253, 254, YMCA Archives; *AM*, Aug. 1918, 958.

84. Atkins quoted in *HB*, Aug. 1, 1918. For trench conditions, see Eksteins,

*Rites of Spring*, 147–55. The best source on the 1918 influenza epidemic is Alfred W. Cosby Jr., *Epidemic and Peace, 1918* (Westport, Conn., 1976). For cigarettes and influenza, see *NYS*, June 11, Oct. 26, 1918; also, *Butte Miner*, Oct. 23, 1918 ("TAKE A SMOKE TO KILL 'FLU'").

85. *AM*, Nov. 1918, 199–200; Sept. 1918, 35. See also Aug. 1918, 939, 946.

86. *NYS*, Oct. 3, 18, June 3, 1918; *Tobacco*, Oct. 17, 1918, 32; May 16, 1918, 30; *NYT*, Dec. 12, 1917.

87. *NYS*, July 15, 1917; May 28, June 22, 1918.

88. Ibid., July 8, Sept. 2, 1917; Frederick A. Pottle, "Stretchers," *Outlook and Independent*, Sept. 18, 1929, 94; Sept. 25, 1929, 130. Many other soldiers commented on the eagerness of civilians to bestow gifts of tobacco. For example, see William K. Dingledine to Mrs. W. J. Dingledine, Dec. 5, 24, 26, 1917, WKD Papers; and Thomas Reid Cole, War Letters, Southern Historical Collection, Wilson Library, UNC, esp. May 20, 1918.

89. *NYS*, June 4, 1918; Klein, *Cigarettes Are Sublime*, 136–37. Cigarettes also served as a medium of economic exchange, one that had higher value, in some circumstances, than cash itself; see *Tobacco*, May 16, 1918, 18; Aug. 28, 1919, 8; Sept. 18, 1919, 5.

90. William K. Dingledine to Mrs. W. J. Dingledine, Jan. 16, 1918, WKD Papers; Erich Maria Remarque, *All Quiet on the Western Front* (New York, 1989; orig. 1928), 10, 38, 51, 96, 146, 152. In one of the most telling scenes in Remarque, the narrator gathers with his comrades in arms one last time. A "dense cloud of smoke" envelopes them. "Where would a soldier be without tobacco?" he wonders (152) (this is sometimes translated as "What would a soldier be . . ."). For accounts of American soldiers demonstrating camaraderie by giving cigarettes to captured Germans, see Stallings, *The Doughboys*, 63, 112. Klein, *Cigarettes Are Sublime*, devotes one chapter to the role of cigarettes in military culture; 135–56.

91. *Hartford (Connecticut) Times*, Feb. 9, 1918; Hutchins quoted in Jesse Mercer Gehman, *Smoke over America* (East Aurora, N.Y., 1943), 570; Dingledine to Mrs. W. J. Dingledine, July 6, 1918, WKD Papers. Dingledine frequently commented on the value of smoking as a distraction from boredom; see his letters to Mrs. W. J. Dingledine, July 5, 1917; Aug. 18, 1918; Feb. 1, 1919; and to Nannie Black, July 9, 1917, all in WKD Papers.

92. Bernard M. Baruch, *The Part Tobacco Played in the War: A Report of the War Industries Board*, in *Tobacco*, Mar. 31, 1921, 1. See also *TW*, Sept. 15, 1920, 8; Werner, "Triumph of the Cigarette," 420; Pierre Schrumpf-Pierron, *Tobacco and Physical Efficiency* (New York, 1927), 26.

93. *Curb News*, Feb. 3, 1919, clipping in BND Papers; *Tobacco*, Dec. 19, 1918, 7; Aug. 15, 1918, 6. Hill quoted in *New York World*, Aug. 11, 1918.

94. *Theatre Magazine*, Nov. 1918, inside back cover; *NYS*, Dec. 15, 1918; *NYT*, Dec. 17, 1921. The *New York Sun* carried relatively little cigarette advertising in April 1917, and none at all for any brands manufactured by the American Tobacco Company. By November 1918, American Tobacco was one of the paper's leading advertisers, with an average of two quarter-page ads for Lucky Strike appearing each week.

95. Woolf painting reproduced in *NYS*, Oct. 13, 1918; photos in ibid., July 8, 1917, sec. 5, 9; Aug. 19, 1917.

96. *Tobacco*, Dec. 12, 1918, 24 (Peace Conference); *NYT*, Jan. 20, 1919 ("No

Smoking" signs); *New York Herald,* Jan. 20, 1919; *Tobacco,* Jan. 23, 1919, 12 (Fisher); *Army and Navy Register,* Aug. 31, 1929, 200 (ration). Fisher later returned to a more cautionary stance regarding tobacco, saying there was much more to say against it than for it; "Should A Christian Leader Smoke?" *AM,* Sept. 1919, 36.

97. *Sacramento Star,* June 13, 1919.

## 4. Milady's Cigarette

1. *The Shield,* Aug. 2, 1920, 4.

2. *TW,* Apr. 15, 1919, 25; Commissioner of Internal Revenue report cited in Richard B. Tennant, *The American Cigarette Industry: A Study in Economic Analysis and Public Policy* (New York, 1971; orig. 1950), 16; Frederick Lewis Allen, *Only Yesterday: An Informal History of the Nineteen-Twenties* (New York, 1964; orig. 1931), 90. The Commerce Department, reporting a 530 percent increase in cigarette consumption between 1913 and 1923, concluded much of it was due to increased smoking by women; *NYT,* Jan. 19, 1925.

3. *Tobacco,* Feb. 5, 1920, 29; *NYT,* Feb. 29, 1920; *Wall Street Journal,* Dec. 8, 1919 (Duke interview); *Magazine of Wall Street,* Feb. 15, 1919, 4.

4. *Printer's Ink,* Feb. 18, 1932, 25; Jeffrey E. Harris, "Cigarette Smoking Among Successive Birth Cohorts of Men and Women in the United States During 1900–80," *Journal of the National Cancer Institute* 71 (Sept. 1985), 475; Michael Vincent O'Shea, *Tobacco and Mental Efficiency* (New York, 1923), 38; Eunice Fuller Barnard, "The Cigarette Has Made Its Way Up in Society," *New York Times Magazine,* June 9, 1929, 6 (tobacco retailer); *NYT,* Feb. 2, 1923; May 12, 1926; June 26, 1928 (insurance underwriters).

5. Boys and Girls Anti-Cigarette League Newsletter, Alice Hyatt Mather, ed., HWW Papers; toothpaste ads in Preston W. Slosson, *The Great Crusade and After, 1914–1928* (New York, 1930), 155–56.

6. *NYT,* Feb. 6, 1920; see also *US,* Feb. 12, 1920.

7. Richard J. Walsh, *The Burning Shame of America: Outline Against Nicotine* (Mt. Vernon, N.Y., 1924), 24. See also Paula S. Fass, *The Damned and the Beautiful* (New York, 1977), 294.

8. For the general economic and political status of nineteenth-century American women, see Mary P. Ryan, *Womanhood in America: From Colonial Times to the Present* (New York, 1979), chaps. 2–3.

9. Margaret Woods Lawrence, *The Tobacco Problem* (Boston, 1897; orig. 1885), 225.

10. Carl N. Degler, *At Odds: Women and the Family in America from the Revolution to the Present* (New York, 1980), 376; Ryan, *Womanhood in America,* 184, 138; "I Struck the Match at Last," Bettmann Archive, Inc., New York City.

11. Nathaniel Currier, "Star of the South," lithograph, 1847, Library of Congress; Russell T. Trall, *Tobacco: Its History, Nature and Effects, with Facts and Figures for Tobacco-Users* (New York, 1854), 4; *NYT,* May 27, 1877.

12. *NYT,* Sept. 6, 1880; Mrs. John A. (Mary) Logan, "The Evils of Cigarette Smoking" (Chicago, ca. 1902), 2, copy in HFF Papers; Lawrence, *The Tobacco Problem,* 244–47.

13. F. W. Fairholt, *Tobacco: Its History and Associations* (London, 1856), 147–48; Richard Klein, *Cigarettes Are Sublime* (Durham, 1993), 46–47; Elizabeth

Biddle, "Cigarette Smoking Among Englishwomen No Uncommon Practice," *NYT*, Mar. 25, 1906. Charles Dickens was bemused to encounter three women in Geneva smoking cigarettes expertly and with gusto in the 1850s; G. L. Apperson, *The Social History of Smoking* (London, 1914), 218–20. Even earlier, a tobaccophile reported approvingly that "[t]he dark-eyed daughters of Spain are great adepts at smoking"; Anon., *The Smokers', Chewer's, and Snuff Taker's Companion and Tobacconist's Own Book* (Philadelphia, 1841), 31.

14. Lithographs reproduced in F. W. Fairholt scrapbook, vol. 3, AC; *New York Standard Union*, May 25, 1895; Edith Wharton, *The Age of Innocence* (New York, 1970; orig. 1920), 76 (see also 165–66); Wharton, *The House of Mirth* (New York, 1964; orig. 1905), 12 (see also 27, 49); F. Marion Crawford, *Marion Darche: A Story Without Comment* (New York, 1893), 203–5, 217, 262 (quote at 204).

15. *Tobacco*, Feb. 1, 1917, 13 (see also *Seattle Times*, Jan. 25, 1917); *CE*, June 20, 1917.

16. Nannie Mae Tilley, *The Bright Tobacco Industry, 1860–1929*, (Chapel Hill, N.C., 1948), 608; M. E. W. Sherwood, "Heroines Who Smoke," *New York Times Saturday Review of Books and Art*, July 21, 1900, 481; *NYT*, Aug. 26, Aug. 28, 1898; *New York Times Magazine*, Sept. 11, 1898. "Sly Cigarette" was written by Ivan Caryll and Lionel Moncton (music) and Harry Greenbank and Aubrey Hopwood (lyrics), and recorded by Tiny Tim on his album *Girl* in 1996.

17. John K. Winkler, *Tobacco Tycoon: The Story of James Buchanan Duke* (New York, 1942), 261–62; Mrs. E. C. Marshall interview with Frank Rounds, Charlotte, N.C., 1963, 42, Duke Endowment Papers, Special Collections Library, DU.

18. Wharton, *Age of Innocence*, 104–5.

19. Klein, *Cigarettes Are Sublime*, 117; Frances Benjamin Johnston, self-portrait, 1896, Library of Congress, Prints and Photographs Division.

20. Emma Goldman, *Living My Life* (New York, 1970; orig. 1931), 141–42.

21. *Reno (Nevada) Evening Gazette*, Jan. 15, 1908; *NYT*, May 9, 1921; Sept. 17, 1912; *Atlantic Monthly*, Apr. 1916, 574. Margaret H. Sanger, founder of the modern birth control movement, did not smoke, but a California newspaper editorialist once described her followers as the sort who did; *Oakland Tribune*, Jan. 27, 1916.

22. Alice Roosevelt Longworth, *Crowded Hours* (New York, 1933), 62–63, 75.

23. *Woman's National Daily*, July 16, 1908, Prohibition Party Series, Temperance and Prohibition Papers, roll 1, 157; *NYT*, Aug. 3, 5, 6, 1910.

24. *Sacramento Bee*, Aug. 19, 1910; Mark Sullivan, *Our Times: The United States, 1900–1925* (New York, 1946), 562; *Life Magazine*, Apr. 12, 1937, back cover. Longworth reportedly received $5,000 for the ad; Charles L. Van Noppen, *Death in Cellophane* (Greensboro, N.C., 1937), 57.

25. *NYT*, Dec. 13, 1912; *Tobacco*, Mar. 22, 1917, 6.

26. *New York Herald*, Mar. 18, 1917. After reading about Mrs. Dudka, a New York City woman said she was considering organizing a Women Smokers' Defense League; *Tobacco*, Mar. 29, 1917, 9.

27. Michael Schudson, *Advertising, The Uneasy Persuasion: Its Dubious Impact on American Society* (New York, 1986), 190; Frances Perkins, "Can They Smoke Like Gentlemen?" *New Republic*, May 7, 1930, 319–20. At the time, Perkins was industrial commissioner for the state of New York.

28. *New York Herald*, July 12, 1908; *NYT*, Dec. 18, 1910; *Tobacco*, Dec. 28, 1916, 13. When another Ritz-Carlton opened in Philadelphia, women were permitted to smoke wherever they liked; *NYT*, Dec. 13, 1912. At New York's Plaza Hotel, on the other hand, women who smoked were firmly asked to either stop or leave; *NYT*, Jan. 9, 1911.

29. *NYT*, Jan. 12, 1908.

30. Ibid., Jan. 8, 21, 23, 1908. The aldermen were spurred to action by reports of an "Ambassador's wife" who lit a cigarette "in one of the most rigid of New York's hotels" with sufficient aplomb that neither the manager nor the maitre d'hotel dared asked her to stop; ibid., Jan. 2, 1908.

31. Ibid., Oct. 11, Nov. 12, 13, 1911.

32. Ibid., Feb. 20, 1905; *Binghamton (New York) Press*, Oct. 15, 1904; *NYT*, Oct. 18, 1904. For William J. Lasher's occupation, see *Broome County and Binghamton City Directory*, 1902. Mrs. Lasher vanished from the public record after her court appearance; it is not known whether she actually served her full sentence or not.

33. *Spokane Spokesman-Review*, Dec. 6, 1911; New Hampshire, *Journal of the House of Representatives* (1913), H.B. 393.

34. Sinclair Lewis, *Main Street* (New York, 1961; orig. 1920), 81; Helen L. Roberts, *The Cyclopaedia of Social Usage* (New York, 1913), 343.

35. *Ohio State Journal (Columbus)*, Aug. 10, 1912; *NYT*, Aug. 13, 1912; Irwin H. Hoover, "Hail to the Chief," *Saturday Evening Post*, May 5, 1934, 14.

36. *AM*, Apr. 1918, 591.

37. For women's support of smoke funds, see *NYS*, Aug. 19, 1917; May 24, 25, 29, 1918; June 2, 4, 1918. The WCTU endorsed a proposal by Anna Howard Shaw, temperance leader and chairman of the Woman's Committee of the Council of National Defense, to ration tobacco at home in order to ensure adequate supplies for soldiers overseas; *NYS*, July 7, 1917; *Boston American*, Sept. 15, 1917; *Los Angeles Times*, Jan. 7, 1918. For the debate over distribution of tobacco to nurses and other women attached to the military, see *Tobacco*, Oct. 4, 1917, 4–5; *New York World*, Oct. 17, 1917.

38. Daniel A. Poling, *Huts in Hell* (Boston, 1918), 14–15.

39. Nina Macdonald, "Sing a Song of War-Time," in Catherine Reilly, ed., *Scars Upon My Heart: Women's Poetry and Verse of the First World War* (London, 1981), 69.

40. *Tobacco*, Apr. 19, 1917, 13 (Chalkadia and Company); May 17, 1917, 13; Dec. 12, 1918, 9 (Strand Cigarette Company); Jan. 29, 1920, 32 (red-tipped cigarettes); Jan. 6, 1921, 4 (importer).

41. Ibid., Feb. 26, 1920, 5 (novelties); Feb. 12, 1920, 32 (percent of holders sold to women); *TW*, July 1, 1920, 16 (vanity/cigarette case). See also *The Shield*, Aug. 2, 1920, 3; Mar. 2, 1921, 3.

42. *Sacramento Star*, June 21, 1922.

43. Josephus Daniels, *Editor in Politics* (Chapel Hill, 1941), 234; Edward Bernays, *Biography of an Idea; Memoirs of Public Relations Counsel Edward L. Bernays* (New York, 1965), 386–87; Tennant, *American Cigarette Industry*, 138–39. Bernays repeated his immodest claim in interviews for two television documentaries: "The Image Makers," from *A Walk Through the Twentieth Century with Bill Moyers*, John D. and Catherine T. MacArthur Foundation Library Video Classics Project, 1984; and "Showdown on Tobacco Road," produced by Terri Randall, Varied Directions Inc., 1987.

44. *TW*, Jan. 1, 1920, 8 (see also Apr. 15, 1919, 13); *Tobacco*, May 20, 1920, 17.

45. "My Mother-in-Law," poster displayed at the Duke Homestead Museum, Durham, N.C.; *Southern Tobacco Journal* ad cited in Tilley, *Bright Tobacco Industry*, 614; "La Turka" ad in *Tobacco*, Dec. 14, 1916, 30.

46. *Printers' Ink*, Aug. 28, 1930, 52; *Life*, June 14, 1917, back cover (Murad ad); *TW*, Apr. 15, 1919, 14 (Helmar ad).

47. Schudson, *Advertising*, 192–93; "Marlboro Makes a Direct Appeal," *Advertising and Selling*, Mar. 23, 1927, 25; *NYT*, Feb. 2, Dec. 2, 1927 (Lucky Strikes); *The Chronicle* (Duke University), Oct. 19, Nov. 23, 1927 (Old Golds). Both Camel and Chesterfield showed women looking on as men smoked; *Time*, Dec. 5, 1927, back cover (Camel); *Outlook*, Mar. 23, 1927, back cover (Camel); *NYT*, Apr. 4, 1927 (Chesterfield). See also Virginia L. Ernster, "Mixed Messages for Women: A Social History of Cigarette Smoking and Advertising," *New York State Journal of Medicine* 85 (July 1985), 336.

48. A Lucky Strike campaign that began in 1932 featured a supine woman, her head pillowed, wearing a slinky gown and platform heels, a blissful expression on her face, with a man seated at her side, both smoking. "Do you inhale?" the ad copy read. "Everybody's doing it! 7 out of 10 smokers inhale knowingly—the other 3 inhale unknowingly." A variation on this theme asked "Do you inhale? What's there to be afraid of?" The message was that women should be inhaling the pure smoke of Lucky Strike. The ads appeared in a wide variety of newspapers and magazines.

49. For example, Barbara Trigg Brown of Richmond, Virginia, remembered that "[h]aving to run my household alone bred in me a sort of independence"; *Richmond Times-Dispatch*, Nov. 13, 1938. For useful interpretations of the impact of the war on women, see Margaret Randolph Higonnet, Jane Jenson, Sonya Michel, and Margaret Collins Weitz, eds., *Behind the Lines: Gender and the Two World Wars* (New Haven, 1987).

50. Tennant, *American Cigarette Industry*, 76–79; *Tobacco*, Apr. 12, 1917, 11, 13. See also Carl Avery Werner, "The Triumph of the Cigarette," *American Mercury*, Dec. 1925, 416–17.

51. *NYT*, Nov. 25, 1928.

52. Maurine Weiner Greenwald, *Women, War and Work: The Impact of World War I on Women Workers in the United States* (Westport, Conn., 1980), 12–13, 32, 92–93.

53. Ibid., 234–35, 32.

54. This analysis is based on Sunday classified advertising sections published May 27, 1917, and May 25, 1919.

55. *Tobacco*, Mar. 1, 1917, 11 (ladder anecdote); July 12, 1917, 26.

56. *TW*, Feb. 15, 1918, 7 (Tobacco Manufacturers Association); *Tobacco*, Aug. 29, 1918, 22, 29 (United Cigar Stores); Oct. 31, 1918, 18; Nov. 7, 1918, 12; Nov. 21, 1918, 12, 22 (influenza).

57. *Tobacco*, May 1, 1919, 10; Dec. 16, 1920, 36. For similar reports about women succeeding in tobacco retailing, see Feb. 13, 1919, 4; Feb. 27, 1919, 14; Mar. 13, 1919, 21; Mar. 27, 1919, 5.

58. Ibid., Nov. 14, 1918, 19; *TW*, June 1, 1920, 26; *Sacramento Star*, June 21, 1922.

59. Allen, *Only Yesterday*, 75. Among the writers who discuss the cultural impact of World War I is Modris Eksteins, *Rites of Spring: The Great War and the Birth of the Modern Age* (New York, 1989).

60. *TW*, Mar. 15, 1920, 14; *Sacramento Star*, Mar. 18, 1921; *Tobacco*, Feb. 17, 1921, 31.

61. *NYT*, Mar. 16, 1919 (canvass); Jan. 9, 1922 (complimentary cigarettes); Jan. 29, 1920 (Woods Theatre); Sept. 10, 1928 (vending machines); Retail Clerks International Advocate, Nov. 1925, 25.

62. G. W. Paschall, "The Cigarette Lady," *Greensboro News*, in *Tobacco*, June 10, 1920, 18; *NYT*, Jan. 14, 1923; Sinclair Lewis, *Babbitt* (New York, 1961; orig. 1922), 116, 121, 126.

63. *NYT*, July 16, 17, 1925 (Detroit streetcars); Feb. 13, 1919, Jan. 12, 1922 (YWCA); July 10, 1925 (Paragon Park); *Tobacco*, May 10, 1917, 11 (athletic club); *Washington Post*, Jan. 14, 1927 (West Point).

64. *Tobacco*, Aug. 19, 1920, 33; *NYT*, Sept 12, 1929; Mar. 9, 1925.

65. *TW*, Apr. 1, 1918, 14.

66. *NYT*, Mar. 16, 1919.

67. *Tobacco*, Jan. 6, 1921, 35; *NYT*, Aug. 19, 20, 1922.

68. Board of Aldermen, *City Record*, Dec. 22, 1921, Jan. 26, 1922, An Ordinance to Amend subdivision 14, section 49, Greater New York Charter. Quotes in *NYT*, Mar. 28, 1922; see also Mar. 29, 1922, 1, 16.

69. *NYT*, Aug. 7, 1922; Apr. 4, 1926; May 14, 1926.

70. Ibid., Nov. 21, 1923; Apr. 7, 1928 (Clark); *CE*, Oct. 12, 1919 (Cole); *NYT*, Apr. 19, 1921 (smoking grandmother; see also editorial, Apr. 21, 1921). For Clark, see also *NYT*, Mar. 17, June 6, 1926; Jan. 26, Apr. 9, May 20, 1927.

71. *NYT*, Apr. 13, 1923; Kansas, *Laws* (1917), chap. 166, secs. 1–5. Cigarettes were not legalized in Kansas until 1927.

72. Sherwood Anderson, *Winesburg, Ohio* (New York, 1960; orig. 1919), 148–49; Lewis, *Babbitt*, esp. 262–63.

73. *Fortune Magazine*, July 1935, 111–16; Robert S. Lynd and Helen Merrell Lynd, *Middletown in Transition: A Study in Cultural Conflict* (New York, 1937), 412, 280. About 20 percent of all women in the *Fortune* survey identified themselves as cigarette smokers, compared to about 50 percent of all men.

74. *NYT*, Dec. 27, 1919; June 25, 1920; Dec. 4, 10, 1921; June 30, 1925; Dec. 27, 1925; Mar. 1, 1926 (women's clubs); Nov. 19, 1929 (Michigan Grange); *Oregon Grange Bulletin*, May 1922, 15; *NYT*, Dec. 28, 1926 (Non-Smokers' League); July 7, 9, 1928 (Boy Scouts).

75. *Tobacco*, Apr. 8, 1920, 11; see also *The Shield*, Nov. 2, 1920, 3; John C. Burnham, "American Physicians and Tobacco Use: Two Surgeons General, 1929 and 1964," *Bulletin of the History of Medicine* 63 (1989), 1.

76. *Oregon Grange Bulletin*, May 1922, 15; *NYT*, Jan. 30, 1924.

77. Frank B. Wynn, "The Physician," *Journal of the Indiana State Medical Association* 14 (1921), 383; Allan L. Benson, "Smokes for Women," *Good Housekeeping*, Aug. 1929, 190–93; *Seattle Argus*, Aug. 6, 1938.

78. *Tobacco*, Dec. 11, 1919, 4; Mar. 4, 1920, 22.

79. *NYT*, Dec. 27, 1925.

80. U.S. Congress, House Committee on the District of Columbia, *Hearing before the Committee on the District of Columbia, House of Representatives, 67th Congress, on House Resolution 7252*, July 27, 1921 (Washington, D.C., 1921), 10, 16; Dr. John Snape, First Baptist Church, Cleveland, Ohio, in *No-Tobacco Journal*, Oct. 1927, 13.

81. Massachusetts, *House Journal* (1922), H.B. 847, "An Act to Prohibit Smoking by Women in Hotels and Restaurants"; quotes in *NYT*, Mar. 7, 1922

(see also editorial, Mar. 8, 1922); *Hearing on House Resolution 7252* (Anti–Blue Law League quote at 19; Johnson quote at 7). Both the Illinois Legislature and the Chicago City Council rejected measures to restrict female smokers; Illinois, *Journal of the House* (1929), H.B. 783; Chicago City Council, *Proceedings*, Mar. 28, 1922.

82. Although the Missouri bill theoretically would have prohibited all public smoking, it was aimed at women. "The woman with the tobacco habit is a more abject slave than the man, just as the woman with the liquor habit goes lower in the scale than the man," its sponsor remarked; *Tobacco*, Apr. 10, 1919, 14.

83. *NYT*, Mar. 13, 1922; Mar. 6, 1924; *The Shield*, May 4, 1922, 1. See also Fass, *The Damned and the Beautiful*, 293–97.

84. *NYT*, Dec. 20, 1925; Antioch College Women's Conference, *Report on the Question of Women Smoking at Antioch, 1925–1926*, 1, 5; Antiochiana file, Antioch College Archives, Yellow Springs, Ohio. Northwestern, Purdue, and the University of Maryland were among other coeducational institutions that allowed male but not female students to smoke.

85. *NYT*, Jan. 22, 1925, Feb. 18, 1926 (Vassar); Nov. 24, 25, 27, 29, 1924 (Bryn Mawr); Dec. 19, 1926 (Smith); Feb. 2, 1927 (Stanford); Fass, *The Beautiful and the Damned*, 297 (Ohio, Rhode Island). Song quoted in J. William T. Youngs, *American Realities: Historical Episodes from Reconstruction to the Present* (Boston, 1987), 127. According to the *Annual Index to the New York Times*, the *Times* published nineteen articles about efforts to ban smoking by female college students between 1920 and 1925, and no such articles between 1926 and 1930. The Antioch College Women's Conference reported that only seven of seventeen colleges included in its study of "the smoking question" banned smoking by women in 1926; *Report on the Question of Women Smoking at Antioch*, 7.

86. *San Francisco Examiner*, Nov. 19, 1927; Susan Ware, *Amelia Earhart and the Search for Modern Feminism* (New York, 1993), 97–98.

## 5. The "Triumph" of the Cigarette

1. *NYT*, July 10, 1928.

2. Carl Avery Werner, "The Triumph of the Cigarette," *American Mercury*, Dec. 1925, 415–21 (quotes at 419, 415).

3. William Haenszel, Michael B. Shimkin, and Herman P. Miller, *Tobacco Smoking Patterns in the United States*, Public Health Monograph No. 45 (Washington, D.C., 1956), 107. By gender, 51.6 percent of men and 34 percent of women smoked cigarettes in 1965; U.S. Department of Health and Human Services, Public Health Service, *Health United States, 1995* (Hyattsville, Md., 1996), 173.

4. Carl A. Werner, *Tobaccoland* (New York, 1922), 106; Idaho, *General Laws* (1921), 385–87; Utah, *Laws of the State of Utah* (1921), chap. 145.

5. Idaho, *General Laws* (1921), 575–78; Utah, *House Journal* (1923), 542; Kansas, *Laws* (1927), chap. 171, 219–23.

6. H. L. Lombard and C. R. Doering, "Cancer Studies in Massachusetts: Habits, Characteristics and Environment of Individuals With and Without Cancer," *New England Journal of Medicine* 198 (1928), 481–87; Emil Bogen, "The Composition of Cigarets and Cigaret Smoke," *JAMA* 93 (1929), 1110–14 (quote

at 1112); Elizabeth M. Whelan, *A Smoking Gun: How the Tobacco Industry Gets Away with Murder* (Philadelphia, 1984), 76–77.

7. Frederick W. Roman, *Nicotine Next* (Evanston, Ill., 1918).

8. *San Francisco Call and Post*, Feb. 13, 1919 (Billy Sunday; see also *Tobacco*, Mar. 27, 1919, 14); *US*, Mar. 13, 1919 (WCTU); *Sacramento Bee*, Mar. 29, 1919; *Los Angeles Times*, Feb. 4, 1919; *CE*, Oct. 18, 1919; *TW*, Mar. 1, 1919, 4 (Wilson); *NYT*, Dec. 27, 1919 (Presbyterians); June 20, 1920 (Baptists).

9. L. Ames Brown, "Is a Tobacco Crusade Coming?" *Atlantic Monthly*, Oct. 1920, 446, 448.

10. *Portland Oregonian*, Dec. 11, 1919; *San Francisco Call and Post*, Feb. 13, 1919; *CE*, Oct. 15, 1919; *NYT*, Feb. 19, 1919. See also *Sacramento Bee*, Mar. 25, May 12, June 7, Aug. 5, 1919.

11. *Los Angeles Times*, Feb. 5, July 2, 1919; *New York World*, Feb. 2, 1919; Apr. 18, 1920.

12. Richard B. Tennant, *The American Cigarette Industry: A Study in Economic Analysis and Public Policy* (New York, 1971; orig. 1950), 143; Jack J. Gottsegen, *Tobacco: A Study of Its Consumption in the United States* (New York, 1940), 198; Kansas, *Laws* (1917), chap. 166, sec. 2.

13. *New York Tribune*, Jan. 25, 1919; *The Shield*, Dec. 1, 1920, 1; *NYT*, Sept. 2, 1923.

14. *Portland (Maine) Herald*, Sept. 15, 1924; *Wilimantic (Connecticut) Chronicle*, Jan. 29, 1924; *Springfield (Massachusetts) Republican*, Jan. 27, 1921 (Welcher); *The Shield*, Aug. 2, 1920, 1–4; Feb. 1, 1921, 2; June 2, 1921, 1; *NYT*, Apr. 3, 1921; *Clean Life*, June 1922, 1, copy in HWW Papers.

15. *Tobacco*, Aug. 7, 1919, 35; *NYT*, May 28, 1919, May 29, 1922, June 22, 1921; Sinclair Lewis, *Main Street* (New York, 1961; orig. 1920), 429.

16. WCTU Annual Meeting Minutes (1887), cc–cci; (1919), 30–31, 89–90; *NYT*, Feb. 29, 1920 (quote); WCTU Annual Meeting Minutes (1921), 94. See also *US*, Aug. 14–28, 1919.

17. "Is There a Movement for the 'Prohibition of the Personal Use of Tobacco by Adults?' A Plea for Fair Play," *World Digest of Reform News*, Apr. 23, 1921, 1, copy in HWW Papers; *NYT*, May 11, 1924; *Topeka Journal*, Jan. 18, 1927; Billy Sunday quote in *Tobacco*, Jan. 13, 1921, 10.

18. K. Austin Kerr, *Organized for Prohibition: A New History of the Anti-Saloon League* (New Haven, 1985), 10; WCTU Annual Meeting Minutes (1924), 123–24.

19. David E. Kyvig, "Sober Thoughts: Myths and Realities of National Prohibition after Fifty Years," in David E. Kyvig, ed., *Law, Alcohol, and Order: Perspectives on National Prohibition* (Westport, Conn., 1985), 5–9.

20. Rev. C. C. Hemtree, Knoxville, Tenn., to Bryan, Feb. 7, 1919, William Jennings Bryan Papers, box 32, Library of Congress.

21. Bryan to John Bryan, Apr. 23, 1917, William Jennings Bryan Papers, box 31; see also Bryan letter in the *Sunday School Times*, June 15, 1907, 299.

22. Michael Vincent O'Shea, *Tobacco and Mental Efficiency* (New York, 1923); Pierre Schrumph-Pierron, *Tobacco and Physical Efficiency: A Digest of Clinical Data, with Annotated Bibliography* (New York, 1927); Irving Fisher, *Tobacco, A Three-Fold Study* (Dearborn, Mich., 1924), 3, 29. O'Shea explains the background and goals of the Committee to Study the Tobacco Problem in *Tobacco and Mental Efficiency*, v–xi.

23. *NYS*, July 10, 1917.

24. *NYT*, Aug. 13, 1921; July 20, 1928. For Edison's support of the smoke fund, see *NYS*, July 25, 1917.

25. *Service League Record*, Mar. 1923; program, First National Anti-Tobacco Convention, Washington, D.C., Mar. 4–5, 1925, both in HWW Papers; Harvey W. Wiley, *An Autobiography* (Indianapolis, 1930), 304. For Wiley's involvement with the ACL, see David Starr Jordan to C. L. Flatter, July 25, 1927, DSJ Papers.

26. Clarence E. Woods, United States inspector of explosives, "Commercialized Scheme of the Tobacco Trust," *US*, Apr. 10, 1919, 7; John B. Huber, "Cutting the Canker Out of Their Constitutions," *AM*, June 1919, 734; Alfred Stokes, "Giant Let-Down," *AM*, Aug. 1919, 910; editorial, *AM*, May 1919, 687; American YMCA Anti-Smoking Poster, 1919, YMCA Archives.

27. *Sacramento Star*, Jan. 24, 1921.

28. Sinclair Lewis, *Babbitt* (New York, 1961; orig. 1922), 58–59, 77, 262 (quote at 59). For depictions of cigarette smoking during conclaves of "the Bunch," see 268–70, 274.

29. *Tobacco*, May 6, 1920, 25; *The Shield*, July 5, 1921, 3; Cook to Charles S. Brown, president of Printer's Insurance Protective Inventory System of Chicago, Feb. 20, 1919, Marshall L. Cook Papers, MHC; *NYT*, Apr. 16, 1924.

30. *TW*, June 1, 1919, 7; Robert Sobel, *They Satisfy: The Cigarette in American Life* (New York, 1978), 88–91; Tennant, *American Cigarette Industry*, 16.

31. WCTU Annual Meeting Minutes (1917), 43; *The Shield*, Dec. 1, 1920, 1–4.

32. *US*, Dec. 23, 1920 (see also *NYT*, Jan. 29, 1921; and *Students' Hand-Book of Syracuse University*, 1898–1899, 44, Syracuse University Archives, E. S. Bird Library, Syracuse, N.Y.); Vida Milholland, "The Fiend Nicotine," *NYT*, Apr. 16, 1922, sec. 7, 8 (see also Milholland, "Tobacco an Enemy of American Progress," radio address on station whap, New York City, ca. 1927, reprinted in pamphlet form, copy in HWW Papers).

33. *Los Angeles Times*, Nov. 16, 1920; *The Shield*, Dec. 1, 1920, 1 (Walton); May 4, 1922, 1 (McRae). Earlier, McRae had vetoed a bill to legalize cigarette sales in Arkansas; the legislature then passed the bill over his veto; Arkansas, *Acts of the Forty-third General Assembly* (1921), 450–54.

34. *Tobacco*, Jan. 29, 1920, 29 (initiative); Oregon, *Thirty-third Legislative Assembly* (1925), S.B. 119; Oregon, *Proceedings of the Senate* (1925), S.B. 119, 202. Cigarette prohibition bills were proposed but rejected in Georgia, Ohio, Texas, Maine, California, Oklahoma, and Arizona.

35. South Carolina, *Journal of the House of Representatives* (1920), 1053, 1096; *Senate Journal* (1920), 50–51, 70; Massachusetts, *House Journal* (1921), H.B. 162; (1922), H.B. 847; *Minneapolis Journal*, Feb. 18, 1922; Maryland, *Journal of the House of Delegates* (1920), No. 27, No. 767; Michigan, *Public Acts* (1919), No. 328.

36. *Congressional Record* 60:3 (Feb. 6, 1921), 2629–35; *NYT*, Jan. 16, Feb. 6, 7, 1921; Milton R. Merrill, *Reed Smoot: Apostle in Politics* (Logan, Utah, 1990), 162–63; Office of the White House, executive order, Aug. 9, 1997.

37. *Tobacco*, June 24, 1920, 17. The *Pittsburgh Chronicle Telegraph* claimed that anti-cigarette bills were intended primarily to discredit prohibition; editorial reprinted in *Tobacco*, July 3, 1919, 3.

38. Idaho, *Journal of the State Senate* (1921), S.B. 134; *General Laws* (1921),

chap. 185, 385–87; *Journal* (1921), S.B. 327; *General Laws* (1921), chap. 262, 575–78. Senator Harding of Oneida County quoted in *Oneida County News (Malad City)*, Feb. 24, 1921. See also *Idaho Statesman (Boise)*, Mar. 5, 1921.

39. John S. H. Smith, "Cigarette Prohibition in Utah, 1921–23," *Utah Historical Quarterly* 41 (1973), 358–72. In 1923, the Utah legislature repealed the ban on the sale and manufacture of cigarettes, but broadened restrictions on advertising to include all tobacco products, not just cigarettes. For a survey of press coverage of the smokers' arrests, see "Utah's 'No Smoking' Signs," *Literary Digest*, Mar. 24, 1923, 14–15.

40. *Sacramento Bee*, Mar. 29, 1919 (Wilson); *Salt Lake Tribune*, Feb. 24, 1923 (half-page advertisement paid for by a committee of fourteen businessmen opposed to the anti-cigarette law).

41. *NYS*, Sept. 2, 1919; *Chicago Tribune*, Jan. 2, 1920; *Daily Pantagraph*, Jan. 19, 1920; *Tobacco*, Jan. 15, 1920, 3, Feb. 12, 1920, 18; *NYT*, Jan. 12, 1920.

42. Frances Warfield, "Lost Cause: A Portrait of Lucy Page Gaston," *Outlook and Independent*, Feb. 12, 1930, 275; Gaston to David Starr Jordan, Jan. 11, 1912, DSJ Papers; *NYT*, Dec. 20–24, 1920; Jan. 17, 1921.

43. Gaston to Jordan, Dec. 24, 1919; James A. Walton to Jordan, Nov. 11, 1925; Jordan to Walton, Nov. 18, 1925, all in DSJ Papers. For Gaston's efforts to organize a new anti-cigarette group, see *NYS*, Aug. 25, 1919, Sept. 2, 1920; and *Tobacco*, Mar. 18, 1920, 22.

44. *Tobacco*, Nov. 18, 1920, 45; *Topeka (Kansas) State Journal*, Jan. 24, 25, 1921; *NYT*, Jan. 24, Jan. 25, Aug. 27, 1921.

45. *Topeka Capitol*, in *Tobacco*, Dec. 9, 1920, 33.

46. Edward Page Gaston memoir, cited in "Lucy Gaston: Liquor, Cigarette Foe," *Harvey Tribune*, Nov. 6, 1966.

47. *Tobacco*, Feb. 10, 1921, 23; *NYT*, May 1, 1921, Jan. 25, 1922. The contents of Gaston's letter to the queen were reported in her obituary in *NYT*, Aug. 21, 1924.

48. Lucy Page Gaston, "War Bulletin No. 1," CTCA Papers, entry 396, box 2; *NYT*, Jan. 21, Aug. 16, 22, 1924; State of Illinois, Department of Public Health, Division of Vital Statistics, death certificate, Aug. 20, 1924.

49. *San Francisco Call*, Aug. 22; *Tobacco Leaf*, Aug. 23; *Chicago Examiner*, Aug. 22 (see also news story, Aug. 2); *San Francisco Examiner*, Aug. 29; *Mobile Register*, Aug. 22; *Idaho Statesman*, Aug. 22; *Ann Arbor News*, Aug. 22; *Daily Pantagraph*, Aug. 21; *NYT*, Aug. 23, 1924. For other obituaries, see *NYT* and *Chicago Daily Tribune*, Aug. 21; *Minneapolis Tribune*, Aug. 22; and *US*, Sept. 4, 1924.

50. Tennessee, *Acts and Resolutions* (1897), chap. 30; *Public Acts* (1919), chap. 32; Nebraska, *Laws, Resolutions, and Memorials* (1905), chap. 181; *Laws* (1919), chap. 180; Arkansas, *Public and Private Acts* (1907), No. 280; *General Acts* (1921), No. 490; Iowa, *Acts and Resolutions* (1896), chap. 96; *Laws* (1921), chap. 203; North Dakota, *Laws* (1895), chap. 32, (1925), chap. 106; Kansas, *Laws* (1909), chap. 257; (1927), chap. 171; Edward Page Gaston to Herbert Hoover, Apr. 25, 1925, Herbert Hoover Library, West Branch, Iowa (Hoover apparently did not save the letter from Henrietta Page Gaston, Lucy's mother; Edward Gaston described it in the letter he subsequently sent to Hoover).

51. James A. Walton, ACL annual letter, Feb. 1, 1937, AZ Papers; Articles of Incorporation of the No-Tobacco League, Sept. 27, 1920, Archives Division, Indiana Commission on Public Records, Indianapolis; *The No-Tobacco League of*

*America: Origin, Purposes, Plans, Methods, Officers, and Directors* (Indianapolis, ca. 1928), 2–3, AZ Papers; C. L. Flatter, Anti-Cigarette Alliance, to David Starr Jordan, July 8, 1927, DSJ Papers; *NYT*, Sept. 20, 1928; May 18, 1929; Aug. 5, 1933. For Pease's obituary, see *NYT*, Oct. 9, 1941.

52. Virginia S. Porter, "The Cigaret," copy in AZ Papers; *Chicago American*, May 16, 1924; *Portland (Maine) Advertiser*, Sept. 15, 1924; *Brooklyn (New York) Home Talk*, Nov. 28, 1929. For the outlines of a typical classroom lecture, see *Cigar, Cigarette or Pipe? Answered Scientifically by the Highest Medical Authorities in the World* (Chicago, ca. 1929), 1–5, 8, copy in AZ Papers. The Kansas State Historical Society holds a collection of 77 lantern slides used by Dr. James W. Fields, a dentist in McPherson, Kansas, in anti-smoking presentations from 1911 to 1939.

53. Thurman B. Rice, *The Hoosier Health Officer: A Biography of Dr. John N. Hurty* (Indianapolis, 1946), 327; *San Francisco Examiner*, Dec. 9, 1927. James A. Walton, superintendent of the ACL of California, complained that a "political machine" had interfered with his efforts to present anti-cigarette lectures in the 1930s; Walton to Anthony Zeleny, Jan. 15, 1938, AZ Papers.

54. ACL fliers, 1929, copies in HWW Papers; James A. Walton to Jordan, Oct. 1, 1930, DSJ Papers; Anthony Zeleny to L. W. Lough, Feb. 3, 1930; reply, Feb. 5, 1930 (Zeleny was president of the No-Tobacco League of America and Lough was general superintendent at the time); Charles M. Fillmore to Zeleny, May 24, 1929, all in AZ Papers.

55. Cather quoted in Warren I. Susman, *Culture as History: The Transformation of American Society in the Twentieth Century* (New York, 1984), 105. Many scholars have pointed out that while the reform impulse ebbed during the 1920s, it did not entirely vanish, as demonstrated by the professionalization of social work and the restriction of immigration, as well as by the prohibition of alcohol. See Arthur S. Link and Richard L. McCormick, *Progressivism* (Arlington Heights, Ill., 1983), 105–13.

56. *Minneapolis Daily News*, Mar. 7, 1922; Zeleny to Arthur Rolle, June 3, 1924; R. M. Manuel, assistant secretary, Greater University Corporation of the University of Minnesota Memorial Stadium and Northrop Auditorium Fund, to Zeleny, Jan. 24, 1928; reply, Feb. 13, 1929; all in AZ Papers. Copies of Zeleny's "sermonettes" are in folders 15 and 16 of this collection. For his career as a physicist, see *Who Was Who in America* 2 (Chicago, 1950), 599.

57. *Congressional Record* 71: 2 (June 10, 1929), 2586–90 (quotes at 2586, 2588). For the influence of religion on Smoot's politics, see Merrill, *Reed Smoot*, 43–80.

58. *Congressional Record* 71: 2 (June 10, 1929), 2589; Merrill, *Reed Smoot*, 164; *NYT*, June 11, 1929. Tobacco was one of about 100 substances removed from the *Pharmacopoeia* in the 1905 revision; *Pharmacopoeia of the United States of America* (Philadelphia, 1905), lxii.

59. Oregon, *Constitutional Amendments and Measures to be Submitted to the Voters of Oregon, General Election, November 4, 1930,* "Anti-Cigarette Constitutional Amendment" (Salem, 1930), 38; *Portland Oregonian*, Mar. 8, 1930; *Oregon Voter*, Oct. 25, 1930, 20.

60. *Portland Oregonian*, June 29, 1930; *The Oregon Blue Book, 1935–1936*, "General Election, November 4, 1930" (Salem, 1936), 178.

61. Tennant, *American Cigarette Industry*, 147; *NYT*, May 19, 1929; *Tobacco*, Dec. 19, 1918, 7; *TW*, Jan. 1, 1919, 22; George Akerson, secretary to President

Herbert Hoover, to Mrs. Ethelyn H. Roberts, director, Narcotic Department, WCTU, Jan. 20, 1930, Herbert Hoover Library, West Branch, Iowa.

62. *New York Tribune*, reprinted in *Tobacco*, Jan. 24, 1918, 11; Susan Stamford, "All Things Considered," National Public Radio, Apr. 25, 1997. Roosevelt's trademark cigarette is memorialized in his official White House portrait, now hanging in the National Portrait Gallery, Washington, D.C.

63. *Magazine of Wall Street*, Feb. 15, 1919, 746; Department of Agriculture figures cited in Tennant, *American Cigarette Industry*, 118, 127, 143; *Tobacco*, Jan. 29, 1920, 32; Mar. 18, 1920, 32.

64. Tennant, *American Cigarette Industry*, 140–44; Federal Trade Commission, *Report to Congress Pursuant to the Federal Cigarette Labeling and Advertising Act* (Washington, D.C., 1985), tables 6–8; *Washington Post*, June 9, 1997.

65. *Tobacco Leaf*, reprinted in *The Shield*, Apr. 4, 1922, 1.

66. Richard Griffith analyzes the Garbo scene in *The Movie Stars* (New York, 1970), 210. A photo of Theda Bara with a cigarette in a scene from *Carmen* is reproduced in David Quinlan, *Wicked Women of the Screen* (Avenel, N.J., 1990), 7.

67. Harris Lewine, *Goodbye to All That* (New York, 1970), 115; Griffith, *Movie Stars*, 72. Valentino demonstrated his smoking technique in *The Four Horsemen* (1921), *The Sheik* (1922), and *A Sainted Devil* (1924), among other films.

68. Edgar Dale, *The Content of Motion Pictures* (New York, 1935), 171–73. *A Woman of the World* is analyzed in Molly Haskell, *From Reverence to Rape: The Treatment of Women in the Movies* (Westford, Mass., 1973), 88–89.

69. *NYT*, Mar. 1, 1922; Oct. 17, 1929. In 1940, Hays again refused to limit the use of cigarettes in films; Jesse Mercer Gehman, *Smoke Over America* (East Aurora, N.Y., 1943), 60.

70. Tennant, *American Cigarette Industry*, 127, 146–47.

71. Egon C. C. Corti, *A History of Smoking* (New York, 1932), 265.

72. Whelan, *Smoking Gun*, 67. See also M. B. Rosenblatt, "Lung Cancer in the 19th Century," *Bulletin of the History of Medicine* 38 (1964), 395–425.

73. Fritz Lickint, *Medizinische Klinik* 24 (1928), 1831 (translation provided in Gehman, *Smoke Over America*, 180); McNally quoted in Patterson, *Dread Disease*, 205; William Wild, "Danger Signals of Cancer," *Hygeia*, Dec. 1926, 699; H. L. Lombard and C. R. Doering, "Cancer Studies in Massachusetts; Habits, Characteristics and Environment of Individuals With and Without Cancer," *New England Journal of Medicine* 198 (1928), 481–87; Ferdinand C. Helwig, "The Growth-Producing Effects of Extracts of Tobacco on Mice," *JAMA* 91 (1928), 150–51 (tobacco as a carcinogen); Eli Moschcowitz, "Tobacco Angina Pectoris," *JAMA* 92 (1929), 733–37 (heart disease; includes a review of the literature); Schrumpf-Pierron, *Tobacco and Physical Efficiency*, 54–55 (inhalation); *NYT*, May 22, 1926.

74. Alton Ochsner and Michael DeBakey, "Smoking Causes Cancer," *Science News Letter*, Oct. 29, 1938, 375; Raymond Pearl, "Tobacco Smoking and Longevity," *Science*, Mar. 4, 1938, 217; *Vital Statistics—Special Reports* 9 (1940), 175.

75. Schrumpf-Pierron, *Tobacco and Physical Efficiency*, 47–48 (smoke as germicide); *NYT*, May 21, 1926 (Mayo); Sept. 24, 25, 1927 (infant mortality); C. S. Butler, "On the Use of Tobacco in Prolonging Life," *Hygeia*, Mar. 1928, 162–63; "Lady Nicotine and the Ladies," unsigned editorial, *JAMA* 93 (1929),

122–23; James A. Tobey, *Cancer: What Everyone Should Know About It* (New York, 1932), 271–72. A physician in Winston-Salem, N.C., found no evidence that smoking had harmful effects on blood pressure, heart function, pregnancy, or lactation; Wingate M. Johnson, "Tobacco Smoking, A Clinical Study," *JAMA* 93 (1929), 665–67.

76. Wolff Freudenthal, "Tobacco, Alcohol, and Cosmetics in Their Relation to the Upper Respiratory Tract," paper presented at the annual meeting of the American Laryngological, Rhinological, and Otolaryngological Society, Montreal, Canada, 1926, in *Laryngoscope* 37 (1927), 217–30 (quote at 218–19). Freudenthal concluded that tobacco and alcohol were not only harmless, if used moderately, but beneficial; as to cosmetics, "They are to be condemned from every point of view" (230).

77. *NYT*, July 10, 1928; Patterson, *Dread Disease*, 208 (see also 206); Ernst Wynder and Evarts Graham, "Tobacco Smoking as a Possible Etiologic Factor in Bronchiogenic Carcinoma," *JAMA* 143 (1950), 329–36. Graham's research convinced him to stop smoking but it was too late; he died of lung cancer in 1957.

78. P. K. Holmes, "Hygiene—Article No. 5: Tobacco," *Physical Training*, Jan. 1920, 116–24; reprinted in *Tobacco*, Jan. 6, 1921, 28–29 (under the headlines "Scientific Consideration of the Effects of Smoking / Possible Benefits / Opposition Often Founded on Prejudice and Misunderstanding / The Real Argument Against the Cigarette, Is It a 'Convenient Smoke?' / Why Physicians Sometimes Encourage the Use of Tobacco / An Informative Discourse"); *TW*, July 15, 1920, 12.

79. *TW*, July 1, 1920, 24.

80. Ibid., July 1, 1920, 12 (Nebraska tobaccophile); 11 (scripts); *Tobacco*, Apr. 21, 1921, 3 (Milwaukee woman); Dec. 26, 1918, 14 (centenarian).

81. American Tobacco Company, "Effect of Subjecting Tobaccos to High Temperatures" (privately printed, 1928), 9, copy in HWW Papers. The pamphlet also claimed that 72 percent of dentists believed smoking inhibited dental decay (6). The slogans are taken from cigarette advertising in newspapers and magazines in 1917 and 1928–29.

82. Joe B. Tye, "Cigarette Ads Reveal a History of Deceit," *Wall Street Journal*, Aug. 5, 1986; unsigned editorial, "Health Appeal," *JAMA* 91 (1928), 1806. The New York Academy of Medicine also condemned the use of medical testimonials; *NYT*, May 5, 1929. The manufacturers of Girard cigars pioneered the use of doctors as salesmen in tobacco advertising with a campaign that began in 1912; *Tobacco*, Jan. 24, 1918, 13.

83. *Smoking and Health: Report of the Advisory Committee to the Surgeon General of the Public Health Service* (Washington, D.C., 1964), 33.

84. *Cigarette News*, June 1929, 2, copy in HWW Papers; *Life Extension Institute Bulletin*, Apr. 1920, reprinted in *US*, May 13, 1920; *NYT*, Nov. 20, 1924; A. L. Warner to Zeleny, Apr. 5, 1929, AZ Papers. The Dartmouth study showed that nonsmokers died at an average age of 69 years, 6 months, compared to 62 years, 7 months for smokers; Charlotte E. Ford, alumni recorder, Dartmouth College, Office of Alumni Records, to Zeleny, Nov. 16, 1936, AZ Papers.

85. Joel Shew, *Tobacco: Its History, Nature, and Effects on the Body and Mind* (New York, 1854), 46–93.

86. Holmes, "Hygiene," 116–17, 122; *JAMA* 93 (1929), 122–23.

87. Zeleny to Pearl, Feb. 4, 1937; reply, Feb. 12, 1937, AZ Papers.

88. Zeleny to Dr. Reed O. Brigham, Oct. 10, 1936 (see also Brigham to Zeleny, Sept. 14, 1936), AZ Papers; Sinclair Lewis, *Arrowsmith* (New York, 1961; orig. 1925), 16; Charles Bulkley Hubbell, "The Cigaret Habit—a New Peril," *The Independent*, Feb. 18, 1904, 376; *Tobacco*, Apr. 3, 1919, 6; 1950 study cited in Charles Marwick, "Many physicians following own advice about not smoking," *JAMA* 252 (1984), 2804. Not all doctors appreciated the gift cigarettes; see *No-Tobacco Journal*, Jan. 1928, 6.

89. Patterson, *Dread Disease*, 208–10; Arthur D. Hirschfelder, University of Minnesota Medical School, to Anthony Zeleny, Nov. 24, 1926, AZ Papers; J. Rosslyn Earp, *The Student Who Smokes: An Original Statistical Investigation* (Yellow Springs, Ohio, 1926), 17; *New York State Journal of Medicine* 17 (Feb. 1917), 55–58. The Antioch study, directed by the director of hygiene at the college, also found nothing to indicate that smoking decreased lung capacity; (16).

90. Patterson, *Dread Disease*, 52–55, 116.

## Conclusion

1. *Wall Street Journal*, June 23, 1997; U.S. Department of Health and Human Services, Public Health Service, *Health United States, 1995* (Hyattsville, Md., 1996), 173.

2. Centers for Disease Control and Prevention, *Morbidity and Mortality Weekly Report*, Apr. 3, 1998, 229.

3. A recent survey on drug use found that 71.8 percent of Americans over age 12 had smoked cigarettes at some point in their lives, but only 28.8 had smoked within the last month; Substance Abuse and Mental Health Services Administration, Office of Applied Studies, *1995 National Household Survey on Drug Abuse* (Rockville, Md., 1996), 89. Former Surgeon General C. Everett Koop set the goal of a smoke-free America by the year 2000 in a speech at the American Lung Association annual meeting, May 1984.

4. "Is It All Over for Smokers?" *Time*, Apr. 18, 1994, 58–62.

5. Norman H. Clark, *Deliver Us from Evil* (New York, 1976), 10–13.

6. *TW*, June 1, 1920, 14; *Tobacco*, May 20, 1920, 3–4.

7. Charles T. White to Wayne B. Wheeler, Feb. 16, 1922, American Council on Alcohol Problems Collection, BHL; WCTU Annual Meeting Minutes (1887), cc–cci; (1919), 30–31, 89–90.

8. *NYT*, May 20, 1923. For cigarette-related lobbying by veterans groups, see *Des Moines (Iowa) Register*, Mar. 14, 16, 1921; *Iowa Journal of History and Politics* 19 (1921), 564; *Tobacco*, July 10, 1919, 18; John S. H. Smith, "Cigarette Prohibition in Utah, 1921–1923," *Utah Historical Quarterly* 41 (1973), 365; and *Topeka (Kansas) Capital*, Jan. 18, 1927. For cigarette advertisements with military themes, see J. Walter Thompson Competitive Collection, Special Collections Library, DU.

9. *Tobacco*, Dec. 5, 1918, 10; Aug. 8, 1918, 18; *TW*, Sept. 1, 1918, 20.

10. North Dakota, *Laws* (1925), chap. 106, 111–15; chap. 107, 112–15; *NYT*, Jan. 8, 1925; *Iowa Journal of History and Politics* 19 (1921), 562–64; Kendall quote in *Tobacco*, Apr. 28, 1921, 25. In legalizing cigarettes, the legislature imposed a sales tax of two cents per package of twenty, in addition to a license

tax of $50 to $100, depending on the size of the town issuing the license; Iowa, *Laws* (1921), chap. 203, 213–16.

11. *Topeka Capital*, Jan. 18, 1927; Kansas, *Laws* (1927), chap. 171, 219–23.

12. U.S. Department of Commerce, *Statistical Abstract of the United States, 1926* (Washington, D.C., 1927), table 175, 171; table 774, 800; Ohio, *Legislative Acts* (1893), 198; D. Gregory Sanford, Vermont state archivist, to author, Apr. 25, 1988. As of 1968, only North Carolina did not tax cigarettes; Alexander C. Wiseman, "The Demand for Cigarettes in the United States: Implications for State Tax Policy" (Ph.D. diss., University of Washington, Seattle, 1968), 2–3.

13. Richard B. Tennant, *The American Cigarette Industry: A Study in Economic Analysis and Public Policy* (New York, 1971; orig. 1950) 15–17; Jack J. Gottsegen, *Tobacco: A Study of Its Consumption in the United States* (New York, 1940), 27.

14. K. Austin Kerr, *Organized for Prohibition: A New History of the Anti-Saloon League* (New Haven, 1983), 15.

15. Hill to Edison, May 18, 1914, published in pamphlet form by the American Tobacco Company, 1914, copy in DU; Hill to *NYS*, Sept. 6, 1919 (see also Gaston to *NYS*, Sept. 2, 1919).

16. *Tobacco*, Apr. 3, 1919, 6; Mar. 4, 1920, 3.

17. WCTU Annual Meeting Minutes, 1889, 130; *Topeka (Kansas) Journal*, Jan. 18, 1927.

18. *Judge*, reprinted in *Tobacco*, Nov. 25, 1920, 8.

19. *NYT*, Sept. 24, 1925.

20. Jeffrey E. Harris, "Cigarette Smoking Among Successive Birth Cohorts of Men and Women in the United States During 1900–80," *Journal of the National Cancer Institute* 71 (1985), 475. This analysis draws from Modris Eksteins, *Rites of Spring: The Great War and the Birth of the Modern Age* (New York, 1989), and from Robert Sklar, ed., *The Plastic Age, 1917–1930* (New York, 1970).

21. Ronald J. Troyer, "From Prohibition to Regulation: Comparing Two Antismoking Movements," *Research in Social Movements, Conflict, and Change* 7 (1984), 54–55; entry on John Francis Banzhaf III, *Current Biography* 34 (Dec. 1973); Richard Kluger, *Ashes to Ashes: America's Hundred-Year Cigarette War, the Public Health, and the Unabashed Triumph of Philip Morris* (New York, 1996), 304–10, 373.

22. G. Decaisne, "The Effects of Tobacco Smoking in Children," *JAMA* 1 (1883), 24–25; Harbour Fraser Hodder, "The Fall of the House of Ashes?" *Harvard Magazine*, July–August 1996, 19.

23. *The Shield*, Aug. 5, 1923, 4; Kluger, *Ashes to Ashes*, 502–5, 552–53, 678–79, 737–39; *Time*, Apr. 18, 1994, 60–61.

24. *Hastings Banner*, Sept. 5, 1918; Kluger, *Ashes to Ashes*, 682; New Hampshire, *Journal of the Senate* (1991), 392, 397; *Statues* (1991), chap. 274 (S.B. 171).

25. *Newsweek*, Nov. 13, 1995, 60; Nader Mousavizad, "Smoke," *New Republic*, Sept. 18–25, 1995, 58; *Vanity Fair*, Oct. 1991, 68–69.

26. "What Happens When You Smoke," *Harper's Weekly*, May 26, 1906, 751; Carleton Beals, "Those Who Have Gone Back," *Outlook*, July 28, 1926, 447; *Tobacco*, Feb. 17, 1921, 20. See also "Prohibition as 'Big Brother' Fails to Win for Blue Laws," *NYT*, May 20, 1923.

27. I. L. Kephart, *The Tobacco Question* (Dayton, Ohio, 1882), 85, copy in

AC; Lawrence Leslie, *The Seer and the Cigarette* (Greenfield, Ind., 1928), 115; Milton Bradley, "Go to the Head of the Class," 1969 edition; Bernardino Ramazzini, *De Morbis Artificum Diatriba* (1713), quoted in Elizabeth M. Whelan, *A Smoking Gun: How the Tobacco Industry Gets Away with Murder* (Philadelphia: George F. Strickley Co., 1984), 36.

# *Index*